Order and Freedom

Literature and Society

General Editor: Herbert Tint

Order
and Freedom

Literature and Society in Germany
from 1720 to 1805

Alan Menhennet

Weidenfeld and Nicolson
London

© Alan Menhennet 1973

First Published by Weidenfeld and Nicolson
11 St John's Hill London SW11

ISBN 0 297 76562 0

Printed in Great Britain by
Cox & Wyman Ltd,
London, Fakenham and Reading

Contents

Contents

Preface

The orientation of this book is literary, but with a special emphasis which distinguishes it from traditional literary history and criticism as they have been applied to our period in many excellent studies. These works cannot be accused of having neglected the relation of literature to society altogether, but it was not their main concern. Our aim here is to make a contribution to the identification and exploration of the border-territory between 'pure' literary and sociological study, an area in which, in spite of the very valuable work which has been done (especially by W. H. Bruford), there are still discoveries to be made. This must be our excuse for the fact that the coverage of eighteenth-century German literature in this book is not exhaustive. Room has had to be made for detailed analysis of selected examples, for we are dealing with complex and shadowy material. Moods, rather than hard facts, must be our starting-point.

The centre of the enquiry is the mental and emotional state of the group of people which produced the works which we study and this, in our case, means almost exclusively the educated and intellectually aware element of the middle class. Even those German authors who did not originate in this class were assimilated into it. It will be seen that the whole study works towards, and then out of this central area, firstly by attempting to draw from an examination of society, seen consistently as the background to literature and thought in general, an idea of the major impulses which are both social and psychological in nature, and relating them to the particular social group with which we are concerned. This is the task of Part I. The rest of the book examines the interplay of these impulses in the literature itself.

That the impulse towards freedom and its natural counterpart, that towards order, should have been particularly prominent in the age of absolutism, Enlightenment and the French

Preface

Revolution is hardly surprising. This was after all the age in which man first felt himself to have been 'born free' (Rousseau) or, in Kantian terms, to be 'an end in himself', but also to be 'everywhere in chains.' The working-out of this realization gave the age a unity which is apparent in Germany, as elsewhere, but in a different way and to a different extent. Political preoccupations were less strong there, and the 'libertarian' impulse less dominant. This is particularly true of the Enlightenment, which is why the German term 'Aufklärung' is preferred in this book.

The traditional scheme of German literary history, namely that of 'Aufklärung' (approximately 1720–70), 'Sturm und Drang' (1770–83 or so) and 'Classicism' (up to the death of Schiller in 1805), seems to fit the facts better than any other arrangement, and is adopted here. This scheme, which posits a serious break in continuity between the 'Aufklärung' and the great golden age of German literature, has its weaknesses, and is objected to by many, whose views deserve respect, especially when put with the vigour and skill displayed by Georg Lukács in *Goethe und seine Zeit*. The problem is too intricate and technical to be capable of solution here. It is hoped that the worst mistakes of crude divisiveness and over-simplification have been avoided, but the interplay between freedom and order still seems to be best represented by the division into three major phases, namely Order (the 'Aufklärung', with those later writers who still lean more towards order than freedom), 'Freedom' (the majority, but not all of those traditionally labelled as 'Stürmer and Dränger'), and 'Synthesis'. This last heading attempts to render the Classical desire to achieve a living unity which does justice to both impulses, what Goethe called 'bewegliche Ordnung' (order in motion).

In the hope that this book can be of use to non-Germanists as well as those whose particular province is German literature, I have tended to quote in English, or, where there seemed to be a literary case for quoting the original, to give a translation in the relevant note. Since the principal subject-matter of the book is a matter of mood rather than concrete fact, the translations sometimes take moderate liberties with the apparent literal meaning of the original, in order to render its inner spirit (the original is, of course, also quoted in such cases). Easily available translations (such as those in the 'Penguin Poets' series) have been called in aid where appropriate. I can only hope that the specialist will be willing to bear with some measure of simplification, perhaps even inaccuracy in the strict view and that the non-specialist will understand that it simply was not possible, in the space available, to remove every difficulty.

Finally, I should like to record here my gratitude to the General Editor of this series for many helpful comments and suggestions.

A.M.

July, 1973

Part 1

The Social and Political Background

I

The Political Scene

The Nation

The question of 'reality' – the extent to which what is written or said corresponds to something incontestably real – is a crucial one in any examination of classical German literature and it intrudes itself at the very outset, long before we can turn our minds to literature in its own right. This is no case of forcing politics into a literary mould, for if we are to describe 'Germany' we must have some idea of what it is. And one of the most important facts of all about eighteenth-century Germany is that, politically, it did not exist.

When we speak of eighteenth-century France or England, we know with a fair degree of accuracy what we are talking about: a nation-state, with a sure consciousness of itself and of its culture. No such clarity exists in the case of Germany. It is true that eighteenth-century people speak of 'Germany' quite frequently. It can be described for the benefit of the curious English reader,[1] even felt to be under threat in time of war, as when the Ansbach poet Johann Peter Uz writes of 'Das bedrängte Deutschland'. But what is being referred to here is the 'Holy Roman Empire of the German Nation'. This latter can, indeed, be located on a map of eighteenth-century Europe. But this provides little consolation: the Empire had become a political ghost, with no power to frighten or impress anyone. As a political system, it probably inspired more levity than loyalty. As Justus Möser wrote in 1781: 'No Curtius among us is going to throw himself into the abyss to save the German Imperial System'.[2] The German nation was a nation without a state, split into a multitude of fragment-'states', very few, if any, of which could lay claim to a corresponding 'nation'. There were home-towns, to use Möser's expression, but there was no actual homeland, no centre which could draw together the threads

3

of German political or cultural life. In discussing the state of the German theatre in 1807, J. G. Seume is constrained to speak of 'the German lands, for one cannot properly speak of Germany'.[3]

From Leibniz, before our period had even begun,[4] to Goethe (e.g. *Dichtung und Wahrheit*, Book VII) and Herder,[5] we find concern about the lack of national unity and content in German life. But none of the various well-meant plans for ameliorating the situation – in which, incidentally, political unification did *not* bulk large – came to anything. It is a sad commentary on the political situation that the nearest approach to a nationally unifying factor which was present in eighteenth-century Germany was the Prussia of Frederick the Great. It is in this context that the cult of Frederick, particularly strong at the time of the Seven Years War, made most sense. Here at last, it could be felt, Germany was once more appearing on the world stage. Frederick was by no means the ideal actor for the part – he spoke and wrote French better than he did German – but he was better than nothing, and certainly came closer to filling the shoes of Arminius than did Joseph II of Austria. The latter state, the greatest of the Empire, was also the least national: 'to be Austrian' says A. J. P. Taylor 'was to be free of national feeling'.[6] Taylor goes on to point out that the aristocrats in Austria and Prussia, even when of German extraction, did not think of themselves as 'German' – a statement which, as we shall see, is broadly true of the nobility over our whole area. Can one, then, speak with any confidence of a German nation and culture in the eighteenth century? Wieland, after all, one of the more pragmatically minded observers of the time, stated, in an essay of 1773 that 'the German nation is not really a nation but an aggregation of many nations'.[7]

It must be admitted that much of the conscious 'Deutschtümelei' of the eighteenth century rings resoundingly hollow, however sincere it may have been in origin. Even Goethe, in the period when 'German' sentiment was strongest in him was only partially successful in creating a 'German' hero in his *Götz von Berlichingen*.[8] And the semi-legendary figure of Hermann, who walks again in many works of eighteenth-century German literature, is a classic example of the living dead, the literary zombie. One has some degree of sympathy with the Germans in their protest – for this is definitely protest-literature, particularly in the 'sixties and 'seventies. Its target could be stated in simplified terms as being the undue dominance in German social and cultural life, above all at the courts, of non-German, specifically, French elements, beginning with the very language in which people expressed themselves. Goethe's aim in *Götz* was, Möser is sure, 'to present us with a collection of pictures from the national life of our forbears and to show us what we would have and what we could do if we could only lose the taste for the prettily polished ('artig')[9] lady's maids and witty menservants of our French–German stage'.[10] It is not just a question of effeminate frivolity; as we shall see a little later, a moral contrast is involved as well. Ironically, Frederick the Great was one of the most Francomane of German monarchs in his tastes, if not his vices. Shakespeare's plays were, for him, 'abominables' and Goethe's *Götz* an 'imitation détestable de ces mauvaises pièces angloises.'[11] The negative side, then, one can understand: it is the positive which seems inadequate.

To the external forces militating against national feeling has to be added the general trend towards cosmopolitanism. In the 'Aufklärung', this appears in such things as Wieland's *Das Geheimnis des Kosmopolitenordens* and *Geschichte der Abderiten*, Lessing's *Nathan der Weise* and Nicolai's criticism of the patriotic fervour aroused by Thomas Abbt's *Vom Tod fürs Vaterland*.[12] The 'Sturm und Drang' was more nationalistic, but Classicism restored the trend with its concept of 'Humanität'. Goethe's idea of 'world literature' is one of its most interesting reflections.[13]

The well-known distich from the *Xenien* of Goethe and Schiller may reasonably be brought forward at this point: 'You hope in vain, you Germans, to make yourselves into a nation: Make yourselves into Men instead, for this you can do.'

Some of the statements already quoted indicate that, while there can be no denying the weakness of German national consciousness as far as a *political* feeling is meant, there was a feeling of 'German-ness' abroad – at least in the relatively narrow, but for our purposes all-important band of society formed by the educated middle class, together with the minority of aristocrats, like F. L. von Stolberg and Otto von Gemmingen, who thought in a 'German' way. This national consciousness transcended local loyalties and was not, in fact, in conflict with them.[14] In the circumstances, the world of letters was naturally the main channel for its expression. Occasionally it was sparked into activity by events. In the Seven Years War, for example, a German prince routed non-German armies. Even those observers belonging to lands not involved in the Austro-Prussian conflict took particular pleasure in the defeats of the French who had, after all sometimes shown a tendency to flaunt their military and cultural superiority over the yokels across the Rhine.[15] The incursion of French revolutionary troops in the early nineties, particularly the occupation of Frankfurt and of Mainz, again roused the German consciousness. Goethe speaks approvingly of the refusal of the citizens of Frankfurt to co-operate with the French,[16] and in newly republican Mainz, in spite of the political benefits brought by the occupation, Georg Forster had to harangue the citizens on the necessity of accepting the French soldiers as their protectors and brothers;[17] if Goethe's description of what happened after the re-conquest of the city in his *Belagerung von Mainz* is anything to go by, Forster's success was limited.[18]

Even before 1770 there is plentiful evidence of a consciousness of and pride in a distinct German national character. The courts and nobles, certainly, were servile enough in their relation to foreign fashion, whether in dress, manners or culture. The protest that this calls forth from the middle class is as strong – though not perhaps as vehement in expression – in the 'Aufklärung' as it is in the 'Sturm und Drang'. Gottsched, the man who is accused by many of having delivered German literature over to the French, in fact shows a robust national feeling. 'We must rise above that slavish esteem for all that which is foreign' he declares in his *Critische Dichtkunst* 'which up to now has been more damaging than beneficial.'[19] Certainly, he encouraged translation and imitation of French classical plays. But his aim, however misguided his method may seem to some, was to extricate the German stage from the morass of irregularity and 'bad taste' in which he found it and render it capable of a regularity of its own. The sturdiness of his national feeling is evidenced by the fact that, much as he dislikes opera for its irrationality, he goes to some lengths to establish that it is a German invention 'in order to humiliate the pride of the foreigners'.[20] Anglomania too was criticized. The 'Aufklärer'

Carl Ignaz Geiger chooses the disguise of a travelling English-man for his satirical pictures of contemporary Germany, and finds fault with the citizens of Zurich, for example, because of their 'Frenchifying affectation', which offends against his idea of true 'Teutschheit'.[21] In a comedy of the same year, however, he castigates imitation of the English from the same culturally patriotic motives.[22]

There is, then, little sense of a political national identity and little chance of a national culture arising on the basis of 'German' personalities or events. A sense of German-ness could be tied, apart from linguistic considerations, partly to social factors and more generally to moral ones. When Uz, in 'Das bedrängte Deutschland', suddenly conjures up the image of Hermann and his victory over the Romans, he is thinking primarily of quali-ties of character. The ancient Germans are conceived as 'unpolished, but fearsome in their freedom' as against their modern equivalents, who are 'weakened by the poison of un-German manners'. Unpolished strength, simplicity, seriousness, fidelity and honesty tended to be associated with the word 'deutsch', their counterparts with words denoting foreignness. Much the same could be said of the conventional distinction between the middle-class 'Bürger' and the nobleman. When Klopstock, in 'Ich bin ein teutsches Mädchen', gives a list of the 'German' virtues, Schubart can use this as the basis for an imagined rejoinder by a 'gnädiges Fräulein' which makes 'German' and aristocratic seem like opposite poles.[23] The so-called 'Rococo', the style which lay closest to the French-oriented culture of the courts, was naturally the one least likely to share this cultural patriotism. Wieland, its foremost practi-tioner, did not welcome the idea of 'leaving the charted paths in order to wander about in the forests with the old Germans'.[24] However, he never denies that there is such a thing as the German national character.[25]

In a vague and indistinct form, much more cultural than political, the idea of a German spirit, even a German 'Volks-geist', was alive in the eighteenth century. Before Herder, indeed, the statesman F. K. von Moser had written of the German 'Nationalgeist' (1765). Herder himself, of course, was the man who gave the German spirit some shape and defini-tion.[26] And in those days, it *was* a matter of spirit ('Geist').

Whether or not because of the practical difficulties involved, there was little thought of turning the spiritual German unity into a political reality. In talking of the national feeling of the Germans of 1848, Namier speaks of a 'linguistic and racial' concept of nationality[27] and – with due caution as to the second of these terms – we could accept this formulation for our period as well, though one would like to supplement it with the word 'cultural'. What one misses is the concern with *power* which Namier discerns in nineteenth-century Germans, even the liberals.[28] Idealism is in full flower, and the more strongly so as the century progresses. As Barnard points out, Herder's approach is characterized by a 'lack of realism', a lack of interest in procedural constitutional machinery and the like.[29] There were a few thinkers who were relatively pragmatic in their approach, such as Lichtenberg or Georg Forster, but even they were not perhaps pure pragmatists and they were certainly not typical. The formulation of the 'Classical' Schiller is somewhat extreme, but it can serve as generally representative of the thinking of the age. Even if the political structure which carries the name, the Empire, were to be dissolved in flames, he writes, 'German greatness will remain'. This greatness is a matter, not of territorial, but of spiritual conquest.[30] And this, in spite of their political impotence and backward social and economic structure, is what the Germans actually achieved in our period. In a period of deep material abasement, German culture became at least the equal of any other in Europe.

The Empire

The imperial eagle is an impressive bird on a coat of arms and even in the eighteenth century the Holy Roman Empire still had some of the trappings of imperial state and authority. There was still an Imperial Diet in Regensburg (Ratisbon) and Imperial Courts at Vienna ('Reichshofrat') and Wetzlar ('Reichskammergericht') which heard and occasionally even decided cases. Goethe, as a budding jurist, went to Wetzlar to study the workings of the Imperial Chamber Court.

These institutions were not quite dead. The courts, for all their weakness and inefficiency in this age of absolutism and 'Kleinstaaterei', did sometimes act as a counterweight to individual autocratic power. They were not used only by the rich,[31] and when the tyrant was not too mighty they could even discipline a prince. Prince Hyacinth of Oranien-Nassau-Siegen was deposed for having sentenced to death a peasant whom he considered a rebel. When it was a question of defending the rights of the rulers, of course, they could act much more quickly. They were prompt enough to send in troops to put down local uprisings at the time of the French Revolution. It is reasonable to assume that they must occasionally have inhibited despots from committing outrageously despotic acts, but likely also that they were less effective in this than the publicistic press, which was quite a lively force in the latter half of the century. What is certain is that there were many occasions on which arbitrary acts of tyranny were neither prevented nor punished. And the wheels of imperial justice ground exceedingly slowly. The courts were starved of the necessary resources to employ enough officials or pay them properly, with the result that bribery was common. It was often necessary to resort to it to get one's case heard at all, such was the backlog of business which had built up: Goethe (*Dichtung und Wahrheit*, Book 8) gives a figure of twenty thousand cases for Wetzlar.

The Diet had been in constant session since 1681 and was now attended by delegates only; its proceedings consisted of the recital of the instructions given to these delegates (which were, of course, subject to revision in the light of events). The only question which was taken really seriously at Regensburg was that of precedence. The financial resources available to the Emperor, *qua* Emperor, were derisory and the fact that the Empire, though still in theory elective, was now *de facto* hereditary in the house of Hapsburg did not make other German rulers any more inclined to strengthen it. Since the Peace of Westphalia, which had set up non-German powers as guarantors of the 'German Liberties' – the liberties of the German princes, that is – and had given these potentates the right to make alliances outside the Empire, all chance of its survival as a healthy political institution had vanished. It was now in the last stage of decline: an antiquated and impotent structure, a patchwork quilt of some three hundred effectively independent states of wildly varying size, shape and constitution.

This system of 'Klein- und Zwergstaaterei'(J. Streisand)

allowed a large number of sometimes very small states to continue in existence against all political and economic logic, all with their own courts and armies, all trying to apply the competitive and restrictive mercantilist system, all extracting border tolls. Biedermann tells us that there were thirty toll-stages between Strassburg and the Dutch border, nine in the short stretch between Bingen and Coblenz. Corn to the value of six to seven florins cost almost as much again to transport.[32] It permitted the survival of a swarm of so-called 'duodecimo' princes, many of whom were truly degenerate, or at least tyrannical and wildly self-indulgent at the expense of their subjects. But it should also be recorded that if the system allowed of a Zweibrücken, whose duke, apparently, thought of himself as an estate-owner rather than a responsible 'father of his people', and was prepared to farm out the whole of his revenues 'for many years in advance',[33] there were also states like Weimar and Baden to set in the credit-column. A conscientious ruler in such a small state could come closer than a 'great' one to realizing that aspect of the absolutist ideal which is enshrined in the conception of the prince as 'Landesvater'. He could know his land and people and preserve a personal, even faintly patriarchal element in the life of the state. In addition, the imperial structure provided a variety of choice and opportunity for the talented and educated man. There was a chance to cross a state border to escape an angry tyrant (as did Schiller) or conscription (Gottsched!) or to better oneself or work in more congenial conditions (Winckelmann in Dresden, Lichtenberg in Göttingen). The system made sure that many people could live part of their lives in a relatively quiet and personalized atmosphere, without political or nationalist distractions and out of the reach of Austrian or Prussian statism and bureaucracy.

It was from this safe distance that most German intellectuals chose to admire the 'enlightened' state of Frederick the Great. Most of the important literary and intellectual achievements of the time were produced in backwaters: Weimar, Biberach, Göttingen, Wandsbeck, and so on. The great thinkers of the age were active in places like Halle, Königsberg, Jena and of course Weimar. The 'provincial' nature of the life led by so many of Germany's great men in the eighteenth century is reflected to some extent in what they wrote. The disadvantages for some

aspects of literature are clear: Goethe himself talks in Book
Seven of *Dichtung und Wahrheit* of the discrepancy between the
'aristocratic dignity' of the 'prince-like' citizen of Rome and the
circumstances of a small-town German scholar. But it is significant that Goethe did not feel any strong desire to leave Weimar
for more metropolitan and exciting places. And the quiet life
can also further certain characteristics in a writer. It can lessen
the impact of the 'great world', to use an eighteenth-century
expression, and turn the mind to nature and to the inner life in
general. If the mind is not atrophied by this situation, it can find
paths to freedom which are no less psychologically real for the
fact that they have little to do with politics.

Viewed from the political angle, eighteenth-century Germany was a sleepy place. There were those of a politically
radical turn of mind who criticized it for this, and others who
had a longing for heroic, 'great' events and sentiments and
bemoaned their absence in German life. 'The state goes
mechanically on its way,' writes Möser, 'and we seek honour
almost exclusively in [official] service or in scholarship'. But
while the fragmented condition of the Empire was undoubtedly
a prime cause of this state of affairs, few influential voices among
thinkers were raised in favour of political unification. Schubart
found great benefit for the individual in the federative situation.[34] Wieland considered that the divided state of Germany
led to greater human and civic freedom and to an equilibrium
favourable to the freedom of the spirit and the unfolding of all
the talents.[35]

We have touched here on the form most consistently taken by
the preoccupation with freedom which is present in German
cultural and intellectual life throughout the century. It comes
out as a desire not so much for political or social upheaval as
for freedom to realize one's capacities to the full. The role of the
state is not so much to shape man's life as to hold the ring while
he does it for himself. Wilhelm von Humboldt puts this forward
in his early political *Ideas* on the delimitation of the powers of
the state (1791). Surprisingly enough, the most influential
philosopher of the German 'Aufklärung', Christian Wolff, had
expounded a view which was not so very dissimilar from
Humboldt's.[36] The Empire did not exist to give this freedom,
but its weak and variegated nature probably did less to take it

away than would have been the case with an efficient centralized absolutist state. 'How on earth', asks Goethe in the first part of *Faust*, 'does the dear old Holy Roman Empire manage to stay in one piece?'. The main reason, of course, is that it suited the princes to keep it in existence as long as they could keep it weak. But for ordinary citizens, too, especially of small states, such a community had something to recommend it. Friedrich Perthes's uncle, for example, a state official in the tiny principality of Schwarzburg-Rudolstadt, sympathized with the ideals of the French Revolution, but he enjoyed a personal relationship with his prince, for whom he would have sacrificed 'both fortune and life' and his nephew, 'born in one of the petty states, had grown up with a true Kaiser-loving heart.'[37] If only the little fish could be allowed to swim peacefully in their enormous pond! But there were too many pike about and when, in 1806, the biggest of all applied the closure to 'the most perplexed and complicated Government, ancient or modern, that ever existed', as a contemporary British observer called it,[38] it was a case, not so much of political murder, as of euthanasia.

Political forms and attitudes

Under the conditions outlined, the predominant political trend of the *Ancien Régime* – towards autocracy – took a number of externally differing forms. There were governments which were ostensibly republican (the Free Cities), there were autonomous country squires and there were ecclesiastical as well as secular states. But in fact, the spirit was the same everywhere. Authority was vested in a single person or in a ruling oligarchy. If the autocrat did not care to govern, effective authority could reside with his chief minister, favourite or mistress. The actual conditions of life of the ordinary citizen depended very much on the character of the ruler – hence the strong emphasis placed by so many political writers on the education of a prince.

The origins of this state of affairs lie well back in history, at least as early as the suppression of the great peasant uprising of the sixteenth century. Many of the issues of the eighteenth century are already raised in the peasants' Twelve Articles, for example the adoption of Roman law, which effectively makes the monarch accountable to no one on earth, the whittling down of personal freedom and privileges, and the iniquitous laws protecting the landowner's game at the expense of the peasant's crops. Nor did the aristocracy represent a serious check on princely authority. The power of the Provincial Estates ('Landstände'), which were usually dominated by the nobility, to exert pressure on the monarch by economic sanctions had been largely eroded and the two sides had settled for a situation in which the prince enjoyed authority and the noble his privileges, and often a 'plum' job in the administrative machine or court establishment. In many lands the Estates seldom needed to be called in full session (Anna Amalia of Weimar only did so twice) and when they did meet they were normally complaisant. Even in Württemberg, where they were of largely middle-class composition (most of the nobles being free knights), the Estates were not very successful in restraining the Dukes Eberhard Ludwig and Karl Eugen. These two, especially the latter, stand out in the rogues' gallery of eighteenth-century German princes for irresponsible self-indulgence and arbitrary and cruel behaviour. It was Karl Eugen who was responsible for the seven-year incarceration of the liberal publicist and minor poet C. D. Schubart, which became a *cause célèbre*, and no doubt for many other injustices which did not do so, because the sufferers were not celebrities. The Estates could do little to check this and when, on one occasion, they remonstrated with Karl Eugen in the name of the 'Vaterland', they were given the most decisive of all German versions of the famous remark of Louis xiv (the ultimate model for all these petty Caesars) : 'I am the fatherland and the image of the Godhead upon earth.'[39]

The common form of the administration of an absolutist state in eighteenth-century Germany was a centralized bureaucratic pyramid, ranging from small 'Ämter' in remote places to the central government, which was normally arranged in some kind of collegiate system. The whole was topped by a Privy Council, responsible to the prince. It was not uncommon for quite small matters to come as far as this, especially in small states like Weimar. Goethe refers to the 'Geheimes Consilium', or 'Conseil', to which he belonged, as 'the ultimate authority, to which all matters come, to which all kinds of business are brought',[40] and the papers printed in his *Amtliche Schriften* bear this out. The prince could thus be in contact with the life of his subjects in quite minute detail. Some rulers allowed great influence to their ministers, as in the case of Kaunitz in Austria or Brühl in Saxony, while others preferred to keep the reins tightly in their own hands, as did Frederick the Great. But whether he ruled directly or not, the prince was always the supreme authority and received extreme respect from his officials.[41] The observance of proper forms and titles was a very serious matter in those days – and not only in aristocratic circles.

The innermost principle of Absolutism had a personal element, in that, in Max Beloff's words, it 'presupposed the hereditary rights of monarchs and was thus still bound up with the contingencies of individual life'.[42] The state was a remote and abstract thought at best for many people and the prince could embody it and make it felt in a personal, if not always a pleasant form. Many princes dealt with a great deal of business personally. There were, of course, wide variations in the amount of time and effort a ruler would devote to such tasks. The daily routine of Frederick the Great in the 1770s, as reported to Wraxall by Prince Frederick of Brunswick, the king's nephew, began at 4 a.m. (five in winter):

He breakfasts quite alone on chocolate; and till ten o'clock he is entirely occupied in transacting affairs of state, which he dispatches in person with rigorous exactitude. From that hour till near noon he goes first to the parade, then walks, or as is more commonly his custom, rides, if his health permit. He returns to the palace of Potsdam, or to 'Sans Souci', before twelve, and sits down to dinner precisely at noon. After the repast he usually remains some time at table, where he unbends himself in conversation with those about him. His afternoon is divided between books and music, in the latter of which he is a connoisseur and a performer. At six, one of his secretaries enters, and reads to him such letters as are addressed to him upon literary subjects or any intelligence relative to that line of correspondence. He dictates his replies immediately. The King eats no supper, but retires to his chamber at nine, and goes directly to bed. Such is his constant mode of life.[43]

Thus a great monarch. Some smaller ones were also conscientious, but not all, particularly not in the earlier part of the century. Pöllnitz describes the day of one of Karl August's predecessors in the Duchy of Weimar as follows:

He wakes early in the Morning, but makes it late before he rises; for he takes his Tea in Bed, and sometimes plays on the Violin. At other times he sends for his Architects and Gardeners, with whom he amuses himself in the drawing of Plans. His Ministers also come to him while he is in Bed to talk upon Business. About Noon he gets up, and as soon as he is dress'd, sees his Guard mount, which consists of 33 Men, commanded by a Lieutenant or an Ensign. He exercises his Soldiers himself and corrects them too when they commit any Fault. This done, he takes the Air, and at two or three o'clock sits down to Table, where the two Maids of Honour, the Master of the Horse, the Major, the Officer of the Guard, and even Foreigners if any happen to be there, are of the Company. The Dinner holds a long while and 'tis sometimes three, four and five hours before they rise from Table. The Glass never stands still hardly, and the Duke talks a great deal, but the Conversation is commonly on Subjects that are not very agreeable. When Dinner is over they drink Coffee, after which the Duke retires for a few Minutes, and then plays at Quadrille with his two young Ladies and the Major; but sometimes he does nothing but smoak Tobacco, and he often retires to his Chamber where he amuses himself with Drawing or else playing on the Violin till he goes to bed.[44]

One does not get the impression of a very energetic ruler.

Karl August, in the age of Enlightened Despotism, kept in close touch with his administration and with the people too, by frequent journeys through his little state – often combining business with pleasure – on which he showed a constant readiness to listen to his subjects' complaints. In addition, after all the various resorts of the administration had been gone through, subjects still had the right to petition him direct. This policy, as Helma Dahl tells us, 'bore fruit' at the time of the French Revolution.[45]

The quality of administration varied enormously from place to place. Prussia was easily the most efficient and had the best civil service. Here, the tireless energy and dedication of Frederick the Great, combined with the emergence of what Hans Rosenberg calls a 'bureaucratic élite',[46] led to better government on the whole, even if taxes were high and freedom (except for the freedom to utter 'as many absurdities against religion as one likes', in Lessing's phrase[47]) not noticeably greater than elsewhere. And even here, the tendency of the ruler to intervene personally could lead to anomalies and injustices. Elsewhere, there were cases of extreme inefficiency and capriciousness. The prince of Oettingen-Wallerstein, so K. F. von Lang tells us, was in the habit of letting the papers from his 'Regierungscollegium' pile up until the spirit moved him to settle a few cases entirely at random. His dilatoriness and capricious method of operation could lead to a situation in which bewildered officials, who had made more than one submission on the same case, were faced with mutually contradictory decisions. Once, says Lang, they were in an agony of doubt as to whether they should hang a certain malefactor, banish him, or merely give him a good whipping, until the offender solved their problem for them by escaping.[48] Against this background, the famous scenes in Lessing's *Emilia Galotti* (Act I) in which we see a petty prince granting a petition at one moment because the petitioner's name is Emilia and at another, off-handedly agreeing to sign a death-sentence 'Gladly, only let's have it quickly', do not seem so far-fetched.

The common run of the numerous tribe of officials was ill-paid and enjoyed only moderate social prestige. As J. H. Merck, an official in Hesse-Darmstadt, put it in the *Teutsche Merkur* of 1780, 'in very modest financial circumstances, one has the secure prospect of not starving'. The cake of prestige and civic influence, he says, is cut up into 'infinitely small portions.'[49] Their status hovered uncertainly between respectability and something not far short of the domestic servant: small princes, in particular, often treated them almost as such. Biedermann quotes from a document laying down the principles of correct behaviour for all subjects (including officials) of the Bishop of Speyer: 'Subjects should comport themselves like servants because the prince of the country is their master and has power over both our lives and our goods'.[50] Other people in the service of such masters – e.g. musicians – were in the same situation. Mozart had to bear a great deal from the Archbishop of Salzburg, and, not possessing the submissiveness (or self-control) of his father, could not endure it. Teachers, many clergymen and others of this approximate station were in a similar position. Servility, or at least the outward appearance of it, was often an art that had to be mastered, if one wished to make one's way in the world.

Princes and nobles were habitually addressed in terms of

exaggerated respect. J. S. Bach wrote thus to Augustus the Strong of Saxony:

> I lay before your Kingly Majesty this trifling work (or proof) of the science which I have been able to attain in music, with the very humble petition that you would be pleased to regard it, not according to the measure of the meanness of the composition, but with a gracious eye as befits your Majesty's world-famed clemency, and condescend to take me under your Majesty's most mighty protection ... etc.

Enclosed with this letter were the *Kyrie* and *Gloria* of the Mass in B Minor. It is difficult to calculate the extent to which this situation sapped the independence of spirit of the artists and intellectuals whose work we will have to consider: probably not as much as might appear on the surface. We shall have to return to this theme in another place, leaving it for the moment with an example from Schiller's *Kabale und Liebe* which seems to sum up the situation rather neatly. The musician Miller loses his temper under the heavy and vicious provocation of the Duke's chief minister:

> Your excellency is the chief authority in the land. But this room belongs to me. If I should one day submit a memorial, I'll pay my humblest respects, but if a visitor misbehaves himself, I'll throw him out – begging your Honour's pardon (Act II, scene 6).

It was not all bad, of course. There were states, particularly in the second half of the century, the period of 'Enlightened Despotism', in which the ideal of a reformed, enlightened absolutism, already present in the thought of the 'Aufklärung' – e.g. in the 'Moral Weeklies'[51] and the political novels of the period, such as von Loen's *Der redliche Mann am Hofe* – was something more than a mere paper formula, even if the patterns of thought of the best of them still fell short of our concept of the proper dignity of Man. It was a more paternalistic attitude than would find favour today. 'The princes tend their peoples like good shepherds' writes the Gotha functionary F. W. Gotter in his *Epistle against Freethinking* (1773). And in a 'Kammerordnung' of 1768, the government of Baden, another enlightened state, considers it to be its duty as 'the natural Guardian of Our Subjects' to teach the peasants modern methods of agriculture.[52] Reform from above was widely held by liberal thinkers to be the only sensible course and it was tried by many, never with complete success, but usually with some. Joseph II of Austria is the outstanding example of the strengths and limitations of this policy. By doing something, at least, to relieve the lot of the hard-pressed, these rulers helped to spare Germany really serious repercussions from the events of 1789 and after.

In discussing the relative lack of revolutionary spirit in Germany at that time, E. Horner, following Karl Immermann, indulges in some speculation about the German national character and argues that the German has 'a natural impulse towards subordination, towards service to the point of self-abnegation'.[53] Such a phrase, with its hint (whether intended or not) of the mood of Götterdämmerung, takes us on to dangerous ground. Certain words and ideas are no longer 'innocent' in German. But it is true that the Germans then, as later, proved themselves a people eminently capable of obedience and respectful towards authority.

Hardly anyone was unaware of the inadequacy of the *status quo*. Wolff recognized it as well as Kant, Wieland as well as Herder. 'The greater and more beautiful part of Europe' wrote Wieland in 1788 'still lies under the pressure of the remains of the barbarian constitution . . . in many of our mightiest realms, the rights of the nation have not been distinguished from those of the throne . . . there are still states in which the source of laws is not reason in general, but the (often very near-sighted) intellect of a single person or of those few people who succeed in gaining control of his authority.'[54] The fervent hope for change is common to all, but nowhere does it take the form of a readiness for change through violence. They see the same facts as did Engels in the next century, but their reaction is less bitterly destructive. Engels writes of 'a single living mass of corruption' and of a 'petty, servile, miserable, small-tradesman's spirit' which 'permeated the whole people'.[55] The revolution foreseen by Wieland is 'a beneficent revolution', proceeding, not from violence, but from 'calm, unshakeably constant persistence and resistance in accordance with duty' (that is, an essentially passive resistance) and achieved 'through the gentle, persuasive and in the end irresistible superior force of reason.' The same general tenor of thought is to be found in Schiller (*Über die ästhetische Erziehung des Menschen*), Kant (*What is Enlightenment?*), or Wolff.[56]

A pendant to this is the positive horror of anarchy which runs through the whole century, from the 'Moralische Wochenschriften'[57] to Schiller's *Das Lied von der Glocke*. Even in the 'Sturm und Drang', the true anarchist spirit is rarely dominant. As to the ordinary mass of people, the evidence is less clear, but it seems that there was no strong revolutionary spirit. Horner holds that they 'almost instinctively closed their ranks in common defence against the threat from outside to their traditional ways' during the wars of the French Revolution and calls their will to rebellion 'infinitely weak'.[58] 'The most that can be said' writes F. L. Ford about Germany in the 1780s 'is that liberals and a small number of radical democrats were beginning to object to the system of small tyrannies in terms which suggest that a revolutionary crisis originating outside the Empire might find a welcome from some elements within it.'[59] Is all this the result of special conditions or of excessive spinelessness? The fragmented state of the nation would have made a revolution on the French model difficult, but not necessarily the rise of a revolutionary *spirit* or the forceful expression of such a spirit – in its own, German way – in uprisings of a more radical nature than in fact occurred. There was repression, true, but hardly as severe as that which obtained, for example, in Imperial Russia, where the spirit of the revolutionary movement, when the political wind began to blow from France, was more radical. Censorship was uneven in its incidence over the whole area: there were some states, like Baden, Brunswick, Dessau and others which had hardly any at all.[60] There was always the possibility of 'marching across the border', as Miller puts it in *Kabale und Liebe* (Act II, Scene 5), if one incurred the wrath of one despot. And in any case, there are roundabout or symbolic ways in which radical revolutionary thoughts can be clearly and even sharply hinted at and private forms of writing in which they can be ventilated. In spite of all this, one's overall impression is that, while the Germans were anything but satisfied with the state of the nation as they saw it, they were less enthusiastic still about possible violent methods of altering it. There was a general preference for a constitutional, most often republican form of government, but the hope was that this would be achieved by evolutionary means. Kant, for example, found that 'no forcible overthrow of non-republican power, however tyrannically that power is exercised, is permissible.'[61]

There was very little, if any democratic spirit abroad. One has to remember that the vast mass of the people were almost totally devoid of education. The tendency was therefore to think of them politically as either downtrodden and passive or, if they were conceived as taking action, as something dangerous, 'the mob', the 'wankelmütige Menge' which Schiller's Queen Elizabeth both despises and fears. It is true that the occasional idealized peasant figure appears in literature, like the 'Bauernbursche' in Goethe's *Werther*, but he is the exception even in the 'Sturm und Drang'. Everyone, or almost everyone, believed in the dignity and majesty of Man, but did not find it embodied in the common people. Even writers of genuinely 'popular' nature and intent like Schubart and Bürger are concerned to dissociate themselves from the 'Pöbel'.

To bring about the ideal, non-violent means were relied on. To change the form of the state without changing the men who inhabit it, says Schiller in one of the most profound political essays of the time, *Über die ästhetische Erziehung des Menschen*, is a pointless exercise. Schiller goes beyond the common idea that one can rely merely on the spread of rational Enlightenment and, on the basis of his analysis of human psychology, proposes art as the potential saviour of the world.

The plea for freedom for the creative human spirit to develop to its full range is one of the outstanding preoccupations of eighteenth-century Germany. If the form it took tended to be generally cultural, this does not make the ideal any the less politically and socially relevant. It does not seem to be out of harmony with the idea of reform from above, but it *is* accompanied by a strong distaste for social disorder and upheaval. The idealist and non-revolutionary path was the one taken, to a greater or lesser extent, by most major German thinkers. It has been said that 'lack of a sense of proportion' is an endemic weakness in the German national character.[62] Without wishing to delve too deeply into racial theory, we can see how such a judgement came to be made. Our period is not without its share of the infinite longings which are sometimes associated, rightly or wrongly, with the German character. One thinks of *Werther*, of *Faust* ('I love the man who desires the impossible' Manto says in Part Two), of some of the more colossal moments in Beethoven who, with Schiller, wishes to 'embrace the whole world' in the finale of the Choral Symphony. Whatever their exact date, all of the works referred to here are in part at least products of the eighteenth century. But this is also an age of control, and those infinite yearnings can always be matched by elements of order: the importance of Law, for example, for Goethe, Schiller and Kant as well as the 'Aufklärer' and in music, the classical side of Beethoven and above all, Haydn and Mozart.

As far as political order is concerned, most thinking men saw the need for change in the long run. It was Goethe, after all, who saw the cannonade of Valmy as the herald of a new age.[63] But most people were far removed from the apocalyptic mood which sometimes grips poets in the face of revolution. Schiller's *Wilhelm Tell* and Goethe's *Hermann und Dorothea* are reasonably representative of the spirit of the period. 'It is not for the German', as Hermann puts it, 'to carry this fearsome movement further and to waver also in this and that direction.' Not only the more comfortably cushioned intellectual objected to the violence of the Revolution. Ulrich Bräker, the 'poor man of the Tockenburg', thunders against the encroaching French 'robber-bands' as 'bloodthirsty Jacobins who would like to upset all order and social relationships so that they might become King of the Castle.'[64] In his typically cautious and balanced survey of 'The present state of the fatherland' (1793), Wieland comes to the conclusion that the position in Germany, imperfect as it is, is not as bad as that in pre-revolutionary France, certainly not bad enough to justify the 'desperate' step of revolution, which could bring in its train 'disorganization, crime and the loss of the present generation.'[65] Freedom at that price would, he thought, be too dearly bought, and in any case, he cherished the expectation that peaceful reform would in due course bring it about. Wieland's summary of the situation in Germany is one on which we might end this part of our study:

The calm which we have enjoyed in the whole of our German fatherland (with a few unimportant exceptions . . .) is strong proof of the good side of our constitution and of the respect which both rulers and subjects have for the laws. But it testifies also at the same time to the steady ('gesetzt') character and good sense of the nation, which is suitably impressed not only by the sight of the triumphs of liberty and equality but also of the immeasurable misery of anarchy, of insecurity of property and life, of the fury of factions, of civil wars, personal vengeance and the whole enormous multitude of crimes and inhumanities of which the revolution in France has been the occasion and with which those triumphs were far too dearly bought.[66]

2

Economic and Social Factors

The general environment

When Schiller, as a newly appointed extraordinary (and therefore unsalaried) Professor of History at Jena, and on the brink of matrimony, was trying to put together his all-important opening lecture on the nature of 'universal history' and the reasons for studying it, he wrote to his friend Körner of the 'terrible stress' ('Drang') under which he had to work to manage even the most superficial preparation, in view of all the other writing which had to be done to provide the money he needed.[1] It is this area – the one in which economic and social factors condition psychological states – that must be our main concern, and it should emerge that their influence was often constricting, even if they were seldom literally crushing, for men of literary talent. But before considering this theme in detail, we should look at least briefly at the national perspective, which shows a not dissimilar pattern. Things were not desperate in most cases, but there was hardly an atmosphere conducive to a mood of ease and harmony, or of energy and enterprise.

Economic conditions did not favour Germany in this period. The seventeenth century had already seen a decline from the prosperity of the sixteenth, and although our century has nothing to match the Thirty Years War the other main adverse factors, the political fragmentation of the country and the swing in the balance of trade towards the maritime nations, continued to work against the German lands. Under 'Kleinstaaterei', the Germans suffered the disadvantages of a centralized absolutist system imbued with the fortress-mentality normally associated with the term 'mercantilism', with none of the compensations provided by the size and scope of a national economy. The German states had failed to evolve an effective financial organization and in particular, an adequate banking and credit system:[2] in short, the conditions for a vigorous economic activity were not present. The great exception, the free city and port of Hamburg, helps to prove the rule. It was prosperous, it had had banks since 1619 and had already begun to attract men of talent and enterprise 'like a magnet' in the seventeenth century,[3] and it was one of the most liberally inclined and interesting places in the whole Empire. This all serves to throw into relief the stuffy and limiting state of affairs in most other places, where enterprise was either small-scale or blighted by the dead hand of state capitalism.

Economic conditions tended to narrow the horizons of the 'Bürger'. A career as a small businessman, a civil servant, academic, teacher or clergyman, none of which categories, in general, enjoyed very high financial or social status, would have been the prospect facing the majority of them. And while this position, once achieved, usually guaranteed freedom from real poverty, many had a taste of the latter in the period during which they were acquiring the necessary training to fit themselves for an 'Amt'. It was during this phase that many of Germany's great writers endured the privations and often exquisite social humiliations of private tutoring which Lenz, one of the sufferers, portrays in *Der Hofmeister*.

From his position on the ladder, the 'Bürger' could look down to the bitter poverty of the peasantry and up to the often opulent luxury of the nobility. In this – on the whole – quite soft-hearted age, there was a fair amount of concern for the former, but little idea of any concerted action which might be undertaken to bring about substantial improvement. The violent upheaval which would have been required to effect a radical redistribution of wealth was, as we have seen, rejected by the majority, and no one had the secret of creating enough wealth to go round. Most observers were not so much callous as helpless and fatalistic in the face of poverty. Improvements, where they were possible, were hardly spectacular and in many of the smaller states, like Weimar, it took all the running that the administrators could do to stay more or less in the same place. Goethe's well-known letter of 17 April 1782 to K. L. von Knebel, in which he describes how consumption at the top of the social pyramid more than accounts for production at the bottom, conveys a strong sense of helplessness. The ideal of a harmonious community, made happy and prosperous in freedom by the reopening of the silver mines, which Goethe portrays so winningly at the end of the poem 'Ilmenau', remained a pipe-dream. He was able to portray such an ideal harmony in a real context only in the inner life of the individual, in figures like Iphigenie and Wilhelm Meister, or in a symbolic form, as in his *Novelle*.

The relief of poverty was a matter for public and – largely – private charity and many individual acts of kindness are documented, not only on the part of the well-to-do.[4] The public provision, e.g., of places where the poor could live and sometimes even work, was inadequate, and beggars were a not uncommon sight. If one could not find a niche in the social structure, life could be cruel and unpleasant, for society could not always find work for idle hands to do. The Devil could, of course, and while Germany could not match the London underworld, it had its share of crime, particularly the highwaymen and robber bands of which Schiller's *Die Räuber* is the most illustrious literary reflection.[5] By comparison with the chronically unsettled and insecure world of the seventeenth century, Germany in our period was a more secure, humanitarian land. The use of torture in criminal investigation decreased sharply, for instance, and brutal methods of execution and punishment became less popular. Yet the gibbet was still a quite familiar sight on German roads, especially earlier in the century: Pöllnitz records having seen a whole avenue of them between Nuremberg and Bamberg.[6] Savage punishments still remained in operation, as for example forced labour of various kinds, such as the 'Schiffziehen' (towing of ships) in the Danube Delta which tended to take the place of the death-penalty in Joseph II's Austria and during which, according to Schubart, men had, in addition to the appalling physical strain and the cruelty with which they were treated, to remain wet through for days on end.[7] There was progress on the economic and social fronts and these were increasingly 'the new times of greater enlightenment and gentle sentiment,' in the words of the Weimar official C. F. Schnauss.[8] But there was a cold, hard world outside the social stockade and much depended on accidentals like birth or the favour or charity of an individual. It is not surprising that the themes of Fate and Fortune are not at all uncommon in eighteenth-century literature.

The often excessive luxury in which many nobles indulged while, in Gellert's words, 'many a pious man starves'[9] was, of course, an offence to any reasonable and humane observer and it was frequently criticized. This is most common among the 'Aufklärer', where the criticism is strengthened by a distaste for excess as such. But this was usually seen as a moral, rather than a political question, whose solution lay in the gradual moral improvement of the human race. There was no lack of awareness of the imperfections of German society, but the attitude adopted towards the problem was largely passive. An excellent indicator is the popular novelist August Lafontaine, who was popular precisely because his outlook is a ragbag of the common attitudes of the middle class. His *Die Familie von Halden* castigates vice at court and the maltreatment of servants by their masters. But it never questions the *status quo*, not even in the most guarded and generalized manner. The insulted and injured have practically no right to take action. Order is paramount and the punishment of evil-doing rests with the 'Obrigkeit'. Where authority cannot or will not act, the individual may, but 'only in a case of the most extreme need'.[10]

A minor passage in Goethe's *Egmont* could be seen as symbolic of the dilemma. In Act II, Scene 2, the Count and his secretary discuss the measures proposed by his steward for raising the money he needs. Egmont rejects these measures because they would bear too heavily on his subjects. And yet he still needs the money, so the steward is to be told to think again . . . One has the same sense that even men of good will are caught up in a cramping vicious circle; the same kind of feeling, perhaps, that prompted Goethe, in the *Italienische Reise*, to record the resolve never again to involve himself in a post in which 'I work myself to a standstill for no result'.[11] After his return from Italy he became, in a way, his own life's work and made his major contribution to the body social and politic through works of the spirit. In the same vein, Wilhelm von Humboldt writes to Georg Forster that a man can make an effective practical contribution ('wirken') in society by virtue of what he is and writes as a private individual.[12] We are on the brink of the famous German

Idealism which is such a bone of contention for historians and political commentators. But there is more work to be done before we can enter that charmed circle.

The classes

The nobility. Class in the eighteenth century was a serious business, and nowhere was it taken more seriously than in Germany. Class-consciousness and class pride were very highly developed among the German nobility and were beginning to develop in a distinctive form in the middle class. Class barriers were not entirely impassable but they were formidable: noble and 'Bürger' did not often mix socially and hardly ever at the altar. Indeed, the middle class opposed to the aristocratic pride of family its own pride in its moral rectitude and did not itself favour socially mixed marriages. When it allowed them as good, this was usually on the basis that the nobility was not losing in dignity, but gaining in morality.[13]

The main positive contribution which the nobility might have made to German life and hence to German culture would have been – nobility: colour, drama, in a word, 'greatness', such as so many German writers failed to find in the reality around them. In the field of music (especially opera) and above all architecture, the nobility can be said to have played an important part along these general lines. The grandiose, yet graceful and colourful was very much part of their taste, and that taste had direct influence on what was produced. But as far as literature is concerned, it was what they *were* and did that mattered, and their contribution in this field was pitifully small. Looking back at the earlier decades of the century in search of an event which might have furthered a 'national' German literature, Goethe can find nothing better than the mock-military 'Lager' held by Augustus the Strong of Saxony at Mühlberg.[14] But if the nobility was not able to contribute greatness to the quality of German life, it was at least able to transmit to it a certain amount of grace, and even glitter. It was not original in this, of course, being essentially the medium through which foreign (predominantly French 'Rococo') manners and culture took some kind of root in Germany. This was not just a matter of literary influences – which of course would not have required a class as mediator – but a style of living, which aroused a certain amount of positive, as well as a strong negative reaction. The great master of the German literary Rococo, indeed perhaps the only German writer who managed to embody the style in a truly successful form, was Wieland, and it is no accident that his most Rococo phase coincided with the period when he was able to get the full feel of it in the milieu of Count Stadion's residence of Warthausen.[15]

This close association with the Rococo is something which the Germans have only recently begun to forgive in Wieland, for it was felt as a kind of betrayal of 'German', 'bürgerlich' qualities. There can be no denying that the facts give some colour to this, as far as the aristocratic associations of the Rococo are concerned. It is one of the most serious aspects, from our point of view, of the immense gulf which existed between noble and 'Bürger' in the eighteenth century. The nobility took its culture almost exclusively from France: it preferred to read French books, see French actors and plays – only small courts, according to Bruford, 'sometimes accepted the services of German players when a French troupe was beyond their means or not easily accessible'[16] – the very language in which it preferred to conduct social intercourse was French. Weimar, with its simpler, more homely and 'German' society, was not typical.

A generally rather arrogant attitude to the unpolished 'German' middle class percolated down even to those renegade 'Bürger' who aped the noble style; at least, this is how it is seen by many a middle-class observer. Gellert, for example, presents such an attitude in the impossible Herr Simon of *Das Loos in der Lotterie*. 'Vive la langue françoise' is his battlecry and he dismisses his guardian, Herr Damon, with the words: 'He's a *bourgeois*. He wouldn't even do for a doorkeeper in France.'[17] In these circumstances, it is not difficult to see how French became the symbol for all the injustice and insults, real or imagined, which the middle class suffered at the hands of the nobility. Even smoothness and grace became suspect, to the extent that, in their most assertive phase, middle-class writers overstressed the rough-hewn nature of the German character. Schiller deliberately presents his heroine's father, in *Kabale und Liebe*, as 'ein plumper, gerader deutscher Kerl'.

At the same time, a certain amount of Gallic wit and polish

did filter through to the middle class. The coarse 'Grobian' was no more suitable as an ideal than the vacuous fop, and the influence of French culture was particularly valuable in combating the former, as was recognized very early on by people like Thomasius. Glittering 'Residenzstädte' like Dresden could not fail to have some influence. The other great Saxon city, Leipzig, the chief centre of the book trade and possessor of an influential university, was Germany's most important intellectual centre until nearly 1770, and was permeated with the spirit of the Rococo. It is characterized in the Saxon 'Kernchronikon' of 'Iccander' by the same word ('galant') as is used by von Gleichen Russwurm to describe the whole French-led Rococo culture, and was thought of as a 'little Paris'.[18] The characteristic word 'galant' appears in a positive sense in the vocabulary of the middle-class writers: Gottsched, for example, expresses the desire for 'galantes und gelehrtes Frauenzimmer' who can help combat the rough *mores* of university students.[19]

They did this without relaxing their disapproval of the nobility as a whole, whose arrogance, in the middle-class view, was matched by an equally egregious immorality: irresponsibly extravagant luxury, sexual promiscuity, dishonesty, idleness and all kinds of other vices. Reason suggests that the aristocrats cannot all have been monsters, and incomplete experience of the reality, together with a certain element of propaganda, will have produced exaggeration and one-sidedness. Goethe, for example, who was in a position to know and judge fairly impartially, rejects the very negative picture painted in the (then) well-known satirical play *Nicht mehr als sechs Schüsseln* (1779) by G. F. W. Grossman.[20] Nevertheless, strictly accurate or not, this attitude is an important fact in itself, in view of the middle-class origin of most German literature of the time; in any case the facts as we have them suggest that, while it may have been an exaggeration, it was not an excessive one. One gains the impression, especially before the onset of 'Enlightened Despotism', of a mad whirl of social gaiety and a serious degree of moral laxity. The court of Berlin under Frederick II lived, it is true, a life of some frugality, but Vienna was not particularly moral, in spite of the efforts of Maria Theresa. An enormous amount was spent on pleasure in the joint electorate of Bavaria-Palatinate under Carl Theodor. Outstanding among other courts for luxury were Württemberg[21] and Dresden, the latter of which we can take as an exemplar.

Saxony needed all its riches to support the two Augustuses, especially Augustus the Strong. True, their expenditure left a considerable architectural legacy (e.g. the Dresden 'Zwinger') and a strong musical tradition behind, but the cost, measured in the sweat and tears of the populace, must have been tremendous. In those days, however, people did not measure in these terms. The absolute prince embodied the majesty of the state and 'magnificence' was a component of this. The poet Johann von Besser regarded 'Magnificenz' as essential to a monarch in his role of 'Statthalter Gottes' on earth.[22] Luxury was also seen as a way of effecting some distribution of wealth. Again, from our specialist point of view, the effect of all this on the cultural landscape of Saxony has to be recorded. It made it into 'La Saxe galante' and it made the Dresden court into one of some brilliance. Saxony was recognized, in the first half of the century, as the leading German land, as far as culture was concerned. Breitinger, for example, allows the province this title, 'especially since the magnificent rule of her royal Elector Frederick Augustus'.[23] Breitinger does not seem to hold the latter's extravagance against him, nor, it seems, did his subjects, for in the 1770's he was still well remembered for 'his magnificence, his affability and the splendour of his court'.[24] Writing much later, J. G. Seume, a non-Saxon, still speaks of the 'brilliant court of the Augustuses'.[25]

A fascinating instance of confrontation between 'Germanic' roughness and sybaritic Rococo is provided by a story told of a visit to the Dresden court by the 'Sergeant-King' of Prussia, Frederick William 1. This strict, authoritarian, sometimes savage monarch was an almost total stranger to the muses and the softer delights in general. Accompanied by the Crown Prince, he was led by his host to a brilliantly lit room, in which a naked woman was suddenly revealed, reclining on a couch (a situation which will not be unfamiliar to readers of Wieland). The Prussian king's presence of mind did not desert him. Whipping off his hat, he covered his son's eyes with it, at the same time ordering him to depart. Then, turning to his host, he remarked coolly 'She is very pretty' and took his own leave.[26]

Amusements and diversions were found a very necessary ingredient of court life and there was often an official with special responsibility for them. Ernst II of Gotha, for example, had a 'Directeur' and 'Sous-directeur des Plaisirs' and even Goethe seems to have helped out in this direction at times in Weimar. Augustus the Strong seems to have been his own provider and to have welcomed any occasion to exercise his inventive talent. Here is Pöllnitz's description of an entertainment devised in honour of the arrival in Dresden of his daughter-in-law:

Upon the Feast-Day, the whole Court appeared at the *Turkish* Palace, in the Habits of *Turks*. The King came in the Dress of a *Sultan*, but without any Attendance. His Majesty was soon after followed by the Princess his Daughter-in-law, with her Ladies. Her Royal Highness, for whom the Entertainment was made, found a body of Janizaries drawn up in the Court-Yard of the Palace. The King receiv'd her at the Entrance of his Apartment, and conducted her into a Hall spread with fine Tapestry, and laid with Cushions richly embroider'd.

The King and Princess being seated, were served by twenty-four Negroes in sumptuous Dresses, with Sherbet, Coffee, and Sweet Meats, in great Vessels of massy Silver; nor were scented Waters, and perfumed Handkerchiefs forgot. After this Collation, they drew near to the Windows to see the *Pillau* (which is the Rice of *Turky*) and the King's Bounty-Money distributed to the Janizaries. This was follow'd by a Comedy, with an Entertainment of Turkish Dances. Then came the Supper, the Guests sitting crosslegg'd upon the Cushions, and the Courses being serv'd up after the fashion of *Turky*, by the Negroes and young *Turks*. While they were at Table, the Company were diverted by the various Leaps and Postures of certain Tumblers and Rope-Dancers. Supper being over, they went into the Garden, which was illuminated with several thousands of Crystal Lamps. There was Tilting, and shooting at the mark, and whenever the Mark was hit, a Sky-Rocket was sent up, which for the time seem'd to sprinkle Thousands of Stars among those in the Firmament. After this, the Company retired into their Palace, where the King and the Princess open'd the Ball, and there was Dancing till five o' clock in the morning, when the Ball was concluded with a sumptuous Breakfast.[27]

The element of fancy-dress in this entertainment is characteristic and revealing.

The Social and Political Background

The German Rococo was once regarded as something in the nature of a Francophile aberration in the history of German literature. Prudery and false patriotism are no longer the inhibiting factors they once were and the Rococo is receiving, if anything, disproportionate compensation for the neglect it suffered previously.[28] The general trend is, however, undoubtedly a healthy one. The Rococo had a contribution to make in respect of colour, grace, wit and above all in the appreciation of form and aesthetic 'play' – 'Spiel' is a key-word for this style. This was very necessary to temper the somewhat homespun utilitarian rationalism which was so strong in the 'Aufklärung'. And it should be remembered that it is the concept of 'Spiel', duly enriched with 'Classical' seriousness, which is later raised to a pedestal in Schiller's *Ästhetische Erziehung des Menschen.*

Apart from frivolity and irresponsible extravagance, another group of failings with which the nobles and their way of life could be charged lay in the realm of the heart: insincerity, dishonesty and the like. 'Welt' and 'Lebensart' were often more important than talent or goodness of heart. The surest way to preferment lay in the ability to please the person in whose gift it lay. This is a stock theme of middle-class social writing and there can be little doubt that it is based on fact. As Herder puts it, in the prize essay *On the influence of the government on the sciences and of the sciences on the government* (written in 1779), a man 'learned to dance in order to become a priest and played the violin in order to become a judge'.

A court society is, of course, an artificial one. As Goethe came to feel, and to formulate in *Torquato Tasso*, it is not a simple matter of black and white. But artificiality is a slippery slope and there is certainly a tendency among observers of the aristocratic scene to see the situation in black-and-white terms, especially when the culture of the heart gained strength in Germany. Imagining that he has been commissioned to sing of 'Friendship and Sympathy[29] at Court', J. H. Merck writes 'But may the song of friendship and sympathy resound in the halls of the despot? Where not even a crack in the wall is left for the dove of simplicity to build its nest? Sound no more, my lyre! There is no ear, no heart to hear you in this place.' Merck was a bad poet, certainly, but an intelligent man, with some experience of court life. Later, Joseph von Eichendorff, a nobleman by birth (though his values were formed by country rather than court life) writes in a similar vein. In the novel *Ahnung und Gegenwart*, he makes his hero say of the court, where Rosa has decided to live: 'The people are different there . . . truth of heart, piety and simplicity count for nothing among them. . . . Somehow I seem to see her stepping, like a Bride of Death, into a great, glitteringly ornamented grave'.[30]

Nor does the nobleman's word appear to have been his bond, at least when he was dealing with the middle and 'lower' classes. Schramm shows how hard it was at the end of the century for a merchant to recover money owed him by a prince,[31] and Seume, in an essay on gaming, one of the chief pastimes of the time, describes a poor craftsman sent away empty-handed and with vulgar abuse ('Lotterbubenausdrücke') heaped on his head by the nobleman whom he had dared to disturb with a request for money owing to him.[32] The 'quality' were in fact by no means always men of solid financial substance. One recalls Lady Mary Wortley Montagu's description of some smaller 'Residence' (i.e. court) towns with their '. . . sort of shabby finery; a number of dirty people tawdered out . . . etc'[33] They were nevertheless riddled with snobbery. Status and precedence were regarded as of the highest importance and it is recorded of one lady, Reichsfrau von Wöllwarth auf Neubronn, that she seriously expected class distinction to be carried over into the next world.[34] Unproductive indolence was another unenviable facet of the nobleman's reputation. Certainly, his favourite indoor pastime (gambling) was not conducive to the public good, and his favourite outdoor one (hunting) constituted a positive menace to the peasant's survival. Game was protected by often very savage laws, and the devastation it wreaked on crops is not difficult to imagine. The nuisance was recognized by many. Even Pöllnitz, who does not seem to be troubled by a very lively social conscience, writes of the profusion of deer in Darmstadt:

This great plenty of Deer is extremely troublesome to the Peasants who are abroad day and night to watch their Fields. The Landgrave and the hereditary Prince are so jealous of their game that they reckon it as bad a Crime as Murder to kill a Deer.[35]

This image of 'foreign' aristocratic vice as against 'German' middle-class virtue seems to have been based on reality, but the factual basis for it became less secure as time went on. Towards the end of the century, the nobility did begin to become 'Germanized' to some extent and to cultivate the virtues that the middle class had regarded as exclusively its own. Some kind of growing together, or synthesis between aristocratic and 'Bürger' ideals, does begin to show itself in the writings of the classical Goethe and Schiller, and aristocratic figures like Wilhelm von Humboldt begin to participate in the main stream of German cultural life. With the rise in standards of education in ordinary German schools, the nobility began to move away from the tradition of segregating its young in a French-dominated atmosphere of private tutoring. In the Romantic generation, nobles like Arnim and Eichendorff have no sense of a difference in kind between themselves and the 'Bürger' and are at least as 'German' as they. The stereotype, black-and-white picture persisted in popular plays and lending-library novels long after the middle class itself had begun to acquire 'aristocratic' vices, such as snobbery, excessive gaming and some degree of luxury.

In the last analysis, any description of the life of the German nobility in the eighteenth century must begin to read like an indictment. When all allowances are made, the entry in the cultural credit-column does not begin to be enough to make up for the debit side. But not to register this credit side would be to suppress an important part of the background to eighteenth-century literature. It seems undeniable that the aristocratic milieu contributed something to the more witty and colourful passages of Wieland's *Pervonte* or *Oberon* or to Goethe's *Wilhelm Meister* and *Wahlverwandtschaften*. When all is said and done, form and atmosphere are vitally important elements in literature, as in other arts, and the great Classics, even at their most serious and 'moral', could not fashion their works in an aesthetically appropriate form out of worthy, honest broadcloth alone.

In fact, as we shall see, the middle class gradually began to assimilate some of the 'richer' elements of the aristocratic culture into its own way of life. We have seen Eichendorff as a critical observer of the nobility, whose culture was no better suited in the early nineteenth century to embody the highest values than it had been in the eighteenth. Yet we can see too, in *Ahnung und Gegenwart*, how it is capable of at least partially seducing him from the aesthetic side: 'He found himself in a numerous and brilliant circle. The many lights, the magnificent clothes, the smooth floor, the graceful remarks which flew to and fro, everything glittered' (p. 693). One catches an echo of a *fête galante*, or of a Mozartian minuet in a brilliant ballroom – in fact, there is a description of a minuet in Eichendorff's story *Die Entführung* which creates a similar atmosphere. However much, and for whatever good reason, the German writers of our period hark back to Greece or Rome or the sixteenth century, they cannot leave their own age behind. There is something of the courtly thrust-and-parry, for example, about the exchanges between Iphigenie and Arkas in Act One of *Iphigenie auf Tauris*. Whatever the nostalgia for the 'natural' and noble grandeur of the classics or the rough-hewn honesty of Hans Sachs, the tone of the eighteenth century keeps breaking through.

The middle class. As will have become apparent already, the middle class had advanced somewhat from its seventeenth-century position of social insignificance and economic dependence. A 'Bürger' could live, in the main, fairly comfortably and with some sense of his own identity and dignity. But if he was wise, he avoided offending the 'great'. If he had especial talent, he might hope to make his way in the world to some extent, but only by particular good fortune and/or the grace and favour of a noble patron could he hope to reach the top. There was nothing like equality of opportunity with the aristocracy; even in the Prussia of Frederick the Great, the higher officer ranks, for example, became the exclusive preserve of the Junkers.[36] In a spectrum as wide as that constituted by this class, of course, there will be considerable variation, but it is certainly true to say that it required an unusual combination of good fortune and the talent to get on before a 'Bürger' could be truly independent or well off. Among literary men and thinkers, such a combination was rare indeed. This was a group of people who were becoming better educated and more socially and politically aware but who were effectively almost excluded from the fields of activity in which these talents might have reached full

35

fruition. They felt themselves, in Professor Palmer's phrase, 'as being above the popular mass but not as belonging to the social élite'.[37]

Such a situation, one might have thought, where an important, large and growing section of the community must have felt strong 'disproportion between capacity and opportunity' (Bruford), must have been an explosive one. Yet there was no explosion. We can study this conveniently in the treatment of social themes in literature and journalism. Social evils are criticized often enough and social injustices clearly resented. But this criticism and resentment almost always stops short of being truly subversive of order and authority, whether political or clerical. The gentle tones of a Rabener, Gellert or Knigge are certainly not those of rebellion. Even more outspoken writers like Bürger, Göckingk ('Die Parforcejagd'), or the young Schiller (*Die Räuber* and *Kabale und Liebe*) do not leave behind a sense of the need for root-and-branch re-structuring of the prevailing *system*, an impression often conveyed by the French *encyclopédistes* at their most urbane. The best-known German secret society, the order of the 'Illuminati', was not revolutionary in the political sense. Indeed, it numbered noblemen and princes among its members.

We are concerned, of course, with the mentality and mood of the middle class. This can hardly be expected to have been static, any more than the social and economic position of the 'Bürger' remained static: in fact, it improved overall as the century progressed. But with due allowance for development, one can isolate constant factors, above all the polar impulses of passivity and aggression, acceptance and rejection. Taking the period as a whole, there can be little doubt that the more passive, more orderly impulse was the stronger.

The passivity of the middle class in the first fifty to sixty years of the eighteenth century has been commented on often enough. 'Leidende Demut' (suffering humility) Biedermann calls it[38] and there were even contemporary observers of a more radical turn of mind who were incensed by the average citizen's willingness to allow himself to be pushed around[39] or his apparently mindless acceptance of the lowly estate to which he was called. C. I. Geiger lashes out against the 'everyday creatures who go mechanically round like cattle in their destined circle and allow themselves to be driven by the same old routine, by habit and self-interest' rather than displaying energy and the power to act and, presumably, to seek change.[40]

Such observers were in the minority. What emerges over and over again as the positive ideal of the 'Aufklärer' in adversity is 'Geduld' (patience) or 'Gelassenheit' (literally, calm: an inner assimilation and overcoming of the hurt through moral resources). The 'sittsame Demuth' of wise Socrates was preferred to the 'Eigensinn' (self-assertive insistence on one's own desires and opinions) of a Diogenes, as Hagedorn formulates it in his 'Satyre von dem unvernünftigen Bewundern'. Clearly, this *could* be the vehicle for, or direct expression of, a cringingly submissive mentality and, no doubt it sometimes was exactly that. But in its truly positive form, that is not what it was felt to mean. Seen positively, it is an affirmation of the overriding principle of Order and is linked with moral worthiness, even greatness. The middle-class painter Wermann in von Gemmingen's *Der deutsche Hausvater* accepts the social difference between himself and the aristocrat, but sturdily asserts that 'as a man', he is the equal of any nobleman. The popularity of this play attests the fact that the image of the middle class which it presents was similar to the 'Bürger's' own view of himself. The earlier 'Moralische Wochenschriften', an even surer guide to the attitudes of the middle class, also combine an endorsement of the prevailing social structure with a readiness to criticize the faults of the aristocracy and a full sense of the worth and dignity of the 'Bürger'.[41] Just like the mature Goethe,[42] Leopold Mozart in his time observed the proprieties of etiquette in relation to his socially 'superior' employer, whereas his illustrious son was more outspoken. But the fact that the father recognized a hard necessity does not necessarily bespeak an inner servility. His letters to his son, in fact, show strong self-control and self-respect. The average 'Aufklärer' would have shared his attitude to the behaviour of the son he strove to guide: 'My son, you are too hasty and hot in all your affairs'.[43]

In serious drama, the passive, sublimely calm hero who is the most common type before 1770, does not entirely disappear during the 'Sturm und Drang', and comes to the fore again in Schiller's Classical plays. There is a particularly interesting case which illustrates very well the ambivalent attitude adopted towards the social order during the period of 'Sturm und Drang' (approximately 1770 to 1783), when Freedom, rather than Order was the watch-word. This is Schiller's *Kabale und Liebe*, which has been taken to constitute a sharp attack on middle-class passivity, as well as on aristocratic depravity.[44] This view is well put by E. M. Wilkinson and L. A. Willoughby in their edition of the play (Oxford, 1945). The issue is the character of the middle-class heroine, Luise. It is argued that her refusal to run away with her aristocratic lover, Ferdinand, and so escape the threat to their love posed by the implacable opposition of Ferdinand's father, arises out of the 'inertia' of the middle class. The reasons she adduces, filial duty and the sanctity of God-given order are seen as indicating her inability to free herself from parentally instilled standards and social taboos, and she is accused of lack of courage. Rather than take action, she prefers to suffer passively. We can agree that the Luise of the early acts of the play is a rather pallid and languishing creature. Yet, curiously enough, the very scene in which she makes the crucial refusal (Act III, scene 4) – and in which Schiller has to make her use a rather weak argument – is also the first one in which she begins to appear at least as forceful a personality as Ferdinand, and from this point on she gains appreciably in dignity and in moral authority and is eventually able to outface even Lady Milford, with a strength born of renunciation. It is an odd way to go about launching an all-out attack on bour-geois passivity! The play seems to wish to express at one and the same time a mood of violence, energy and activity, and an admiration for heroic, apparently passive suffering.

The 'Stürmer und Dränger' were considerably more dynamic and activist in temper than the 'Aufklärer'. Yet this generation produced works – particularly plays – which contained violent and revolutionary *passages*, but were rarely radically revolution-ary as a whole. They, and even more the Göttingen writers ('Göttinger Hain') who stand between 'Aufklärung' and 'Sturm und Drang', combine fighting words about freedom with a streak of often sentimental passivity. J. M. Miller strikes a blood-curdling note in his song of 'The Angel of Death at the bedside of a dying tyrant', but in his very popular novel *Siegwart* positively revels in the martyr-like acceptance of undeserved suffering by his heroes and heroines. J. A. Leisewitz writes strong indictments of despotic tyranny in 'The midnight visit' and 'The pawning', but his *Julius von Tarent* juxtaposes activism (in Guido) and passivity (in Julius) like oil and water. Later, in the so-called 'Weimar Classicism', the pendulum swung back towards calm and acceptance of limitations (e.g. Goethe's 'Grenzen der Menschheit'), even before the disenchantment caused by the violent turn taken by the French Revolution.

Seriousness, sentiment blended with rational control and moderation, and a domestic, inward and essentially unpolitical turn characterized the outlook of the German 'Bürger' in our period. His life-style tended to be quiet. The virtues he cherished were modesty, honesty and industry, and he did not normally dress himself or furnish his house with the flaunting ostentation and luxury of the common run of aristocrat. 'If I come into a finely furnished room,' says Court-Chaplain Schneeberg to Jung-Stilling, 'and find a man who is expensively dressed, I don't bother myself about what class he belongs to, I expect a bottle of wine and sweetmeats. But in a middle-class ('bürger-lich') room, where the man is dressed in middle-class style, I expect no more than a glass of beer and a pipe of tobacco.'[45] With time, a number of aristocratic vices, including the car-dinal sin of pride, did become increasingly prominent in the middle-class mentality. Friedrich Perthes, for example, found, as a bookseller's apprentice in Leipzig, that the pride of the merchants' sons was an impassable barrier to social intercourse with them,[46] and even priests were not immune. Pastor Stoll-bein, in *Heinrich Stillings Jugend*, insists that the peasants take off their hats to him while yet a great way off, objects to eating with the 'mob of peasants' at a christening, and when he suffers a heavy fall replies to Johann Stilling's expression of concern with the 'heroic' words: 'Mind your own business, you lout!'[47] The special vice of the eighteenth century, gambling, also took hold among the 'Bürger'.

On the whole, though, the middle-class virtues were not yet swamped, and they could be said to have been given their apotheosis in the great Classical literature and thought of the last decades of the century. Not that one can simply call this the *direct* expression of middle-class morality or sentiments. That is to be found much less alloyed in the plays of Schröder or Iffland and the art of Daniel Chodowiecki, which present reality, but never with a drastic or complicated approach. They affect rather a 'domestic' mood, with a tinge of simple sentiment and idealization. In Goethe and Schiller, who were not popular favourites, the middle-class reality – which had many virtues but also a certain dullness and spiritual limitation – was transcended, or perhaps one should say, transmuted.

The peasants and artisans. The peasantry is an easily identifiable group: the line between middle and 'lower' is more difficult to draw in the case of the artisans. We are concerned, of course, not to make a distinction by actual occupation – though it often amounts to the same thing – but to determine the educational status and the material and psychological state of the group of people concerned. The people with whom this section sets out to deal are those whose situation may not, technically, have been serfdom, but was not far removed from it economically and socially. As well as poorly-paid and underprivileged craftsmen (such as Jung-Stilling, during his period as a hand in the tailoring trade), this group includes the vast tribe of lackeys and servants. Such people worked long hours for little reward and enjoyed, on the whole, little respect. They were often thought of and treated as 'subjects', neither fully free, nor fully human. For all his acceptance of the brotherhood of man in abstract theory, the educated middle-class observer found it difficult to accept such people as brother men in practice. The playwright and poet C. F. Weisse, for example, who spent a period in a rural area as a tax official, is not impressed by the natural humanity of his companions. He calls them 'half-men'.[48] He feels isolated, deprived of companionship on the spiritual and intellectual level.

It was broadly impossible, of course, for these people to acquire the education and intellectual development necessary to make them fit companions for Weisse. Schools, in the country particularly, were poor in quality for the greater part of the century (though here, as in so many other fields, the efforts of reforming and charitable and public-spirited men brought about considerable improvement later). One needed to be strong in character and fortunate as well as gifted to break out of the charmed circle, as a tiny minority actually managed to do. Jung-Stilling is a case in point. Born with talent and a strong inclination towards the world of learning, he was constantly having to resign himself once more to earning his living – and not much of a living at that – with the tailor's needle until a generous patron gave him more congenial conditions to work in and the time and financial support to learn and read. He recounts, with a typical touch of Pietistic 'Empfindsamkeit', how he felt the change on the occasion of a journey home to see his family:

> . . . he considered how miserable and poor he had been when he set out from home, whereas now he had more than enough money, fine clothes and other necessities. This made him so soft at heart and so grateful to God that he could not forbear from weeping . . . he had now grown up tall and slim, and had on a handsome dark-blue suit of clothes, and fine white linen . . . and now he looked gay and blooming, because things were going well for him.[49]

The sense of release from an almost intolerable pressure is clearly discernible.

How much talent remained mute and inglorious there is no means of knowing, but one assumes that there was a great deal. Friedrich Perthes, as a bookseller's apprentice in Leipzig, had to work twelve hours a day and was not paid enough to be able to benefit from the 'good society' it had been hoped he would find in that sophisticated city. He recounts how, had it not been for a good upbringing and the moral support of one acquaintance, he might easily have lost the desire for higher things and slipped into the 'dissipated' way of life of his fellow apprentices.[50] For the vast majority of this social group, and particularly for the peasantry, the horizon of life was bounded by the struggle for existence.

The picture of the common people that we see in the literature of eighteenth-century Germany is rarely a portrait of the reality. It is usually conditioned by some convention such as the Enlightenment ideal of natural moderation or the 'Sturm und Drang' vision of simple, unspoiled 'natural' humanity. The 'Bauernbursche' in Goethe's *Werther* is an example of the latter, and it is instructive to note how little or no suggestion of crudeness is allowed to intrude. When a relatively realistic approach to country life appears, as when Wieland paints a portrait of the country bumpkin Pervonte, the gap which the educated middle-class writer feels between himself and the common run of the populace becomes clear. Wieland's ideal is the Pervonte of the ending, cleaned and tidied up, and endowed (from a magical source) with civilized rational good sense.

The injustices and hardships suffered by the common people could offend against the rationalist's sense of right and wrong and touch the sentimental heart, and no doubt many a 'Bürger' felt rather proud of his superiority to the nobleman in that he recognized, as Miller puts it in *Siegwart* (Vol. 2, p. 256), that peasants were 'also human beings'. But there were few who were prepared to carry ideas of the brotherhood of man to the stage of raising one such to their own level, as did Lichtenberg in his marriage. There was sympathy for the 'Volk', but not for the 'Haufen', the masses. The picture painted by Pöllnitz of the Bohemian peasants in the early years of the eighteenth century is probably extreme (their lot, like that of Hungarian peasants, was particularly hard) but is probably closer to reality than the Wahlheim idyll of *Werther*:

> ... miserable to the last degree ... often not a bit of bread to eat ...
> always trembling and humble (because of their constant subjection)
> ... The severity with which these people are ruled is really terrible,
> but 'tis as true on the other hand that gentle usage has no effect on
> 'em ... blows are the only way to make them good for anything.[51]

One can imagine the brutalizing effect of only a mild version of this.

Thought of in terms of a real political and social force, the so-called lower classes could only be conceived of as a threatening volcano. We have already mentioned the antipathy to democracy which characterizes the age. Portraits of the 'people' in political contexts are almost always negative or at least disrespectful: the gullible and mercurial mass so easily swayed by a demagogue in Goethe's *Egmont*, for example, or the 'women who became hyenas' in Schiller's picture of the French Revolution in *Das Lied von der Glocke*. Even in the *Damokles* of F. M. Klinger, a writer whose political reflections show a decidedly radical trend, the people, for whose freedom the hero fights and dies, are but a frail and fickle support. One is aware of a certain distrust of the people such as existed elsewhere too, for example in England. George Rudé quotes a letter written to the *Gloucester Journal* in 1709: 'Are my apprehensions of tyranny of government equal to those I have from the licentiousness of the people?[52] Even if corresponding eighteenth-century German observers do not, on the whole, voice apprehensions as deep as these, that does not mean that their attitude to the common people was more 'democratic'. It simply reflects the fact that the situation on the political and social front in Germany was much quieter than was the case elsewhere.

3

Society and the Writer

We shall be trying, in Part Two of this book, to follow the themes and preoccupations which have emerged from the consideration of society into the field of literature, considered in its own context. The present chapter will attempt to throw some light into the border area between society and literature proper. We are concerned here with writers purely *as* writers; their feelings and general psychological state as they go about the business of creating literature. The first step, clearly, must be to examine the material and spiritual conditions of authorship.

Neither brilliant social standing nor great financial reward could be expected in our period from even a successful activity in the field of serious literature. It was an even more risky step to devote one's life to the theatre, and while music, particularly through opera and related entertainments, had the *entrée* in aristocratic circles, it was not so very easy to make one's living by it: the warning example of Mozart is always before our eyes.

There was, as might be expected in a body politic which had so many heads, no effective law of copyright in the German lands. English authors were much better protected.[1] In Germany, piracy was rife. The battle against it went on from about the mid-eighteenth century until well into the nineteenth. The most that even Goethe could achieve was a number of grants of 'privilege' to his works in specific lands. That this was inadequate protection in the fragmented Germany of the eighteenth century is immediately apparent. Combined with the lack of a real public on English lines, this meant that Sir Walter Scott, for example, made almost half as much on his novels alone in a single year as Goethe received from his main publisher, Cotta, in the whole of his literary career. Scott 'earned more from literature in three years than Goethe in all his long life'.[2] Serious writing was rarely a sufficient source of income for the support of a wife and family.

In general, a patron (such as Klopstock had in the King of Denmark) or an official position or other regular job was essential to a writer's financial security, and even then did not always guarantee a life free from the basic worries. What was certainly not available, except to the very fortunate, was the ability to be a 'free' writer in the full sense of the word: a man, that is, who is not only a writer first and foremost but is free also from the depressive psychological effects of poverty, dependence or some other external pressure. Certainly, the opportunity to cultivate oneself and one's art at leisure, such as Goethe says was given him by Duke Karl August of Weimar,[3] was granted to few indeed, and even to be a favoured poet at court was no bed of roses, as *Torquato Tasso* shows. The majority of writers could echo the words of the 'Magister' in Nicolai's *Sebaldus Nothanker* (Vol. 1, 1773):

Where is the German land in which the German scholar can live as a scholar? Where is it possible, without particularly favourable circumstances, to find the leisure which a writer needs if he is to excel in his art? The best, the most desirable fate we can expect is some official position ['Amt'], in the expectation of which we must starve if we have no patrimony to put into acquiring it and in which, when we have achieved it, we forget scholarship because of the great mass of official work.[4]

A classic example of the destructive potentialities of this situation is that of G. A. Bürger, a poet of real ability who, apart from a few ballads, never really managed to do his talent justice. He had had to use up his patrimony to acquire the post of 'Amtmann' (legal official on a landowner's estate) in Hanover, and had then found that his salary was not sufficient to support him and his family unless he was unduly grasping in the matter of fees. He had to write, therefore, to supplement his salary, but found himself in a vicious circle where the heavy burden of official work made it impossible to devote enough time and care to his writing.[5] When, as a Professor at Göttingen, he later fell ill, his situation was even worse. He was not paid his salary because he could not teach, and the combination of a more pressing need to write with the psychological impossibility of doing so is graphically described in his letter to the Classics Professor Heyne of 16–17 March, 1794. Against this background, it is easier to understand the elements of rhetorical hysteria and self-pity which spoil much of his work. It is to the credit of others that the element of strain in their writing is less dominant than in Bürger, though fair also to say that few suffered from an equal burden of financial and personal problems.

Nor was literary eminence necessarily a gateway to high position or social prestige. At the height of his Olympian grandeur, when foreigners were making pilgrimages to Weimar for his sake, Goethe's decision as Director of the Court Theatre was overruled in favour of the Duke's mistress in the affair of the 'chien d'Aubry'.[6] The author of the well-known idyll *Luise*, and translator of Homer, J. H. Voss, was asked to walk beside the valet in a prince's funeral procession,[7] just as Mozart had to dine at the same table as the Archbishop of Salzburg's valets. 'Many a man of quality' writes the Hesse-Darmstadt official J. H. Merck 'would blush if it became public knowledge that he had offered hospitality to this or that man of letters.'[8]

Only a small minority of German writers and thinkers were economically and socially secure by virtue of their parentage. Many were the sons of Protestant clergymen, not, on the whole, a prestigious or well-off class. G. A. Bürger's father, for example, had an income of only 160 Thalers. In dealing with the 'great' and powerful, they were rarely able to dispense with a certain obsequiousness of manner. And if one wanted to get on, an 'insinuantes Wesen', as Karl Philipp Moritz calls it,[9] was a great advantage. 'Flattery is slavery for German souls' says J. M. Miller in his poem 'Abschied' (1773), but there is no doubt that it was part of the atmosphere of eighteenth-century social life, and that writers indulged in it as well as others. The crucial point is whether they were slaves at heart. It is true that Herder writes in 1779:

It is not the best sign of the relation in which the sciences and government stand towards one another that the former are such objects of contempt for the latter and can hardly contain themselves for sheer veneration if a Maecenas condescends actually to write a single sheet or a book. Such a slavish attitude is unheard of in other countries.[10]

Yet such a passage is as much a testimony to inner independence as it is to servility. Schiller who, as against Herder, explicitly rejected the French Revolution, was nevertheless not thrown into an ecstasy of 'Devotion' by the mere title of Prince. On a letter by a certain Prince August (of Gotha?) which Goethe had sent him to read, he comments, in his letter of 29 November 1795: 'It has a lot of good humour in it, for a prince, particularly.' He wonders whether the Prince may not be able to make it possible for him to print in *Die Horen* a translation of Diderot's *La religieuse* – 'when a Prince is involved, the first thing that always occurs to me is whether he can be useful in any way.'

Nor is the self-control which had to be exerted in these relationships necessarily a negative or morally debilitating quality. The maintenance of respect carries with it, for the Classicists at least, important social and moral virtues which do not kill, but rather enhance inner freedom. Goethe's rejection of 'Apostles of freedom' in the *Venetian Epigrams* (No. 51) is made on the basis of their self-indulgent egotism. 'If you wish to free many, dare to serve many' he says, in an echo of the penultimate stanza of 'Ilmenau', where he counsels free acceptance of limitations on his personal freedom to the Duke.

Whether or not it was a product, ultimately, of social conditions, there can be no doubt that there was a strong positive ethos of self-control through most of our period. It would not have been thought admirable to make some equivalent of a rude gesture to a magnate, however intrinsically unworthy he was of respect. The imperfections of these 'gods of this world' were often noted, and there is much serious criticism of 'Hofschranzen' and the like. But to deny respect to the aristocrat in his representative capacity, his 'Stand', would seem to have been felt as a direct attack on the social order, which the middle class had no wish to make. J. E. Schlegel has an interesting passage in his *Abhandlung, dass die Nachahmung der Sache, der man nachahmet, zuweilen unähnlich werden müsse* (1745). He illustrates his argument by the fact that the reality of the life of heroes and of high society is often less perfect than the common concept of them leads us to expect, but that the artist's job is to imitate the concept, not the reality. 'It is right,' he says, 'that we should be prevented by respect from seeing the human being in the gods of this world. Duty itself approves of our false concepts of our rulers, because they further our obedience, and the preconceived ideas that we have of the great ones of the world are happy for us, because we would account ourselves less happy, if we thought of those who are above us as our equals.'[11] One recalls that even the recalcitrant Miller in *Kabale und Liebe*, when he is trying to eject the President, expresses a willingness to accord him full respect when he meets him in his capacity *as* President. To assume that absence of rebellion means mere servility is too facile. The real test is the spirit in which these men wrote, the degree of conviction they could give to themes like freedom, moral dignity and so on, and this evidence certainly does not condemn them.

Another, and most important respect in which the German writer was at a disadvantage by comparison with his French or English compeers was that of his public. Not only was this not large enough to set him free from dependence on a patron or other source of income, there was none of that interchange and interaction between writer and public which can be so useful. Writers lacked the sense of communicating with a potentially critical and potentially appreciative audience. One has an impression of German authors producing their works on a number of little islands in the midst of a vast, indifferent ocean. Complaints about the German reading public are frequent. Breitinger bemoans its low aesthetic level in the early 1740s,[12] and in spite of all that had occurred in the interim the Classicists were still doing so in the 'nineties. Herder, in the *Humanitäts-briefe*, states that German literature has never had a proper public: 'the greater part of the public does not know them (the best writers) and does not give them a place in its heart'.[13] Goethe speaks with some affection, in his letter to the composer J. F. Reichardt of 3 March 1790, of the honest, solid qualities of the Germans, but is even more forthright about their aesthetic limitations. 'Our public,' he says, 'has no idea of what art is.'

According to Schubart,[14] the great mass of German readers restricted themselves to 'Hauspostille' (a devotional book for home reading), hymn-book and calendar. Those who aimed higher might well stop at popular novels or plays which combined entertainment with routine moralizing at the level of the average man. The only writer of our period who had both popular appeal and high spiritual aspirations is Jean Paul Richter, and it was in all probability his great weakness, his streak of sentimentality, which worked the trick, just as a sentimental reading of the book rather than a deep appreciation of its literary merits had given Goethe his one great popular success with *Die Leiden des jungen Werthers*. Even during the 'Sturm und Drang', German literature in the eighteenth century was literature of the intelligentsia for the intelligentsia.

The lack of a metropolis, of a cultural centre where the cream ('Ausbund') of the nation could come together and interact, as Bodmer had put it in the preface to his *Critische Abhandlung von dem Wunderbaren* (1740) and which is still bitterly lamented by Herder in the 'nineties,[15] only served to aggravate this feeling of isolation. The sense of a link with the 'real' life of the nation could not be present with the same strength as in other lands.

This is mirrored in the literature of the time. The tendency to seek a setting in far-off times and countries – ancient Rome, Jerusalem (*Nathan der Weise*), Greece, Italy, Spain, the Netherlands, sixteenth-century Germany – is symptomatic. Even a novel like Goethe's *Wilhelm Meisters Lehrjahre*, in which the hero is firmly involved in a contemporary German setting, does not impress as truly realistic. How many of the descriptions give a sense of solidity, how many of the characters have the kind of tangible presence which is so abundant in Fielding? Philine is such a character, but there is no other of any prominence and Philine has at best a subsidiary status.

Goethe accepted the name of 'Realist' and never ceased to preach the necessity of maintaining contact with reality, but could not live by realism alone. *Faust* also shows a response to the everyday in scenes like 'Vor dem Tor' and in the Gretchen episode, but it shows even more powerfully the pull towards the transcendental. The novel *Die Wahlverwandtschaften*, which has a 'real' German setting, is a very unrealistic masterpiece. And the importance which Goethe's study of nature, his science, had for him is perhaps more than anything to be explained by the way in which it reconciles sensuous actuality and abstract truth. It is the point of contact between the empirical and the transcendental as appears, for example, in his concept of the 'Urphänomen', which combines the three main ways of perceiving truth: ideal, real, and 'symbolic'. It was through his scientific work that Goethe found himself, for the first time, experiencing a fellow-feeling with Kant, which he expressed in the essay *Einwirkung der neueren Philosophie*.

The Social and Political Background

It was the 'Aufklärung' which brought German literature closest of all in the eighteenth century to putting down deep roots in this world. It directed men's eyes away from 'unnatural' ideals to the common run of life, and in its comedy in particular it did achieve some kind of reflection of social reality. But however hostile the 'Aufklärer' are to illusions and 'romantic' extravagances, a schematic, abstract quality adheres to their portraits of the world around them. Their reality is true to 'nature' as they conceived it, but, as we shall see, that concept was severely limited. Their characters tend to lack solid flesh, their settings to be colourless and neutral. There were few practical realists among them: Lichtenberg, perhaps, or C. F. Nicolai, the 'common empiricist' who was such an inveterate critic, and such a butt of the Classicists.[16]

Lichtenberg and Nicolai were among those who rejected Goethe's *Werther* on its first appearance, the latter going so far as to parody it in a novel, *Die Freuden des jungen Werthers*. Goethe's novel is a drastic demonstration of the fact that, to some extent at least, the mind and heart can be independent of external reality. *Werther* was no doubt not the first work to show this path to freedom – poets, above all Klopstock, had already discovered and made use of it, the idylls of Gessner and the whole pastoral convention of the 'Aufklärung' and Rococo pointed in this direction, and novels of ideas and personal 'Bildung' like Wieland's *Agathon* (1767) showed a broadly similar tendency. *Werther* had a special force and authority, and probably gave a decisive impulse. At any rate, the culture of mind and heart was dominant from this point up to the end of the century, and even more so in the Romantic Movement which followed. Politics and social reality were very much secondary: it was recognized, of course, that each man was involved in them to some extent, but they were not of absorbing interest in themselves.

Ordinary reality was more often than not thought unworthy of the central place in literature. It was left to some Romantics to suggest that one could dispense with it altogether, but the urge towards transcendence is implicit in the 'Aufklärer's' generalized concept of 'Nature' and in the Titanic and infinite longings of the 'Sturm und Drang' and is consciously formulated by the 'Classical' Schiller: 'The poet and artist must have two attributes, he must rise above mere reality ('das Wirkliche') and remain within the realm of the sensuous' (letter to Goethe, 14 September 1797).

In what kind of relation, therefore, does this literature stand to contemporary social reality? The latter clearly could not constitute for the majority of serious writers an adequate medium for the expression of their highest thoughts and preoccupations. They tended to cut themselves off from it in practical life and to use it as a platform from which they could soar to true 'Humanity', or to metaphysical and religious truths. Nowhere else was the interest in 'pure reason' so strong, nowhere else did men take such a deep interest in the abstract principles of aesthetics.

A dearth of practical politics was accompanied by an abundance of political theorizing; no less a thinker than Kant rejects the view of the 'Praktiker' on the grounds that while they know a great deal about individual men, they know little about Man ('den Menschen').[17] We are talking, of course, of that German Idealism whose culmination, in Hegel's theory of history and the state, is well-known; the 'Classical German Philosophy' whose demise is proclaimed by Engels but which might even be argued to have left its mark on Marxism. Freedom, justice, a happy and harmonious life, these were constant preoccupations of 'Aufklärer', 'Stürmer und Dränger' and 'Classics', but the discussion always has a tendency to move into the theoretical. The real events and issues do not dominate in novels and dramas which deal with such situations.

Even such a consistent exposer of illusion as the 'Aufklärer' Johann Carl Wezel, in his 'black' novel *Belphegor* (1776), in which the idealistic hero is subjected to such a concentrated course of disillusionment that he becomes a misanthrope, returns constantly to the search for a metaphysical formula. This is in marked contrast to the hatred of metaphysics which informs *Candide*, the model for Wezel's work. The novel is dominated by reflection and discussion; the factual, narrative and descriptive parts are flat and thin to a degree, the characters devoid of independent life, the humour rudimentary. Intensity of interest, and colour and animation in the prose are only achieved when the general 'meaning' of it all is under discussion. To achieve some degree of freedom and happiness, the three main characters have, as the 'raisonneur' Fromal puts it, to 'separate ourselves from our race'[18] and to live with their slaves (whom they never call by that name) in an ancient, idyllic relationship which is 'the least in esteem and the greatest in happiness, the peaceful way of life of the patriarchs, of the poetic land of Arcadia and of the countryman in the zones where freedom reigns'.[19]

This breathes the spirit of escape-literature. The popularity of the theme of withdrawal from the 'great world' or simply the practical social world, in order to cultivate one's inner self and one's own happiness, cannot be overlooked by the most superficial observer of eighteenth-century literature. The passage in Lessing's *Minna von Barnhelm* in which Tellheim proposes to Minna that they retire to some Arcadian country spot, the patriarchal ideal of the 'Sturm und Drang' – e.g. *Werther* and *Götz* – and many other examples, come easily to mind.

The real life which surrounds these writers can hardly be called inspiring. They belong to a group which is becoming progressively better educated and more aware of itself, but which is not yet fully independent, socially or economically. Their possible field of practical activity, as Georg Forster put it,[20] is 'narrow', particularly with the fragmentation of Germany into abnormally small states. Practical reality offers little in the way of great events or issues in which they can involve themselves. Small wonder, then, that observers say that 'conditions in the little states had turned men in upon themselves'[21] and talk directly of 'escapism',[22] especially when Schiller, for example, writes such things as this:

> In des Herzens heilig stille Räume
> Musst du fliehen aus des Lebens Drang
> Freiheit ist nur in dem Reich der Träume
> Und das Schöne lebt nur im Gesang.[23]

That external conditions gave an impetus to the Germans to seek fulfilment elsewhere than in reality is not doubted. What seems uncertain is whether one can call this the sole, or even the primary cause of this tendency. Other eighteenth-century literatures do not share this anti-realism, even though conditions are not so very much better outside Germany. There is no reason to suppose that low life in Germany was much more intrinsically dull than in England nor that the German writers, had they wished to, might not have acquired knowledge of it. But there is nothing to compare with Smollett, Defoe or even the description of the brothel in Richardson's *Clarissa*, a subject which the author doubtless does not describe for its own sake but which he nevertheless makes very real. There is nothing in contemporary German art to correspond to Hogarth or Chardin, though subjects would undoubtedly have been available to those who sought them. The most prominent Germans in the history of eighteenth-century art-history and painting are Winckelmann and Mengs, hardly men of a realistic turn of mind.

One cannot explain this phenomenon away with a simple reference to special conditions: and there is no certainty that the Germans would have found what they sought in a unified state which had progressed further, socially and economically, than the rather exaggeratedly retarded condition described by Lukács.[24] Schiller, in the poem 'Shakespeares Schatten', rejects the protests of those who object to his desertion of the bourgeois milieu in favour of the heroic. The world of 'parsons, commercial counsellors, ensigns, secretaries or majors of hussars' cannot contain what he wants to express and he refuses to join the Schröders and Ifflands in imitating 'eure Natur, die Erbärmliche'.[25] But another mentality *is* able to derive aesthetically satisfying literature from such a milieu: the novels of Jane Austen deal with nothing for which an equivalent could not have been found in Germany. Her world is hardly noble or pretty – witness her rogues' gallery of snobs and vulgarians. Yet how much more 'real' are her characters and settings than those of, for example, Goethe's *Die Wahlverwandtschaften*, a novel of a stature at least equal to that of *Mansfield Park* and set in a similar milieu.

It would be wrong to leave the impression that the Germans were unaware of, or indifferent to the unsatisfactory nature of life in their country, or that their attitude towards it was that of the ostrich. If their withdrawal was an escape, it was conceived as an escape to reality, not from it. There *was* a tendency to a kind of make-believe emotional life, which often manifested itself in a vague, self-induced melancholic state. But, with few exceptions, the major writers and thinkers of the eighteenth century recognized this danger and were able to overcome it. It is only a very minor element, for example, in the work of Klopstock and was an even less powerful force in the other major 'Aufklärer'. Goethe undoubtedly felt the pull in this direction at the time of writing *Werther*. But, as we shall see later, that very work contains and overcomes it, and *Tasso* describes it with an objective and critical understanding. In the section dealing with Plessing in the *Campagne in Frankreich*, Goethe expresses a clear rejection of it, together with the conviction that the cure lies in turning to 'nature' and to practical life.[26] Wilhelm von Humboldt was certainly an idealist to a large extent, but as Kessel shows, he consistently respected reality, refused to accept speculation which was detached from observation,[27] and felt that ideas must be 'tied to reality'.[28] Schiller writes a horrific description of the fate of the 'Phantast', the false idealist who completely abandons the world of sensuous reality, at the end of *Über naive und sentimentalische Dichtung*.[29] He welcomes the opportunity of acquainting himself with low life through Rétif de la Bretonne's *Cœur humain dévoilé* (letter to Goethe of 2 January 1798) and, with all his love of the ideal of humanity, is aware of man's material needs. In a distich headed 'Dignity of Man', he writes: 'No more of that, I beg you. Give him something to eat and somewhere to live. Once his nakedness is covered, the dignity will come of itself.'[30] The idealistic withdrawal was not always mere flight. Useful, constructive and helpful practical activity '(Tätigkeit') is the great moral ideal of the Classicists.

At the same time, even a practical reformer like Humboldt, in his essay on Goethe's *Hermann und Dorothea*, sees a necessity for the imagination to idealize reality. Man, he says, seeks to establish his control over the 'incidental' world around him: 'thereby alone does he confirm the fact that he belongs to a better land than that of actuality, namely the land of ideas.'[31] Schiller speaks of emancipating art from 'servile imitation of nature' (to Goethe, 29 December 1797). At no time in the eighteenth century is reality rejected as subject-matter in literary theory or practice, but it rarely if ever seems sufficient in itself. It did not contain truth wholly, but man would be hopelessly lost if he attempted to divorce himself from it. It could not satisfy the spirit, but the spirit could not exist apart from it.

So we have an oscillation between two poles in our period, and an attempt in the Classical phase to achieve a synthesis in this, as in other fields. Schiller, in his treatise *On Naive and Sentimental Poetry*, ends with an examination of the realistic and idealistic attitudes and an attempt to reconcile them, which is not strictly necessary in the context of the essay. His underlying preoccupation – the relationship between himself and Goethe – breaks through. The problem of reality is one which occurs often in his correspondence with Goethe, and it is instructive to note how both are concerned to wed reality to higher significance. Schiller sees it as his problem to avoid loss of contact with the real, which is why he is ready to welcome Rétif's book 'in spite of all the repellent, flat ("platt", i.e. falling below "true human nature", not "poetic,") and disgusting elements in it'. He needs dramatic themes which contain both the real and the ideal, and feels that themes from history are safer, because 'it is one thing to idealize the realistic and quite another to realize the ideal' (to Goethe, 5 January 1798).

As for Goethe's view of reality, Schiller must have been delighted to read, in a letter from Frankfurt of 16 August 1797, of 'some kind of sentimental element' which his friend had noted in the effect certain objects had on him. Goethe calls these objects 'symbolic'. These things are individual cases which 'stand as representatives of many others and have a certain quality of totality in them'. Goethe, who is on his way to Switzerland, promises himself 'a fine harvest' from cultivating this mode of observation of things which are not poetic in themselves and noticing 'not so much what is remarkable as what is significant ("bedeutend") about them'. Schiller explains this phenomenon by saying that when an object is 'empty' of sustenance for the spirit, the thinking mind has to approach it from the 'symbolic' side and so make from it 'a language for Humanity' (to Goethe, 7 September 1797). The observer's 'Gemüt' (mental and spiritual sensitivity) is the crucial factor, not the object. Nothing, apart from the experience of the poetic itself, so purifies the spirit of what is empty and common ('gemein', another word for mere reality) as this way of looking at things. This theoretical use of the word 'symbolic' is not necessarily quite the same as the use modern criticism would make of the word, but the two are related and it is not too surprising that, especially in such an integrated mentality as Goethe's, techniques at least very close to true symbolism emerge: in much of the later poetry, for example, or *Die Wahlverwandtschaften*, the *Novelle*, or the second part of *Faust*. In the more intellectualistic mentality of Schiller, the search for the symbolic – in poetry at least – leads to something more contrived and synthetic (e.g. *Das Lied von der Glocke*). Hölderlin is closer to Goethe in this respect, but his imagery is more often clouded by irrational and subjective forces than Goethe would have liked. He is hardly a Romantic, but he shows a certain trend in that general direction.

The German temperament and conditions favoured what, to an outside observer, might appear to be a 'Romantic' mentality, one which tended to turn from objective reality to the ideal, and inner worlds. Even the 'Aufklärung' is relatively tentative in its realism. What marks the eighteenth century off, in the German context, from Romanticism proper is the containment of this trend. A balance, some kind of hold on objective reality is maintained, or at least intended. When there is confusion or flux, it is because this balance has failed under strain. And there is no doubt that there were strains on eighteenth-century German writers, which in some produced the quality which we shall see Schiller calls 'überspannt'. The German 'Innerlichkeit' and idealism were not produced by the conditions alone, but they were fed by them and the absence of a lively and colourful public life made it all the more difficult to achieve the balance to which we have referred. Great things were done by many, but perhaps only Goethe escaped the effect of strain entirely. And it cannot be an accident that Goethe was one of the few who did not have to worry about money.

Bürger and Schiller give us two contrasting, but related views of this situation. In his submission to the Hanover 'Landesregierung', to which reference has been made, Bürger writes 'Oh, how often one sees a man limping and criticizes him or mocks him without considering where the shoe may be pinching and whether it is his fault.' (The submission, dated 1784, is a general reply to complaints made about him and not restricted to the quality of his literary work, though this is an important factor, which Bürger himself brings to the fore.) In March 1789 he writes to F. W. L. Meyer of the 'pure impossibility' of being noble in one's sentiments without money in one's purse.

Schiller, the man who castigated Bürger so severely for his lack of self-discipline, himself had experience of the cramping effects of poverty and later, when his material fortunes had improved, of crippling physical disease which often made writing difficult or impossible. He composed *Wallenstein*, for example, against great odds, which made the serene grandeur of the finished work all the more impressive. The point made by Bürger is not alien to his mind. Writing to Goethe (on 17 August 1797) apropos of a number of other authors in whom he sees failings similar to those he discerns in Bürger, he says:

I would like to know whether these Schmids,[32] Richters[33] and Hölderlins would have remained so subjectivistic, so unnaturally strained ['überspannt'], so one-sided under any circumstances; whether the fault lies in something basic ['primitiv'] or whether the lack of aesthetic sustenance and influence from without, combined with the obstacles provided by the empirical world in which they live have had this unfortunate effect, given their idealistic tendency. I am very much inclined to believe that the latter is the case and even though a man of happy natural constitution can win through in spite of all, it nevertheless seems to me that many a useful talent goes to waste in this way.

Schiller, then, mentions two environmental factors: possible lack of aesthetic stimulus and guidance – the sort of thing which he and Goethe enjoyed in the 'nineties, which Goethe had had with Herder in Strassburg and perhaps Lessing with Mendelssohn and Nicolai in Berlin, but which was otherwise rare – and the obstacles of material circumstances. He posits a connection with psychological factors: undue subjectivity, lack of the broad, balanced view and a certain strain, a tendency to the unnatural and to exaggeration, to taking an idea beyond the bounds of sense and truth, all of which can be contained in the concept 'überspannt'. It is the danger which he recognizes for himself in *Über naive und sentimentalische Dichtung* when he talks of the possible failings of the 'sentimental' poet and idealist. The poet he says, must aim at 'the absolute, but only within the limits of the human'.[34] If he strays beyond the limits of 'the concept of human nature', he falls into 'Schwärmen', the endemic failing of 'Überspannung', which corresponds to the 'Phantasterei' of the false idealist. This latter leads, as he puts it in a drastic passage at the end of the treatise, to complete loss of character,[35] to the fall into a bottomless pit.

One feels that Schiller had looked into this pit. As a poor young writer, a refugee from his homeland with no secure base, he had indeed managed to produce plays which, if not by any means perfect, were aesthetically meritorious and were certainly full of sincere and convincing nobility. But no one could claim that these plays were free from elements of 'Überspannung'. *Don Carlos* included, they are full of excessively hyperbolic rhetoric, intense but strained emotion, and characters just within the bounds of verisimilitude. Not one of them is a satisfactory dramatic unity on the realistic level. Without a measure of good fortune – the Danish pension which enabled him to stand back and breathe freely for a while and devote himself to the study of philosophy, and the unique opportunity of constant interchange of opinions and experience with Goethe – it is debatable whether he would have achieved as satisfactory a balance as he in fact did. The tendency was in his basic natural constitution – one thinks of the overstrained emotionalism which struck his schoolmates in Stuttgart – and the fact that the tendency to over-idealize was not entirely repressed in the later Schiller, in spite of the insights of the 'nineties. With the experience gained from *Wallenstein* fresh in his mind, he resolved to avoid freely invented subjects because they might be his 'Klippe' but significantly, after his second masterpiece, *Maria Stuart*, which had built solidly on historical foundations, he moved to free invention (*Die Braut von Messina*) and wholescale tampering with history (*Die Jungfrau von Orleans*, in its weaker parts possibly the most 'überspannt' of his classical productions).

Another most instructive author from this point of view is Jean Paul, whose early years of struggle against poverty, like his major works, belong to our period. In most of these, the problem of the relation of ideal to reality is central and the sense of strain is very strong. A typical work is *Schulmeisterlein Wuz* (1796), a 'kind of idyll', in which reality and fancy, idyllic charm and humour and intense melancholy are in continual collision. Jean Paul's most nearly objective distillation of his experience of poverty and small-town life comes in *Siebenkäs* (1796–7). The hero is cheated out of an inheritance and thereby condemned to a life of pinching and scraping. A man of intellectual capacity and spiritual awareness, he is harnessed to a wife of good heart but narrow mental and spiritual horizons. Eventually, by feigning death, he escapes from this situation, but before then, the author shows him combating grey reality with his only weapon, an outlook compounded of imagination and rather capricious humour. Total depression is avoided by Siebenkäs's ability to 'play with the world around him and clothe it in webs woven within himself',[36] but the whole is ballasted with a very real melancholy; and even when the lawyer's skill with a gun has earned him a little money at the shooting contest, we know that this will be but a brief respite. 'But how long, you joyful soul, will this forced blossom remain hanging on your life?' Jean Paul asks, in a characteristically tortuous metaphor.[37] At times, he allows his hero a holiday from the dreary world of everyday, but even in passages of hope there is a tendency to strained rhetoric and to a certain sagging in the rhythm. Such a passage occurs on pp. 60–61:

Und als eine zuckende Puppe neben ihm noch in der halben eingerunzelten Raupenhülse hing und ihren Blütenkelchen entgegenschlief – und als das Seelenauge der Phantasie von dem Grummethaufen in die Abendpracht des Heumonats hinüberblickte – und als jeder vielfarbige Baum gleichsam zum zweiten Male blühte – und als die bunten Gipfel wie vergrösserte Tulpen einen Regenbogen auf den Duft des Herbstes zogen: – so jagten nun nur frühere Mailüfte dem flatternden Laube nach und wehten unsern Freund mit bebenden Wogen an und stiegen mit ihm auf und hielten ihn empor über den Herbst und über die Berge, und er konnte über die Berge und Länder wegschauen und siehe, er sah alle Frühlinge seines Lebens, die für ihn noch in Knospen lagen, wie Gärten neben einander stehen und in jedem Frühling stand sein Freund![38]

This passage attempts to soar clear of sordid reality: the impression it makes, however, is one of strenuous, but unavailing effort. It talks bravely of spring, but has not purged away the atmosphere of autumn; and its long sequence of 'und als' clauses, each of which seems almost to droop with exhaustion as the intonation falls at the end, have an effect which is more elegiac than exciting.

Universal longings and imaginings in a severely restricted milieu (poverty in a small town), this was Jean Paul's own early experience and he never entirely broke free from it. In a way, if one does not drive the parallel too hard, this could be taken as epitomizing the whole German scene and its dichotomy between transcendental ambitions and restricted reality. It is a situation which has its literary, as well as social dangers: strain, exaggeration, empty rhetoric, faults to which not all German writers have fallen victim, but which tinge a great many, including some of the more important. These dangers can be avoided, as they were, for example, by the engaging and unassuming Matthias Claudius, but only at the price of a severe limitation of literary and philosophical aims. Or they can be met and overcome, and then an effect can be obtained which is both real and transcendental. Such moments are rare in the period of 'Aufklärung' which, by and large preferred limitation and safety, but there are some in German literature after 1770, as for instance the climax of the 'Classical Walpurgisnacht' in *Faust*, Part Two, which can stand comparison with the sublimest in Beethoven.

Part 2

Order

Part 2

Order

4

The 'Aufklärung' as an Age of Order

If ever a generation created God in its own image, it was that of the 'Aufklärer'. Order was an integral part of their very being, and they saw it throughout the universe. The music of the spheres was a music of clarity and proportion, like some of Haydn's music, perhaps. And so, in his rendering of the creation-story of *Genesis*,[1] J. P. Uz shows God as the all-wise, benevolent planner, certainly a figure of some greatness, who spreads his hand over the abyss and 'draws the ends of the unborn world', but without any of the mystery inherent in the conceptions of a Böhme or Blake. The creation takes place in an orderly manner, culminating in the appearance of man, 'the witness of thy greatness ... so that there should exist a being capable of rational enjoyment of what thy grace has produced.'[2]

The spirit of the 'Aufklärung' is one of confidence and it is this which chiefly distinguishes it from the Baroque. Admittedly, the Enlightenment owed much to seventeenth-century thinkers in Germany, as elsewhere. But in so far as these men – Thomasius, Leibniz and the others – already possessed the faith in man, and hence in reason, which characterizes the 'Aufklärung', they were no longer truly men of the Baroque. That part of Leibniz's thought which it could assimilate became gospel for the 'Aufklärung': the *Théodicée*, particularly, became a textbook for a whole tribe of philosophical poets.

This confidence extends to the whole universe, physical and moral. Man is created in order that he may be happy, in order to be happy he needs only to be virtuous and to be virtuous, he needs only to employ his reason correctly. Nature is inherently rational and good. 'Vice', says Gottsched, 'is a capacity for acting contrary to the law of nature.' Evil actions arise out of false judgement.[3] Pleasure (as long as it is indulged in with the

63

moderation which nature demands) is therefore a lawful and valid pursuit and the doctrine of original sin becomes, in effect, a dead letter.[4] Holiness was now measurable by an essentially human yardstick. It was a target one could see, and feel one had hit without divine assistance. God might be necessary in philosophy, but many felt that he was less so in practical life.

This irreligious trend was rather less strong in Germany than elsewhere in the eighteenth century. The process known as 'secularization'[5] had a strong impact on German cultural life, certainly, but much genuine religious feeling remained, even in the 'Aufklärung', in people like Gellert, Claudius and Klopstock, not to speak of Pietism, of Hamann and the 'Sturm und Drang', and of the important part played by religious feeling in the whole emotional and intellectual life of Goethe.

The question of beauty is the one bedevilled most of all by the problem of individual taste, and anyone wishing to bring law and order into this wild land is urgently in need of an objective standard and a strong controlling authority. The 'Aufklärer' thought he had found his standard in the concept 'nature'. Nature, says Sulzer, 'is the artist's guide and teacher'. It is the basis of any idea of generally valid rules, which were of vital consequence to the 'Aufklärung'. Nature conceived as an agency or cause, Sulzer states, is 'nothing else than the Highest Wisdom itself. . . . Therefore, the theory of art cannot be anything other than the system of rules which can be deduced, by exact observation, from the processes of nature.'[6]

But what is nature and where is it to be found? It seems to offer us a sure clarity but, instead, it leads us round in a circle in which nature is truth, truth reason, and beauty is merely the word which embodies these things in the aesthetic context.[7] Of these four, the only one of whose existence we can be sure from experience is the reason. Can we find a sure base here? Certainly, the reason, with its logicality and orderliness, appreciation of clear purpose and consistency, has a particular authority in the 'Aufklärung'.

In matters of taste as well as of cognition and morals, reason is thought of as a consistent and sure guide to truth. Bodmer believes that if all reasoned correctly, there would be unanimity of taste.[8] The 'Aufklärer' talked often of good taste, by which he meant, not something freely individual, but the fruit of the proper rational understanding of nature. Perhaps that is why this generation became involved in so many heated disputes about issues (e.g. correct style) in which the theoretical positions of the disputants do not seem to us to be so very far apart. Tolerance in matters of religious belief was a watchword of the age, but this did not extend to matters of taste. Here, the exact truth of 'nature' was involved and the supreme arbiter was not feeling, but reason. Reason, being one and indivisible for the 'Aufklärer',[9] could lead, strictly speaking, to only one answer. Lessing, for all his lithe argumentation, was as dogmatic in his desire to reduce tragedy to a single unitary principle as Gottsched had been before him. Wieland, whose rationalism is less strict, nevertheless will not allow true freedom to individual taste. He recognizes that it is impossible to lay down a simple set of mechanical rules for artistic excellence. But he is far from thinking that all tastes are equal or that beauty is a subjective matter. Democritus, his spokesman in the *Geschichte der Abderiten*, demands that feeling, which is certainly necessary, be nevertheless an 'educated feeling',[10] and while he rejects arbitrary rules, still accepts that there *are* rules, namely those which 'flow from the nature of the thing itself'.[11] It is still a question of studying an object, something outside oneself, and 'imitating' it. The degree of true freedom allowed to the creative artist is still relatively small. Even Klopstock can talk of 'rules'. In the Introduction to his *Geistliche Lieder* he says that 'every kind of poetry has its own tone' and lays down rules for the different kinds of religious poem.[12] Both concepts, 'nature' and 'reason', as used at this time, tell us very little of themselves. They lead us back to the inner feelings of their users, to the spirit of order and moderation.

Nature is a useful word by means of which the 'Aufklärer' hypostatizes his love of order, rational purpose and propriety. Sulzer formulates it thus:

Nature never acts without an exact purpose. . . . In the arrangement of parts, it always proceeds in such a way that everything, down to the most trifling detail, appears as a whole, existing in and by itself. The parts are always placed in the most harmoniously balanced relationship to one another and similar parts are always symmetrically positioned.[13]

From the example which he gives in *Der Biedermann* (Band I, Blatt 1), in which freaks, albeit an undeniable reality, are designated as unnatural, it becomes clear that by 'nature', Gottsched means the norm, or, in his own words, 'something intelligible, orderly and rational'. What 'rational' means to the 'Aufklärer' becomes clearer with the succeeding sentence. Nature is 'something comprehensible'. Writers are exhorted to 'follow in its footsteps'.[14] This is, in essence, the 'nature' which the aesthetic theory of the 'Aufklärung' desires the artist to 'imitate'. For Lessing, too, nature is characterized by rationality and order. In his discussion of the mixture of comic and tragic in Spanish drama, of which he disapproves, in sections 69 and 70 of the *Hamburgische Dramaturgie,* he is brought up against the fact that such a mixture occurs in real life, in nature. Since for him too, 'nothing which is an imitation of nature can be at fault', he would seem to have trapped himself. He falls back on the constitution of the human mind, on what it can and cannot grasp. In essence, the nature the artist has to imitate is that of the reason or, to be more precise, the intellect, for it is clear from what Lessing says that what the intellect cannot grasp, and therefore control, the aesthetic sense as conceived by him cannot appreciate. Similarly, in the thirty-fourth section, he will not allow a dramatic character who is a mass of inner contradictions and inconsistencies, not because such a person might not exist, but because it runs counter to the nature of Nature, which is always consistent, purposeful and rational.

The literary theory of the 'Aufklärung' is a garden laid out on very straight lines. Those human faculties which tend to obscure the straight lines, and which one associates with freedom, are not cast out of the Garden of Enlightenment, but delivered over to the keeping of a wise but firm custodian, who keeps them properly clipped and confined. This controlling faculty can be given different names in different contexts, but is generally best rendered as the intellect, and more particularly that aspect of the intellect which sees the rational patterns in the mass of data presented by the senses and imagination, the relationships, similarities and connections, and which 'Aufklärer' call the wit ('Witz'). The business of poetic creation is best thought of, for the 'Aufklärer', not as direct personal expression of experience (this would, of course, savour too much of freedom!), but as the activity of the wit. The poet is a kind of creator,[15] but within limits. The nature of the subject he chooses to 'imitate' and the genre in which he chooses to work have their set style and rules. In a well-known passage, Gleim says:

You will deceive yourselves if you draw conclusions about the morals of poets from their writings. They characterize themselves, not as they are, but as the kind of poem they are writing demands that they should be.

A poet, Gleim continues, writes 'only to show his wit' and adopts 'the particular system which gives him most opportunity for being witty.'[16]

Klopstock himself, the poet of inspiration, says of poetic invention that it consists in 'combining what is already there in a new way'.[17] The intellect maintains its hold on the creative imagination through the principle of 'probability'; that is, an invented character, object or action, even if not provided direct by the nature around us, must remain commensurate with the basic laws of nature. As we shall see, this proviso robs the ideas of Bodmer and Breitinger on 'the wondrous' of much of their apparent emancipating force.

Two main dangers threatened the tidiness of this formal garden. The imagination, universally admitted as essential to poetic excellence,[18] could take a path opposed to that of reason and so could the emotions, which were also formally recognized, following Horace,[19] as necessary to the achievement of the proper effect on reader or audience.

The theorists who seem to offer most freedom for the imagination are the Zurich writers, Bodmer and Breitinger. In advocating the principles of the 'Wondrous' and the 'New',[20] they say things which seem logically to challenge the hegemony of the intellect and 'nature'. Breitinger could call the poet a creator (in the sense that he makes perceptible to the senses things which are not naturally so perceptible). Bodmer also talks at times in terms which suggest the liberation of the imagination. Yet he is hardly consistent in theory, and the practical application also undermines that first impression. Could Bodmer seriously have spent so much time, in his treatise on the Wondrous in poetry, laboriously trying to square details of

Milton's *Paradise Lost* with the principle of probability,[21] if he were genuinely convinced that the poet's fancy should be free?

Breitinger maintains better control than his colleague. Probability never relaxes its hold on the Wondrous in his discussion. To achieve its end at all, art cannot tell the truth plain and unvarnished. It can appeal to the reader's interest and imagination best through the 'New', i.e. what is striking and out-of-the-ordinary, the Wondrous being simply the extreme form of this. But it only 'seems' to stray from the path of truth[22] and its form and laws are in fact based either on actual, or on 'possible' truth.[23] But no truth is conceivable (i.e. 'possible') for the 'Aufklärer' which is not rational and consistent, these qualities being the essence of his concept of God. Any imagined world which is 'possible' will be ruled by nature, which appears in the world of the imagination as probability. And sure enough, we find Breitinger saying that the Wondrous is in fact 'disguised probability.'[24] The leading strings have been loosened somewhat, but the control is still there and any attempt at true freedom will make us only too clearly aware of them.

The current of emotionalism within the 'Aufklärung' is best represented by Klopstock, who also seems to give a strong impulse towards freedom. He emphasizes dynamic and not purely rational factors to a much greater extent than most of his contemporaries. He speaks of 'moving the whole soul'[25] and demands genuineness of feeling and 'exactly true expression of passion'.[26] At the same time, he believes that a stage of 'coolness'[27] is necessary after the subject has been emotionally experienced, and that calm ('Ruhe') is an essential 'counsellor'.[28] And as he stops short of a 'Sturm und Drang' position here, so he does in the case of the concept of genius. The ideal conditions for genius, he writes in the *Gelehrtenrepublik*, are those in which 'sensitivity of emotion is somewhat higher than liveliness of imagination, and sharpness of judgment is higher than both of these'.[29] This seems to bring us round once more to something akin to 'wit'. Certainly, while Klopstock is willing to trust sentiment further than many of his contemporaries, he is not willing to free it from rational control. The principle of order once again escapes serious threat.

The 'Aufklärer' is not totally at his ease as the foregoing remarks may have suggested. His calm depends to a considerable extent on limitation: on the elimination or strict control of disruptive elements. One of the most dangerous of these is excess. Nature, as he conceives it, abhors an extreme, even the extreme of free thought. The 'Aufklärung' frowned on freethinking, whether religious or political, and one of the worst sins in its calendar was 'Schwärmerei', a straying beyond the bounds set by reason and nature which could invalidate even nominally admirable motives and sentiments, and make them 'false'. Musarion's remark: 'No excess, my friend, if you please'[30] could serve as a motto for the whole 'Aufklärung'. Whatever the sphere of activity, 'happiness and enjoyment lie in the middle position', as Hagedorn puts it.[31] To stray beyond the bounds set by nature and reason (i.e. the mood and taste of the 'Aufklärung') is to involve oneself in 'Schwärmerei', such as the 'false heroism' detected by Lessing in some martyrs,[32] or in such a stylistic fault as bombast ('Schwulst'). Socially, true happiness and, indeed, true freedom lies in being content ('vergnügt') with a modest competence and enjoying peace of mind, which is never to be found in the rich man's marble halls. The trick is not to expropriate the expropriators, but to avoid contact with them, and flee their haunts.

The non-revolutionary implications of this philosophy of limitation, which is universally shared by the 'Aufklärer', are immediately apparent and lead us naturally to a consideration of the 'passivity' and 'timidity' with which the eighteenth-century German 'Bürger' has often been charged, particularly in his capacity as 'Aufklärer'. There is no doubt that this is one side of the coin. Whether it be in avoidance of the social and political implications of a theme, in the adoption of a posture of calm, unresisting endurance ('Gelassenheit') rather than resistance to the evil man, or in a general lack of dynamism in its taste, the 'Aufklärung' gives plenty of examples to support this charge. Gellert is a particularly good example of it; one could hunt for hours and in vain among his writings for a truly subversive word, and the same is true of his literary taste.

The most revealing instances of this trend in the 'Aufklärung' occur in its attitude to heroism. It had a taste for the heroic and sublime as such, but a certain kind of heroism was no longer acceptable: the kind which could be described as 'hard' in quality, whether the physical heroism of the warrior or the superhuman willpower of the Stoic. Both violate the central 'Aufklärung' principles of reason and 'nature'. Condemnations of the first type of hero are easy to find, from the Ulfo of J. E. Schlegel's play *Canut*, who seeks a false glory in irrational defiance of a benevolent monarch and in battlefields covered with corpses, to Lessing's rejection of the grim endurance of 'barbaric heroes' in the opening sections of *Laokoon*.

But while rejection of Stoicism as such is common practice among 'Aufklärer'[33] it is not always easy to distinguish between the standard 'gelassen' hero of the 'Aufklärung' and the Stoic ideal. The main area of difference seems to be that Stoic heroism is seen as a paper heroism only, positing an unnatural ability on the part of the will to overcome pain. It is an exaggeration – something the 'Aufklarer' instinctively rejects. Yet at the same time it is an exaggerated form of an attitude which he deeply admires. Wieland's Musarion, after having exposed the false pretensions of the Stoic *philosopher*, makes it clear in the third Book that she has great respect for the Stoic *ideal*. The typical hero of the 'Aufklärung' is someone who suffers, steadfastly and without resistance, and often without complaint. It is made clear that he does in fact feel pain, but greater emphasis is usually placed on his freedom of spirit and greatness of soul. Active, often antisocial 'greatness' was disapproved of, as in the case of Ulfo, or of the wicked servant Betty in J. B. Pfeil's *Lucie Woodvil*, who ranks herself among the 'great spirits' but is set in perspective by the 'sublime'[34] figure of the virtuous Amalia.

A time was to come when mere 'Gelassenheit', at least as practised by the 'Aufklärung', was not felt to be enough. Even when his activist 'Sturm und Drang' phase was over, Schiller felt the need to demonstrate a spirited will in his characters. They end in their own, more dynamic version of acceptance, but they are not without inner fire. Thus Maria Stuart, in her confrontation with Elizabeth in Act III, Scene 4, casts aside 'lamb-hearted calm' and 'suffering patience'. The Self is given some right to rebel against constraint, even if in the end it freely accepts what necessity decrees. For the 'Aufklärung', however, this spark of self-assertion was not felt to be necessary. And calm acceptance was by no means thought of as 'lamb-hearted'. Both the hero and the figure of Medon in von Cronegk's *Codrus*, for example, are models of iron constancy, heroes designed 'not to be pitied, but to be admired', in the words of Elisinde.[35] The masterly inactivity of this type of hero is constantly held up for admiration and endowed with moral sublimity, even saintliness, as in the case of Lessing's Sara Sampson, whose readiness to forgive is described as 'divine' (Act IV, Scene 5) and whom Mellefont later formally canonizes.[36]

This concept of heroism, then, does not lack strength, nor is it fair to deny it some measure of the spirit of freedom, even if an inner freedom has to be settled for. It is not simply an expression of cowed resignation to the limited economic and social situation in which the average 'Bürger' lived, even if it clearly implies some degree of acceptance. He could maintain his self-respect. The heroic is one of the main channels available to his sense of independence and is sometimes coupled with a theme of national political freedom (as in Uz's 'An die Freiheit', or Weisse's *Die Befreiung von Theben*), though always in such a way as to avoid too specific a relation to actuality.

Freedom is a figure that the 'Aufklärer' can conjure up but cannot face in an undiluted form. He believes in freedom of thought, in a critical approach to revealed truth, he even believes that the peasant too is a human being and that serfdom is wrong in principle. But he does not take this to the extent of rejecting, or even seriously thinking of rejecting, the established order. Gottsched, for example, will not condemn the institution outright and even gives some rules for humanitarian treatment of serfs.[37] Orderliness is a prime characteristic of the most typical thinker of the age, Christian Wolff, and the appreciation of it, indeed positive joy in it, is well expressed by Nicolai when, in his autobiographical sketch 'Über meine gelehrte Bildung', he explains why Wolff had such a strong influence on him. The cause, he says, in a phrase which can sum up the theme of this whole chapter, was 'the uncommon orderliness, clarity and distinctness which reigns in these works'.

5

Rationalism

G. E. LESSING

All 'Aufklärer' are rationalists in the broad sense, but some are fiercer in their devotion to reason, and narrower in their conception of the scope which it allows to imagination and feeling, than others. It is this trend, sometimes confused with Enlightenment as a whole, which the term 'Rationalism' is here used to distinguish. Rationalists in this sense, whether limited or gifted, rigid in thinking, like Gottsched, or flexible, like Lessing, are united by certain tendencies. Their love of clarity and good sense, and their distrust of obscurity, fancy and enthusiasm, are stronger than those which obtain in Rococo and Sentimentalist writing and thought. They have a positive love of system, of philosophical and theoretical argument and the like. It was in the men in whom this trend was predominant that the almost mathematical clarity of Wolff's philosophy met with most sympathy. Gottsched, for example, solves philosophical problems like theorems in his *Weltweisheit*.

The point of disagreement, as Lessing says, is often the most enlightening, and the attitude of various 'Aufklärer' to the major authors and works of the emergent 'Sturm und Drang' will help to clarify our differentiation. The Sentimentalists, as one might expect, feel most sympathy with the new generation. Klopstock, who 'doubted a little' whether Lessing and he could be friends,[1] and who rather disliked critics in general, certainly felt that Herder was sometimes led, by his love of images, away from 'real truth', but nevertheless singles him out for special approval 'because it is your very strong feeling that makes you a critic.'[2] Wieland, in his essay on Goethe's *Götz von Berlichingen*, did not endorse Goethe's departure from traditional forms but recognized the talent of the play and expressed the wish that

Germany had more such 'monstrosities'. Lessing called the play 'Wisiwaschi' (rubbish).[3]

Matthias Claudius, who combined solid, simple common sense with a fresh, rather naive humour *and* emotional sensitivity, certainly disapproved of the hero's suicide in *Die Leiden des jungen Werthers*, and found 'a lot of good sense' in Nicolai's parody. At the same time, his acceptance of the power of love to 'go all through you and jump and bother you in every vein and sport with your head and your reason'[4] is something we do not find in the Rationalist Nicolai. The latter recognizes the poetic brilliance of the novel, and many good qualities in Werther himself,[5] but a thing he cannot accept, and which Goethe, for all his awareness of the pathological elements in Werther, insists on, is the limited authority of the voice of common-sense reason and 'experience' when confronted by a strong individual emotion. Werther is not a mere self-indulgent melancholic of the type represented by Schmidt in the novel itself.

Nicolai, in *Die Freuden des jungen Werthers*, makes Werther a 'weakling', presents his gusts of emotion as comic, and places him infinitely beneath an Albert, who, through the exercise of 'a little cool reason',[6] can renounce his claims on Lotte with no apparent agony of soul. The emphasis on coolness ('Kälte') is particularly strong with the Rationalistic stream of the 'Aufklärung'. Wieland, for all his reservations about Sophie von Laroche's *Geschichte des Fräulein von Sternheim* (a novel which shows some emotional individualism and won favour among the 'Stürmer and Dränger'), and for all the 'Kälte' which made him see the heroine as a 'singular' person, is nevertheless partially won over by the appeal to the heart: 'all my cold-blooded philosophy could not hold out against the truth and beauty of your moral portraits; my heart became warm . . .'[7] One would not wish, then, to place Wieland or Klopstock in quite the same box as Nicolai and Lessing, even if their particular boxes are all contained within a bigger one labelled 'Aufklärung'.

A liking for order and logicality was common to all 'Aufklärer', but that of the Rationalists was particularly deep. This could amount to an excessive puritanism, which attempted to reduce more or less to vanishing point all the elements which might cloud order and trouble common sense. Thus there were those, particularly writers and critics of the Gottschedian persuasion, who were implacably hostile to opera, or frowned on the use of verse in comedies, or wished to banish Harlequin from the stage. Lessing, another Rationalist, mocks at the attempt to do this in his seventeenth 'Literaturbrief'. The only important proponent of this brand of draconian Rationalism is Gottsched, and its spirit may be studied in his *Critische Dichtkunst*. Others had greater confidence and flexibility, or at least the intelligence to see the ridiculousness of the position towards which the rigorists were tending: art driven too far towards pure reason and logic must deny its nature. Lessing, whom we will be examining in detail later, is a representative of the relatively liberal wing of Rationalism, but even if he flirts occasionally with things which Gottsched would have regarded as inclined to threaten the dominance of the reason, he always stays within the boundaries which are here being marked out.

Regularity of form has a particular attraction for the Rationalist, not by virtue of the qualities of deliberate stylization, detachment from mere everyday reality, and idealization which caused the Classical Goethe and Schiller to turn once more to the neo-classical French drama,[8] but because of the satisfaction and pleasure it affords to his sense of order and purpose. For all his lambasting of Voltaire in the *Hamburgische Dramaturgie*, Lessing was on the whole closer to him in spirit than he was to Shakespeare, whom he praised with a sincere appreciation of his great dramatic talent, though unappreciative of the non-classical aspects of his drama.

In poetry, the Rationalists are the least inclined to break away from the restrictive, but inherently neat and symmetrical alexandrine line, and they tend to sheer away from the rhythmical subtlety and variation, or exploitation of the evocative and associative power of language, which Wieland and Klopstock display to such great effect. Haller, for example, owes most of his poetic effect to bold, inventive thought and metaphor.

Haller is a particularly interesting example of Rationalism in literature. Easily the most important Rationalist poet, he was also an eminent scientist, and a man of serious and passionate temperament, with a definite religious streak in his character. His life was darkened by failure to achieve the position of real influence and effectiveness in the administration of his native republic of Berne which he dearly wished for, and even more so by domestic misfortune.[9] And yet, though there is at times an undeniable sense of strain in his poetry, he remains consistently Rationalistic both in thought and poetic technique. The Rationalistic mentality, then, is not automatically destroyed by these seemingly disruptive forces: it manages to contain, if not to assimilate them. It may well be that the effort of containment is a prime cause of the peculiar intensity which distinguishes Haller's work. Haller is also the outstanding practitioner, in his time, of a genre which has particular affinity to the Rationalistic mind, namely the 'Lehrgedicht', or philosophical poem. Here, the tendency to favour thought rather than emotion, imagination or mere delight, which can be seen in the predominance of philosophical discourse over action in the Rationalistic novel, and in many aspects of Rationalistic drama, comes closest to being reconciled with the demands of poetry. The other verse forms favoured by Rationalists, the fable and 'moral' tale, were less likely still to lead to a truly poetic use of language.

The novel was a form wide open to misappropriation to non-literary Rationalistic ends, and the 'Aufklärung' produced a large number of novels in which characters and story are subservient to the expression of opinion or to didactic moralizing. Nicolai's *Sebaldus Nothanker*, which, as the author himself states in his preface, is much more concerned with opinions than with life, is a fair example of the genre. The basic framework, adapted from the traditional form which was not always permeated by a serious spirit and hardly ever by an orderly one, is that of the more or less labyrinthine fortunes or 'events'[10] of a central character. To the Rationalist, this is not interesting enough in itself to justify a work of literature before the throne of reason. Some of Lessing's reviews in the *Berlinische Privilegierte Zeitung* in the early 1750s may be quoted as evidence of this approach to the genre. Lessing considers that what he calls 'the wondrous element in the novel',[11] by which he must mean the involved concatenation of unusual events which constitutes the intrigue of a typical novel of the time, needs control and justification. Of the *Geschichte eines Kandidaten*, which he considers the first worthwhile novel to have been written in Germany since Gellert's *Schwedische Gräfin*, he remarks: 'The author narrates, portrays and makes moral reflections in such a way as to please the reader of good taste'.[12] Reviewing the *Begebenheiten des Mylord Kingston*, he notes that the 'labyrinth' of the hero's fortunes is well handled: 'the events always contain some good moral, the intrigue is coherent and the dénouement unexpected and instructive.'[13]

With Lessing, we have arrived at the point at which Rationalism achieves its highest literary expression, in the areas in which it is most natural that it should be able to find a fruitful *modus vivendi* with literary criteria and values, namely criticism and theory, and the drama. That the former was a popular and flourishing activity has already been made clear. As for drama, comedy was the genre in which the earlier 'Aufklärer' were most successful and if no tragedy of any great merit had been produced before Lessing, it was not for lack of interest and endeavour. In both, the approach adopted reflected the dominance of Rationalism in that phase of the 'Aufklärung': the plays were French-orientated, regular in form and organization and biased towards intellectual and utilitarian values. Comedy tended to attack 'vices' by satirizing them as folly, tragedy aimed at the same moral effect by presenting them from their destructive side and pointing to the contrast with virtue. Lessing began in this pattern and never entirely broke with it.

Lessing was, first and foremost, an intellectual. To attempt to fit him into the traditional moulds of dramatist, theoretician, philosopher or theologian is to do him a disservice. True, he wrote important works which, to be classified at all, need to be placed under these heads. But this often obscures the essential under the superficial. Discussion, rather than the subject under discussion, is often the important thing. Discussion cannot live without some kind of material to feed on, but while the precise theme cannot be a matter of indifference, it is not necessarily crucial to the quality of the argument. Lessing could be as much himself, and as great, in vindicating Cochläus ('but only in a trifling matter', as he himself says), as he is in canvassing an ingenious interpretation of the doctrine of the Trinity.[14]

Lessing's own protestations that he is 'not an imaginative writer' ('Dichter'; cf. the final section of the *Hamburgische Dramaturgie*), 'not a theologian', and so forth, should be taken more seriously than they often are. He was in many ways the intellectual's intellectual, an almost pure example of the type, for whom argument is its own reward. His superb intelligence, brilliant wit and absolute mastery of German prose style almost blind us at times to his limitations – his almost total lack of poetry, for example. Whatever the intellect can do is within Lessing's capacity, and he was the first German for a very long time to show how wide a range is covered by this phrase. For just as there is a logic of the imagination, so there is an imaginativeness of the intellect which enables it to obtain some kind of grasp on things which are strictly outside the scope of its experience. It was this which enabled him, though of an essentially untragic nature, to progress as far as he did in the field of tragedy.

This imaginative quality has sometimes led observers, impressed by such things as Lessing's praise of Shakespeare, or his talk of the genius, to say that he transcended the 'Aufklärung' at some points at least. Such a view rests either on an equation of 'Aufklärung' with totally insensitive Rationalism, or on a reading of Lessing's words in the spirit of a generation later than his, encouraged, perhaps, by the respect shown for Lessing by writers like Herder and Goethe. Without in any way wishing to detract from the importance of what Lessing wrote on Shakespeare, we must point out that he saw him entirely in terms of the dramatist and dramatic art as conceived by the 'Aufklärung'. Shakespeare's characterization, for example, is described in the terminology of the conventional theory of imitation of nature. Othello is not a unique product of titanic creative genius, as he appears in Herder's famous essay on Shakespeare, but 'a complete textbook' of the 'sad passion' of jealousy.[15] In creating (in *Hamlet*) a ghost which really chills our blood, Shakespeare is not so much the writer whose powerful imagination and sensitivity break down the inhibiting barriers of Rationalism, but the technician who understands the tricks of the trade ('Handgriffe') necessary to make us accept something of whose real existence we have doubts.[16] Lessing does not leave the shelter of the Aristotelian umbrella to consort with Shakespeare; rather he draws him under it.

Rationalism, in Lessing, is not afraid to face the problems of the irrational and potentially disorderly: whether they were truly mastered is a moot point, for he gives little evidence of ability or at least willingness to experience them inwardly. His reaction to *Werther*, in which he speaks contemptuously of the 'modern' kind of hero, the product of the Christian era, who is inwardly so soft as to become the prey of his emotions, is one indication of this. We need not suppose that Lessing was not possessed of a feeling heart but there is no strong evidence that he was ever possessed by consuming *personal* emotion. The totally unconvincing nature of the expression of such emotion in his plays supports this view. One expects some relaxation of control, but what tends to occur is either a calculated rhetorical set-piece, or a relatively cool, plain statement.

It is a different matter when the emotion is conceived in a general, still human but not truly individual context. This is where we find the Lessing who made such an issue of 'Mitleid' in his theory of tragedy,[17] who even states at one point: 'The man who feels most pity is the best man.' It could be argued that this is the most natural channel for emotion to take in the man who is temperamentally Rationalistic. For here, it is under some kind of control and is not necessarily in conflict with the reason or disputing its supremacy. The idea of hot passion swamping cool reflection, which is well expressed in the negative image applied to Odoardo in *Emilia Galotti* – 'ein brausender Jünglingskopf mit grauen Haaren'[18] is a very uncongenial one. A cool head with a warm heart, however, is a different matter. Cool thinking about warm subjects – which really only works on the general plane – is something to be welcomed. When considering the various ways of 'Thinking about God' put forward by Klopstock in the *Nordischer Aufseher*, Lessing very characteristically reverses Klopstock's order of priority. He much preferred the path of systematic abstract thought, which Klopstock considered relatively dry and unproductive, to that preferred by the other writer, in which the more non-rational faculties play a crucial role in bringing about the most fruitful state of mind.[19] This 'abandonment of oneself to one's feelings' he emphatically rejects.

Lessing's own speculations on religious subjects are all in the Rationalistic vein and generate heat only in a polemical situation, such as that of the *Anti-Goeze*. His discussion of pity in the context of dramatic theory is clever and for the most part coolly calculated. The letter of 29 November 1756 to Nicolai is a particularly good example. Here, Lessing divides tragic pity into three stages. The one to be aimed at, as we might expect, is the middle one, which is defined as the stage of 'tears'. This is the stage at which there is neither too little, nor too much pity. The suffering character is endowed with enough virtue to attract the pity of the right-thinking observer, but if this morally admirable element reaches the pitch at which rational appreciation gives way to enthusiastic admiration, Lessing's enthusiasm wanes in proportion. He actually speaks of weighing ingredients in the balance in order to achieve the 'Kunststück' (technical skill or trick) of arousing the tears of an audience.

The Sentimentalist playwright, such as Klopstock in his *Der Tod Adams*, sets out to win pity and admiration for his characters by displaying their beauty of soul. No doubt, Lessing would have claimed the same quality for the heroine of *Miss Sara Sampson*, but it is rather beauty of mind that she conveys, with her inexhaustible stock of high-minded sentiments and her analytical discourses on herself and her situation. It is true that, on its first performance, this play had a success of sentiment with its audience. It took the tide of Sentimentalism at the flood. But the witty nature of its language (e.g. Mellefont: 'How wretched it makes me that I have not the heart to make you more wretched still', Act I, scene 7) is a great barrier to emotion, as is the strong element of contrivance which it shares with all Lessing's plays. It is emotionally *affecting* only in odd and awkward moments like the intervention of Mellefont's little daughter in Act II, scene 4. Lessing, in fact, is not at his ease in handling this character, and removes her from the action as soon as he decently can.

There is a good deal of the safer sentiment of the healthy, robust 'Bürger' who enjoys feeling moral, as long as his emotion is sanctioned by the reason. Waitwell, the faithful servant, is a constant source of such sentiment. Virtue and sensibility are perfectly blended in him. Yet he too is infected by the wit of his only begetter. When Sara, for example, expresses fear that reading her father's letter will give her pain, he replies: 'Pain, Miss, but it will be pleasant pain.'

Just as Lessing's outstanding intellectual qualities allowed

him to go beyond the relatively naïve tragic theory of the
Gottsched school without overstepping the bounds of Rationalism, so they gave him a similar extra flexibility in tragedy itself.
And although he took the genre seriously and strove to succeed
in dramatic terms, it is at the intellectual level that his later
tragedies are most rewarding. It is the tragic *problem*, rather than
the characters in themselves, which seems to interest him most:
one has the feeling, particularly in *Emilia Galotti*, that the
catastrophe is the motivating force behind the characters. And
the problems which Lessing sets himself are hard ones for the
'Aufklärer', who wishes to feel that he lives in a good and
ordered world. This is no rejection of the basic principles
on Lessing's part. It is in his nature to seek difficulties, for the
sheer pleasure of overcoming them without recourse to the
irrational. So to arrange matters that, without any deviation
from the accepted norms of probability and human nature,
the unlikely is seen to be entirely explicable and 'natural' – this
is perhaps the highest triumph for the Rationalist and his
principle of order. Seen in this light, *Emilia Galotti* can make
sense.

The problem is a particularly daunting one: a father has to
kill his own daughter. Lessing discusses the subject first in a
letter to Nicolai (21 January 1758), which leaves no doubt that
the difficulty of the subject attracts him. He even intends to
add to the difficulty, by removing the story from its ancient
Roman context and making of it 'a middle-class' Virginia. The
political aspect inherent in the original can also be dispensed
with, he feels. What is left, with all its hideous problems of
motivation, seems to him 'beautiful'. But this beauty is intellec-
lectual. If we can *feel* the situation as well as think it, we recoil
a little from Lessing's enthusiasm.

The final version of the play, completed much later, shows the
same basic impulse. The pity we feel arises out of the contemplation of the situation and the pleasure out of our realization of the
immense skill which has gone into calculating the characters
and events so as to bring matters to precisely that point. The
heroine, for example, is a nicely calculated dramatic *character*,
but not an entirely convincing *person*. We are asked to see her as
a girl who is pure enough to win the love of an Appiani, and to
wish to marry him, yet of so strong a sensuality that in the fifth

act, she gives up the struggle against the Prince in advance, whose virtue is at one point so irresolute that she cannot admonish the Prince when he declares his love, yet who is later so bold as to attempt suicide and when that fails, to taunt her father into killing her. All this is comprehensible from the point of view of the exigencies of the plot, but it makes the achievement of any significant degree of identification with the character very difficult.

One of the most striking manifestations of the spirit of orderliness in Lessing is his almost dogmatic insistence that tragedy is concerned purely and simply with arousing pity in the audience. This seems to arise, not out of a taste for simplicity, but, at a deeper level, out of the radical nature of his Rationalism. So many kinds of tragedy have been written that one despairs of a completely satisfactory definition, but it does seem that in most cases, tragedy gives us some experience of and adopts some kind of attitude to an area which lies above, below and beyond the well-lit, well-ordered sphere of our 'normal', controlled existence. Certain events and experiences seem to suggest that another dimension can and does intervene in that existence with disruptive, often drastically disruptive effect: perhaps, if we allow a great width of interpretation to the word, we can call it the transcendental dimension. Various forms of tragedy deal with this phenomenon in various ways, some religious in origin, some using secularized forms of religious views, some rationalistic in the wide sense of the term. But the Rationalism which we are dealing with in Lessing's case wishes to go further and assimilate what seems at first sight an external phenomenon into the 'normal' context. He wishes to *humanize* tragedy, even at the risk of losing the grandeur which comes from the confrontation with something transcendental. I am not saying that Lessing consciously set out to do this, but the formulation does seem to fit various attitudes of his.

Lessing is not the first Rationalistic 'Aufklärer' to be driven by this impulse, of course. It informs Gottsched's interpretation of the *hamartia* of Aristotle's theory as an aberration of the reason in the hero. One can see it in the very common insistence that whatever happens, 'die Vorsicht' (Providence, the concept which embodies the conviction of the time that the system in which they live is secure, purposeful and right) cannot be at fault. It can be implicit, too, in the move towards an assertively 'bürgerlich' kind of tragedy, of which Lessing was one of the great supporters. Obviously there are various motives involved here, but in Lessing's case one cannot help feeling that the aim of bringing tragedy down to the merely human plane is a crucial one. In the fourteenth section of the *Hamburgische Dramaturgie*, he argues that the only important thing is that one feels as similar as possible to (and therefore as capable as possible of feeling sympathetic pity for) the characters. What he is in fact excluding – by implication at any rate – is the element of possibly overwhelming greatness, the great issues and principles which a character of rank might represent, the great and transcending events in which he might be involved.

When, in the *Hamburgische Dramaturgie* (Stück 75) he first substitutes 'fear' for 'terror' as a translation of Aristotle's *phobos*, Lessing has taken some of the sting out of tragedy, but he is not satisfied with that. In a brilliant passage, in which mastery of style and rhetorical skill in arrangement still cannot conceal the absence of real argument and proof, he claims that what Aristotle meant by 'fear' was in fact the fear that what is happening to the tragic hero could happen to us, in fact, just another aspect of pity, 'pity applied to ourselves'. It is entirely in harmony with this point of view that he should render Aristotle's purgative *katharsis* as a purification of our ability to feel pity. Lessing certainly taught the Germans to criticize drama and think about it in more flexible and fruitful ways, but his actual conclusions about tragedy, fortunately, did not become current. Had later dramatists written in his spirit, it would have meant the death of tragedy before its time. Instead, all the elements which he had attempted to drive out were restored, even the great world of kings and princes, for reasons well stated by Schiller in the prologue to *Wallenstein*.

The spirit of order is, as we have said, a strong factor in this tragic theory of Lessing's. The area in which one is most inclined to think of Rationalism as potentially disruptive is that of religion, and Lessing is one of the most active of Rationalists in this field. That he was out of sympathy with orthodox Christianity and critical of it is well known. Our main concern is to determine how strong is the willingness to destroy the old

Christian structure, and none of the negative evidence, even taken in isolation, suggests that he would have been ready to face the disappearance of the church with equanimity, if it left a vacuum.

In the important letter to his brother Karl of 2 February 1774, Lessing leaves no doubt of his dissatisfaction with orthodox Christian theology, and of his even greater dissatisfaction with the neology of Semler and his kind, who are merely trying to graft rationalism on to the old system. Of the two, he prefers the latter and indicates that it should not be thrown away (as dirty bathwater) until one is sure of being able to substitute something better. In a second metaphor, he equates the old theology with a crumbling building standing beside his own house (that, presumably, of eighteenth-century 'philosophy'). He is willing to help demolish the other building, but not to shore it up (as Semler is doing), because it threatens the safety of his own. This might seem to indicate an immediate willingness to destroy, but could also be interpreted as the desire to leave well alone and let nature take its course. Certainly, the spirit of his last and most important work on the subject, the *Erziehung des Menschengeschlechts*, is clearly opposed to the continued authority of Christianity as a revealed religion and looks to a future when supernatural help and sanctions will not be necessary, but it is at most evolutionary. The arrangement and style of the work reflects a liking for stable and ordered structure as well as a feeling that change must come. There is a measure of respect for the structure established by the revealed religion, even if the implication that the reason is essentially independent of it is quite clear. The formula of the history of religion as a process of education, the adoption of which was originally prompted by the desire to produce a reply to the aggressive Deist Reimarus, is one which preserves the essentials of Enlightenment, but at the same time avoids a destructive clash with the existing structure. It might be as well to leave the matter there, as far as Lessing is concerned.

There is one other major aspect of Lessing which we need to consider: the element of laughter in his character and work. Here too, the issue of freedom naturally arises. Pure humour inevitably threatens to obscure clear, orderly distinctions. If not controlled in some way, it blows where it lists and can upset, or produce odd distortions in the best-laid plans of careful thinkers. In literature, the emancipation of laughter demands an aesthetic form free from utilitarian or strictly Rationalistic considerations. That Lessing had humour there can be no doubt. At the same time, his Rationalism was strong and flexible enough to contain this element also. Free laughter does not need rational sanction. For Lessing, it was never as free as that. In reviewing a comic novel called *Der deutsche Don Quichotte* in 1753, he grants the author 'a very comic wit' and 'an imagination which is uncommonly rich in droll images'. But 'the trick of concealing serious morality among these' is lacking and the laughter aroused is therefore 'unfruitful' and likely to repel the man 'who does not wish to laugh for no reason'.[20]

A little over a decade later, he finished his best comedy, *Minna von Barnhelm*. The previous comedies he had written had all been comedy within the basically satirical (i.e. rationally directed) scheme of the earlier 'Aufklärung'. *Minna* shows a number of deviations from that model in that it reflects the greater flexibility of Rationalism in the mature Lessing and allows more scope for serious emotion on the one hand and for less narrowly satirical laughter on the other. These two elements, in somewhat one-sided form, are brought into honourable conflict through Tellheim and Minna respectively and eventually into a reconciliation, in which each recognizes something of his or her own limitation and the other's different worth, and the uniting of hero and heroine in marriage becomes something more than just the ritual conclusion of any comedy.

But it is not a comedy which emancipates laughter. We have no contemporaneous theoretical discussion of the issues involved. But certain very important words which are put into the mouth of the heroine in Act IV, Scene 6 could almost serve as a concentrated statement of Lessing's attitude, with the proviso that the reference to seriousness should be interpreted with a deeper appreciation of Tellheim's point of view than Minna probably has at this point. Tellheim, a deeply virtuous and honourable man, has suffered a grievous injury to that very honour. Being also – as are so many men of this type – an exceedingly proud man, he cannot shrug off the injury and has fallen into a state of black melancholia. Minna who does not realize how deep-rooted the disease is, tries to laugh him out of it. 'You are disposed to laugh,' he says with cold dignity, 'I regret that I am not able to laugh with you.' 'But what have you got against laughter?' she replies. 'Can't one laugh and be very serious at the same time? My dear Major, laughing is a better way of staying a reasonable being than sinking into irritation.'[21]

So the rationality of laughter and the usefulness of comedy are clearly implied.

This is spelled out in more formal theoretical form later, in the *Hamburgische Dramaturgie* (sections 28 and 29). Lessing here proceeds as he often does, first amusing himself by exposing the limitations of the naïve, Gottschedian form of Rationalistic utilitarian theory (we are not 'cured' of a certain 'vice' by seeing it presented as folly), and then 'saving' utilitarianism, just as the baby seems to be in danger of disappearing in company with the dirty bathwater. Laughter, like pity in the tragic theory, is thought of as a human capacity ('Fertigkeit'), which needs to be strengthened, refined and purified. Comedy, by making us laugh and teaching us to laugh at the 'right' things, makes better men of us.

If we return to *Minna* with this Rationalistic position in mind, we appreciate that, while the balance is much less crudely tilted towards one side than in the straightforward satirical comedy in which the voice of reason drowns that of 'folly', the satirical form still provides the basic pattern. When all allowances are made, Minna's view is healthier than Tellheim's and while the play cannot and does not ride roughshod over his very deep feelings, it would be a poor look-out for their future marital harmony if he cannot be seen to have realized the exaggeration of his Prussian sense of honour and come round to something closer to Minna's point of view, as he does when he shows his willingness to tear up the letter which outwardly restores that honour so that he may possess her.

The last stage to be considered is that in which Lessing allows humour to play, though not to play with true freedom. There is too much witty, exactly calculated intellectual control for that. Gaiety there is in plenty, but however sprightly the pace and however sparkling the style, the movement takes place along the neat, straight lines of Rationalism rather than the gracefully meandering ones of Rococo, the style of play *par excellence*. This is most apparent in Lessing's attempts in the Rococo genre of 'Anacreontic' poetry. There is much cleverness and wit, too much, in fact, for the achievement of the feather-light touch and smooth flow of the Rococo style. The jokes are too often the kind which depend on the play on words (e.g. in 'Antwort eines trinkenden Dichters': 'One can certainly drink too much, but one can never drink enough'). A fine example of the difference is Lessing's treatment of the standard Rococo situation, the discovery of the beloved asleep. Wieland is very fond of this and always handles it well, building up an atmosphere with controlled sensuousness and tinges of emotional and imaginative sensitivity, through which his ironic humour plays with detachment and grace. Lessing's presentation is almost totally lacking in atmosphere, and runs to a wit which is stimulating to the intellect, but hardly relaxes or frees the mind. He describes the lover, who gazed at Laura and 'felt far too much to be able to feel clearly, to be able still to feel how much he then felt'.[22]

The most perfect expression of playful wit in all Lessing's writings occurs in a letter written to Nicolai on 22 October 1762, asking him to buy some books at an auction. The actual request takes up little space and the rest of a long letter is made up of a series of parenthetical excursuses – an analogy between correspondence and commerce suggested by the word 'Briefwechsel' ('Wechsel' meaning both exchange and a bill of exchange), a second digression full of clever conceits, jumping from idea to idea as the words suggest them, and a long imaginary letter to Madame Nicolai, discoursing on various aspects of the married state, as they might affect her willingness to let her husband go to the auction. At one point, he exclaims 'I must be addled in the head today to be dashing off remarks like this without consideration'. On the contrary: the dashing-off of remarks as the fancy takes him is the very carefully considered and calculated formula by which the whole letter is put together. It makes the impression of spontaneity, but its very spontaneity is dictated by and controlled by the intellect. It is both a pleasure and an effort to read. Lessing seems here to have visualized a free play of the fancy, but his madness has too much method in it for us to say that he has achieved it. There is too much wit, for one thing, for true relaxation, as in the rather taxing second digression, in which Lessing eventually arrives at the paradox 'and so I gain as I lose', by dint of saying that the reference books he can now buy, so that he can look up things he has forgotten, contain more than he has in fact forgotten. The more brilliant the *wit* becomes, the more we are inclined to feel that the *humour* is a little forced.

Lessing represents the literary peak of pure Rationalism within the German 'Aufklärung'. Looked at in the general European context, it can perhaps appear a little timid and provincial, or unduly scholarly, even a little metaphysical in character. Or it could be called more solid and substantial, more constructive than is the case elsewhere. Whichever emphasis one prefers, it seems undeniable that it is especially strongly imbued with the spirit of order.

6

ROCOCO

C. M. WIELAND

The term 'Rococo' is familiar to the general reader from the
history of art and architecture, whence it was borrowed by
German literary critics and historians – as was its historical
predecessor, 'Baroque' – to render a style and a set of attitudes
which were present in the writing of the 'Aufklärung' from the
outset (e.g. the lyrics and light tales of Hagedorn), became prominent in the so-called 'Anacreontic' school of the forties and
fifties and reached full fruition in the work of Wieland from
about 1760 to 1780. In literature, as elsewhere, the term represents a style and mood which are clearly related to the Baroque.
but equally clearly distinct from it. The intense, often agonized
rhetorical mood, massive proportions, unsymmetrical structure
and disturbed lines of the Baroque style are replaced by something lighter, more balanced and more self-assured.

In many fields, the Rococo took over forms or practices from
the Baroque, but it always applied them in a way which reflected
its stronger attachment to this world and its values. It was a
style which was more human in spirit and scope. Even in the
case of architecture, where the two styles are much closer to
one another, so much so that V. -L. Tapié can say that Baroque
'slides' into Rococo in Balthasar Neumann's church of Vierzehnheiligen,[1] the difference can be noticed. There is a clear
trend away from the monumental towards a more graceful
style, one which is better suited in fact to secular purposes.
Among the various literary genres, Rococo is most at home in
the Anacreontic lyric or verse-tale, ranging from the frivolous
'conte' (as in Wieland's *Comische Erzählungen*) to works with
epic pretensions, like the same author's *Oberon*.

This latter poem demonstrates the fact that Rococo writers
did not feel themselves debarred from attempting serious, even

heroic themes, while remaining within the Rococo style. Wieland combines chivalry with humour and fairy tale in *Oberon*, and narrates the whole in a basically light tone. In the end, his success is less than total: one has the impression of a graceful ship laden with a cargo which is slightly too heavy for it. Even so, the work is certainly not a failure and the same could be said of the novel *Geschichte des Agathon*, which also attempts to combine the light and the serious. The more purely humorous *Don Sylvio von Rosalva* may succeed more completely at its level, but it is a lower level.

A Rococo tragedy would, of course, be a contradiction in terms, but one is surprised by the poor showing of this style in literary comedy. Marivaux, after all, shows that a comedy of gay and artificial grace is possible. But whatever the reason, the Germans cannot match his sensitive and elegant handling of *commedia dell' arte* forms, even if some interest was shown in them by playwrights and theorists, including Lessing.[2] As far as the stage is concerned, the Rococo achieves its best work in the field of 'Singspiel' (e.g. C. F. Weisse, with works like *Der Teufel ist los*) and of operetta. This leads us naturally to recognize the fact that the German Rococo reached its highest peak in Mozart. And in this case, the combination of grace with seriousness is achieved in masterly fashion, in the music, if not always in the libretti. No definition of a style can contain genius completely, but it is surely better to extend the scope of 'Rococo' to include *Don Giovanni* and *Die Zauberflöte*, as it should be able to include Watteau, than to attempt to describe them as examples of *opera seria*.

Rococo literature is polite literature and – even when written by and for 'Bürger' – still in a sense courtly literature, which reflects in some measure the polished manners and elegant gardens and palaces of those aristocratic circles in which we moved for a time in Part One of this book. This is the world of *fêtes galantes*, of pastoral amusements and polished social intercourse, in which there is a conscious and deliberately chosen element of play. Rococo partakes in large measure of the nature of a game and it has its methods of ensuring that the passions can be indulged, but cannot become destructive, just as a game has its rules and its referee. The tone and style of a Rococo work will normally ensure that such dangerous things are not taken absolutely seriously. The presiding goddess and god of this world are Venus and Bacchus, but they are shorn of their more demonic attributes. In Watteau's *Departure from Cythera*, for example,[3] the canvas is dominated by the presence of Venus. But while this is far from being a merely light or frivolous picture, the nature of the passion as reflected in the expressions and attitudes of the figures and in colour and line is a far cry from the 'Vénus toute entière à sa proie attachée' of *Phèdre*. In treatments by artists of lesser spiritual scope, Venus assumes almost the nature of the Dresden china figures which are another typical product of the Rococo.

Since free play – within limits – is of the essence of Rococo, some degree of liberation from the restrictions imposed by the spirit of strict order is necessary. The German Rococo tends in general to be less disruptive than the French. Goethe observes perceptively in *Wilhelm Meisters Wanderjahre* that whereas the eighteenth-century French writers had been 'destructive', Wieland was no more than 'teasing' ('neckend'). At the same time, Wieland and his colleagues allow themselves liberties which would have made the true Rationalist feel uneasy. To achieve the requisite lightness of tone, some relaxation of strict Rationalist standards of morality is needed, though only in the context of the Rococo game. Similarly, there must be a relaxation in the field of the imagination. The Rococo writer must be able to let the fancy roam a little.

One thinks immediately, of course, of the Romantic Movement and it is true that there are points at which the two overlap, notably in the matter of their interest in fairy-tale themes. But the differences are more striking. The Rococo achieves its particular aims without breaking through the limits of the 'Aufklärung', though it does often risk more than the narrow Rationalism of that period would have been prepared to endorse. The result is a compromise form, characterized by the search for a balance between freedom and order, in which the fear of disrupting the latter is all too often stronger than the impulse towards the former. Both the Rococo writer and the Romantic deal in kinds of unreality. Both might appear to be 'escaping' from the reality of everyday. But while the Romantic either disregards actuality, or plays with it ironically, out of a basically serious purpose, namely to remain true to the values of the higher reality with which it is often directly in conflict, the Rococo writer *accepts* that actuality more or less at its own valuation. His play is at most a *holiday* from everyday reality, whose rules and laws have not lost their validity. When necessary, so that freedom shall not become truly disruptive, we can be reminded of their continuing existence and force.

While the Rococo is therefore not necessarily merely superficial and frivolous, it lacks, indeed it cannot afford, the truly deep seriousness which often underlies even the most apparently light-hearted of Romantic writing. In dealing with love the Rococo poet or novelist might well allow a measure of real physical and even spiritual attraction, he will allow flirtations, references to sensual gratification, even to heroic love, but he will avoid the absorbing seriousness which we find in a Romantic treatment, or, for that matter, in Heinse's *Ardinghello*. In another context, he might allow the distinctions of social class to fade into the background, but we never have the sense that the pillars of society are remotely threatened. Emotional involvement on the part of author and reader is never total and the intellect remains supreme.

Nothing alarms the Rococo writers so much as loss of control. Even Wieland does not approve of relaxation of control in his characters, which he associates with 'Schwärmerei', that state of domination by the non-rational faculties which no 'Aufklärer' could condone. His presentation of the moment in which Musarion is threatened by this state (Book III, lines 1156 ff.) shows his awareness of the dangerous attraction it contains:

> Die Nacht, die Einsamkeit, der Mondschein, die Magie
> Verliebter Schwärmerey, ihr eignes Herz, dem sie
> Nur lässig widersteht, wie vieles kommt zusammen,
> Das leichte Blut der Schönen zu entflammen![4]

The sensual, emotional and poetic factors are blended here in an effective evocation, but the word 'Schwärmerei' is itself a built-in safeguard and the mood is not allowed to acquire too much momentum. In the very next line, Wieland tells us that his heroine was still in conscious intellectual control. ('war ihrer selbst gewiss'). One can imagine the scorn which a genuine Romantic might feel for such a capitulation to reason.

Few Rococo poets allow the physical aspects of love any real scope. The Anacreontics content themselves with hints, whose effect is largely neutralized by playful wit. When Wieland presents beauty of a potentially overwhelming fascination, it is only in moments of moral danger for his heroes, as in the confrontations between Huon and Almansaris in *Oberon*. When sensuous beauty is presented in a positive light, static effects are avoided: all is animation and flowing grace.

Pleasure is a good in itself for the Rococo as long as it is not disorderly. It must be contained within the framework of a state of serene and balanced enjoyment in which all is harmonious good-will and men can come together in relaxed, but still rationally controlled 'Freude' or 'Vergnügen'. For a satisfactory artistic realization of this ideal, we have to wait until the mature work of Wieland, but it is there in Hagedorn (e.g. 'An die Freude') and Uz, who even gives a philosophical statement of it in his *Versuch über die Kunst, stets fröhlich zu sein*.

Moderation is the foundation-stone of true pleasure for the Rococo. The serious and non-radical spirit of the 'Bürger' still lurks under the courtly sophistication of the style. True pleasure, says J. N. Götz, is to be found 'between virtue and reason.'[5] Uz, in 'Die Trinker', rejects with horror the Dionysian image of Bacchus: when possession replaces self-possession, he will 'flee faster than the sand before the whirlwind'.[6] There is no German equivalent of any stature for *Les Liaisons Dangereuses* or *Tom Jones*. Wieland who, as it was, earned considerable opprobrium for his alleged moral laxity (for example, from the Klopstock-worshippers of the 'Göttinger Hain'), nevertheless retained enough moral seriousness to win the qualified approval of Klopstock himself, and even of so stern a moralist as Schiller.

The same principle of moderation in freedom informs German Rococo practice with regard to the irrational world of the fancy. The fundamental 'Aufklärung' belief that literature should improve as well as entertain continues to exert a strong influence, even in contexts of apparently frivolous play or of free fantasy. The usefulness of rational gaiety is often stressed by Rococo writers in reply to stern moralistic critics, as for example in Wieland's introduction to Part Two of *Don Sylvio von Rosalva*, in which it is stressed that the hero's adventures correspond to 'the course of nature' and the claim is made that even if the book does no more than 'clear the dust out of the heads of busy people in their hours of relaxation', it will be 'a thousand times more useful' than one which simply reiterates the old moralistic commonplaces. A desire for more freedom, colour and movement is noticeable, but so is the desire to retain those pillars of rational stability, nature and moral justification.

As in outlook and subject matter, so in literary form, the Rococo introduces greater fluidity and flexibility without falling into disruptive irregularity. Metrically, Rococo poetry has more variation and movement than its Rationalistic counterpart. It favours more varied stanza-forms, less solid and heavy rhythms and uses the long, four-square alexandrine, when it uses it at all, in combination with shorter lines, where its effect is to give rounding and stabilizing without unduly impairing the flow. Poetic form and language are handled with a view to achieving grace, euphony and atmosphere rather than incisiveness or profundity of thought, but this never occurs to such an extent that one could speak of the emancipation of these elements from the authority of reason and meaning. Just as moderation plays a vital role in the Rococo philosophy of life, so it is an important factor in the achievement of the correct stylistic balance and, accordingly, the great model is Horace, whose flight, as Hagedorn puts it, is 'wisely free'[7]: free enough, that is, to achieve the poetic aims of the Rococo, but not so free as to undermine its rational control or offend against its moderate taste. The ideal is a harmonious balance of rational and sensuous, of mind and emotion, in which the two sides co-exist amicably, with the constant understanding that ultimate authority rests with the first half of the partnership.

The combination of pretty nature-scene and clear if undemanding thought in Hagedorn's piece 'Der Morgen' can fairly be taken as representative of the general trend. A modest ambition is expressed in a modest form. The ideal is a gentle pleasure, 'free from pride and cares', a parallel for which is provided by the natural setting which the poet describes. It is pretty, but the natural beauty is kept at an unspectacular and generalized level. The only touch which suggests forcefulness or passion is the reference to bloodstained pathways in the description of the hunt, which is there to enhance, by contrast, the tenderness which animates Phyllis's 'sanfte Brust'. The verse

manages to be simple without being plain, and to achieve a
smooth flow without loss of stability. Stanza two is a good
example:

> Die Hügel und die Weide
> Stehn aufgehellt,
> Und Fruchtbarkeit und Freude
> Beblümt das Feld.
> Der Schmelz der grünen Flächen
> Glänzt voller Pracht,
> Und von den klaren Bächen
> Entweicht die Nacht.[8]

The design of the poem has a neat symmetry, with a measure
of variety. A landscape is put before us, lit by the morning sun
and peopled with living creatures and then, in the third and
fourth stanzas, by humans following contrasted activities.
Sound and rhythm are characterized by gentle variety and
movement and add a pleasant colouring to the tone of the
whole, without remotely threatening to distract attention from
the main thread of the poem's message.

Rococo is, much more completely than any other trend of the
'Aufklärung', a matter of *style*, of tone and atmosphere. Too
much seriousness, too much emphasis on content, militates
against the achievement of its precious balance. This is why
one is inclined to sympathize with Alfred Anger when he
maintains that 'Scherz' (an attitude of light, gay humorous-
ness), as opposed to the intellectual faculty of 'Witz', is the
factor most characteristic of this kind of writing. All writing of
the 'Aufklärung' is intellectualistic to some extent, but that of
the Rococo, by comparison with that of Rationalism, lacks a
cutting edge. There is a tendency to relax from the satirical
towards the humorous trend, as for example in Wieland's *Don
Sylvio von Rosalva*, where the crazy fairy-tale of Biribinker, which
has a rational, even utilitarian purpose, namely to expose
irrationalistic 'Schwärmerei', often approaches the mood of
sheer fun. It is mastery of tone and mood rather than cleverness
which is decisive here: this is not the gaiety of wit, such as we
saw in Lessing's letter to Nicolai, referred to in the previous
chapter. That letter is light-hearted and inventive and entirely
dominated by intellect. Lessing's imagination moves with quick-

silver speed, but this speed cannot blind us to the fact that it is not free or relaxed. The style is all brilliance and sharp edges, whereas Wieland's is more flowing and engaging and not directed so exclusively to the intellectual faculties.

In the social field, the Rococo, like Rationalism, is anything but radical. The relative de-politicization of Beaumarchais' *Mariage de Figaro* in the Da Ponte-Mozart opera,[9] or the ethos of contented obedience exuded by Gleim's songs for simple people,[10] are symptomatic of this. Contentment with his lot is a fundamental part of the German Rococo writer's outlook: not that this meant that he was unaware of inequalities and injustices in society, or of the limitations on his real freedom. Nor did it mean that he did not resent these things: references to courts and courtiers are by no means always complimentary in those aspects of Rococo writing which comment in this field. One thinks, for example, of Wieland's *Pervonte*, where the pride of the heroine Vastola and even more, of the noble circles from which she originates, contrasts unfavourably with the good sense and wisely modest demands of the hero. This modesty, in fact, is the key to the whole Rococo attitude. It is the measure of what Engels saw as the 'philistine' capitulation to the *status quo*, of most of the great men of the age, including Goethe.[11] Seen from another angle, it could be said to reflect the decision that it would be both futile and wrong to fight against it. It is also a measure of the limited freedom achieved by the Rococo: by rendering, or at least declaring himself spiritually independent of material riches, the truly wise man can live in contented ease, though he almost always has to escape from the 'great world' into the conventional pastoral landscape in order to do so.

In the final analysis, it is doubtful whether this escape was successfully achieved by many, or for long. Local tax officials like C. F. Weisse,[12] or civil servants in the government of an unpredictable petty tyrant, as was the case with Uz, lived in a restrictive, repressive atmosphere and this must have had some effect. Sometimes this appears simply in the lack of the ultimate panache which the more invigorating air of other climates might have helped to bring about. It cannot be an accident that many German authors were unable to rival the French in capturing the tone of confident social badinage on the courtly level. Many of them are at their most poetically effective in passages hinting at private feelings, or rendering the delicate atmosphere of the natural setting. The final stanza of Uz's 'Du verstörst uns nicht, o Nacht' even gives us a foretaste of Goethe:

> Murmelt ihr, wann alles ruht,
> Murmelt, sanftbewegte Bäume,
> Bey dem Sprudeln heischrer Fluth
> Mich in wollustvolle Träume.[13]

Sometimes, this relative lack of independence manifests itself in a more rhetorical way, as in the same poet's 'Der Weise auf em Lande' ('The Sage in the Country'). Uz announces at thed outset his intention to 'flee' into the arms of idyllic nature from the 'press' of city and court, but while he can manage a happy, easy mood for a time, he cannot put the darker picture entirely out of his mind and soon breaks out in a passionate denunciation of the mad scramble for wealth and position and the injustices meted out to the weak in the 'great world'.[14]

The ideal state, for the Rococo, is not excitement, but a contented peace ('Ruhe'), most often to be enjoyed in a modest country retreat (e.g. Uz: 'Der Weise auf dem Lande'). There, the German finds it easiest to hold the balance between too little and too much. This equilibrium involves too great a limitation of the area of experience to be entirely satisfactory. The impulse towards order is still too much of a dominating influence. At the same time, a loosening of the leash is welcome and the literary achievement of the German Rococo, at least in Wieland, can command respect.

Wieland's social and personal experience taught him the value of balance, and the ability to control enthusiasm. If we add to this a good, if not outstanding intellectual capacity and a high degree of receptivity to sensuous beauty and grace, we have almost the ideal person to embody the outlook of the Rococo. The negative side is also present: the tendency to draw the line too narrowly in deciding what is safe experience and thus to make the sphere within which balance is achieved too restricted to be permanently satisfying to the human spirit. The quest for balance is the main theme of Wieland's mature work but when a successful balance is achieved, as in *Musarion* or *Don Sylvio von Rosalva*, our enjoyment is alloyed with a slight sense of emasculation of the forces involved, and of restriction of the horizon. When he is more inclusive in his coverage of life, as in the novels *Geschichte des Agathon* or *Geschichte der Abderiten*, the effect is more open-ended and less harmonious.

It is typical that, try as he may, Wieland finds it impossible to produce a really satisfactory picture of the serene balance which is his ideal in the wide-ranging philosophical context of *Agathon*. The portraits of Aristippus (Book IX) and Archytas (Book XI) have a palely theoretical flavour and in each case, Wieland makes the sage's serenity dependent on the enjoyment of an equable temperament and fortunate circumstances.

The quality of serene gaiety ('Heiterkeit')[15] which Wieland tries to show in Aristippus and which is essential to the Rococo balance, is indissolubly linked with the relaxation of the stern philosophical frame of mind in a state of play, and those works which cultivate this state are also the most happily balanced. Unfortunately, while Wieland feels the need to blend play with philosophy, he has not mastered the art of doing so in a truly integrated form. The attempt to do so is apparent in almost all his Rococo works, even in the crazy fairy-tale *Der neue Amadis* (through the character of Olinde), but the most he achieves is an equilibrium, whose rather calculated nature he strives to mask by constant movement and oscillation between the two points.

The verse tale *Musarion* (1768) is the work best suited to illustrate these various characteristics. It traces the progress of the hero, Phanias, through illusion and disillusionment to eventual balance under the tutelage of natural experience, helped by the guiding hand of the wise, beautiful and – most important – charming Musarion. It is neatly constructed in three books which correspond, though not with too rigid an exactness, to the stages of his development. The expression of the Rococo mood and outlook which Wieland consciously strove for in this work[16] is achieved through the grace, melodiousness and ironic detachment of the narration, through embodiment in the character of Musarion herself, and through direct articulation by her.

The description of Musarion (Book I, lines 145 ff.) illustrates the tone and technique of the work, as well as its philosophical position.

It begins with a bantering reference to Venus:

> Was hilft Entschlossenheit?
> Im Augenblick, der uns Minerven weiht
> Kommt Cytherea selbst zur ungelegnen Zeit.

In his easy, detached narrative style, Wieland then moves into another of the classical allusions of which he is so fond:

> Zwar diese war es nicht, doch hätte
> Die Schöne, welche kam, vielleicht sich vor der Wette,
> Die Pallas einst verlor, gleich wenig sich gescheut.[17]

The reference to the Judgement of Paris, naturally a favourite Rococo theme, helps to further the desired atmosphere, and to guard against too great an immediacy of impact.

The use of varying patterns of rhyme is a feature of the whole tale, and is characteristic of the stylistic technique of Wielandian Rococo. But Wieland always maintains that fairly strict control which is the basis of the moderate freedom of the Rococo style. A gentle movement is desirable, but there must be nothing too violent. Expectancy is never allowed to develop into tension, nor relative complexity into confusion, and the balanced patterns of the couplet, interlacing (a-b-a-b) or embracing ('umarmend', i.e. a-b-b-a) rhyme, form a stable basis, on which the structure rests securely. Rhythmically and metrically, there is variation within a framework of regularity, and little changes of pace and accentuation prevent the poem's smoothness from becoming monotonous. These variations are not such as to disturb the reader: they are those of a bright and graceful conversational flow, corresponding to the tone of the language used. Tone and content blend perfectly in the description of Musarion:

> Schön, wenn der Schleier bloss ihr schwarzes Aug' entdeckte,
> Noch schöner, wenn er nichts versteckte;
> Gefallend, wenn sie schwieg, bezaubernd wenn sie sprach:
> Dann hätt' ihr Witz auch Wangen ohne Rosen
> Beliebt gemacht, ein Witz, dem's nie an Reiz gebrach,
> Zu stechen oder liebzukosen
> Gleich aufgelegt, doch lächelnd wenn er stach
> Und ohne Gift. Nie sahe man die Musen
> Und Grazien in einem schönern Bund
> Nie scherzte die Vernunft aus einem schönern Mund;
> Und Amor nie um einen schönern Busen.[18]

The conceptual basis of this portrait is quite clear. Two sides, reason and beauty, are linked together in an alliance. The presentation skilfully concentrates on activity and movement and together with the smooth, yet lively and varied rhythm, creates as its end-effect the quality which is closest to Wieland's heart: not beauty, but charm ('Reiz'). This is not so much a quality in itself as the effect of the balanced simultaneous action of several qualities. There is something here of the artificiality of the Rococo, the art of the juggler whose quickness makes us forget that the pretty coloured balls are not necessarily in any meaningful relationship with one another. It is balance by constant adjustment. Round and round the theme Wieland goes, balancing one element with another, and one feels that he could go on for ever without truly harmonizing the two sides of his equation. Can 'Stechen' (sting) and 'Liebkosen' (caress) ever be wedded together? Is 'smiling as it stung' ('lächelnd wenn er stach') a formulation which removes the opposition between its two component parts? We are forced again to speak, not of harmony, but of equilibrium, just as Wieland himself, in his dedicatory letter to Weisse, speaks of the 'equilibrium between enthusiasm and coolness of mind' in his heroine.

The final summation of *Musarion*, the portrayal of the state of rest and peace achieved by Phanias, brings out the extent to which limitation and even negation are involved in the ideal balance. The ideal is described, once again, in elegant, flowing verse, tinged with discreet touches of poetic sensitivity, using a pretty (but never remotely Romantic) natural setting. A system of checks and balances operates throughout. Phanias is neither rich nor poor. His estates are given a 'quiet' charm by 'modest' art, midday drowsiness steals upon him by a 'little' stream. Middle-class moderation is raised to a cult. The philosophy of charm, in which he is now a believer, is one which teaches contentment with a restricted lot: what Nature and Fate bring are enjoyed 'contentedly' ('vergnügt') and the rest is 'gladly done without'. The world is seen as 'neither an Elysium, nor a Hell': no world, certainly, for uncompromising idealists, and the satisfaction with which the whole picture is imbued does not lack a tinge of complacency. Characteristically, Phanias's idyllic little cot is undisturbed by politics, by 'the civil storm which constantly disturbs Athens'. Once again, the positive pre-supposes a negative.

In return for the limitations freely imposed on himself here, Wieland does achieve gains which are not to be despised. He has managed to find an area for the educated but socially and politically under-privileged citizen which may not have every-thing but which has qualities of beauty and civilized urbanity and is certainly habitable. That there are higher things than what this work has to offer us, we know, and Wieland himself knew. He hints, at times, at something of the kind; in the passage, for example, in which Musarion conjures up the great classical ideals of heroism and self-sacrifice associated with names like Aristides and Leonidas (Book III, lines 1271 ff.). It would defeat his own purpose, of course, to develop the theme further here. In other places, he even gives these ideals a more central position: as, for example, when he brings the great chivalric virtues into harmony with eighteenth-century morality and humanism in *Oberon*.

In this, his nearest approach to a genuine epic, a fairy-tale theme and atmosphere are blended – if with only qualified success – with a truly serious moral theme. But the work fails to sustain the deeply serious heroic tone for very long. The trans-parent but perceptible preserving fluid which always encloses a work of the Rococo is present here too. The 'immovably firm spirit'[19] of the heroic moral theme is overlaid by more graceful and flowing lines and the festive ending, in which virtue is rewarded by Oberon and Titania, is more reminiscent in its tone, colouring and motifs of the culmination of some piece of elaborate Rococo stagecraft than of a deeply serious finale such as Schiller has, for example, in *Wilhelm Tell*.

In *Agathon*, we have an attempt to solve, within the framework of the development of the hero's character and outlook over a long period, the same general order of problem as we have seen in *Musarion*. But in the novel, we are dealing with a character of greater depth and scope, with a wider range of experience. Politics and religion are not excluded on this occasion, nor is the degree of enthusiasm in the hero's character necessary to make him a participant in these fields. There are many more per-plexities than in *Musarion* and whereas Phanias slides easily enough into his blissful state of balanced calm, Agathon has not achieved the same state of contentment even at the end. Wieland has allowed more of himself, his own interests (which included the political), and his experience of the world to enter into the picture.

Even so, he has not forsworn the control and limitation of the Rococo. It may take Agathon a long time to master the 'enthusiastic tendency' in his soul[20] which in Book Ten still makes him harbour revolutionary thoughts against the tyrant Dionysius, nor does Wieland deny that there is good in his emotionalism and idealism. But he certainly believes that these tendencies need to be tempered and if he does not fall a victim to cynicism, Agathon is definitely a much 'cooler' personality at the end. In addition, this book too is wrapped protectively in the Rococo manner, which is always able to introduce a tinge of playfulness or detachment if the atmosphere seems to be becoming too serious, as in the episode in which Agathon is reunited with Danae (Book XI).

The German Rococo, then, combines a certain amount of freedom with a rather greater amount of order. It has some achievements of real aesthetic worth to its credit and it embodies a spirit of civilized balance and tolerance which commands some respect. But if the limits of its tolerance are somewhat wider than is the case with Rationalism, so that feeling and imagination are given more room for manoeuvre, they make their presence felt soon enough to remind one that this style, too, belongs unequivocally to the Age of Order.

7

Sentimentalism

F. G. KLOPSTOCK

Some may be inclined to question the appropriateness of classifying the writers who will be discussed in this chapter under our present general heading of 'Order'. It is certainly true that Sentimentalism is more difficult to distinguish from 'Sturm und Drang' than was the case with the writers we have examined hitherto. Not only do Herder and the young Goethe have a great respect for the outstanding Sentimentalist poet Klopstock; a whole group of close contemporaries of Goethe, most of whom belong to the so-called 'Göttinger Hain' wrote in a manner which was closer to Klopstock's than to Goethe's.

This Göttingen group, in fact, can help us, largely by virtue of its very proximity to the 'Sturm und Drang', to draw the line of which we have just spoken. They and those like them, such as Leisewitz and Gerstenberg, often seem, like the 'Stürmer und Dränger', to question the validity of rules. Like them, they speak much of freedom, and flaunt their emotions, often in a highly rhetorical manner. Yet the comparison forced upon us by their temporal proximity to the 'Sturm und Drang' reveals in every case a measure of restriction that the latter movement would never have countenanced. Their cult of inspiration lacks the 'Sturm und Drang' insight into the independent validity of the individuality; their talk of freedom and criticism of tyranny remains generalized, as was that of the 'Aufklärer'; their emotion rarely goes beyond the traditional and general. And their energy is often more apparent than real: many of them share Klopstock's tendency to the contemplative, rather than the dramatic mood.

Their attitude to the dramatic form is in fact a very good guide to their position. Only Leisewitz and Gerstenberg used this form at all. These two are more problematic than the others, and do stand genuinely between the two camps. But both *Julius von Tarent* and *Ugolino* can be linked with Sentimentalism in the way which, in spite of the character of Guido in the one and the gruesome theme and often fiery language of the other, they shrink back from absolute self-assertiveness and activism. Guido is dominated, eventually, rather than dominating and the prevailing atmosphere in *Ugolino* is one of passive suffering. Sentimentalist drama proper is passive and static in quality. The energy in Klopstock's *Hermann* dramas resides in the language rather than in any action, and the Biblical dramas indulge in lyrically inclined reflection on the suffering of the central figure.

The true emotion, in this Sentimentalist approach, is tied to a *state* of the character, and arises out of contemplation of that state. Melancholy is the state which lends itself particularly well to this approach and it is very popular in Sentimentalist poetry and that of the 'Göttinger Hain'. Gentle, often moonlit mourning for love unrequited, lost or even in some cases not yet arrived, all of which make one think immediately of the early Klopstock, are popular with the 'Hain' poets. Another type of ode or elegy often met with among the latter is the fantasia whose main purpose is simply the cultivation and enjoyment of an indistinct mood. No emotional energy is involved, indeed the intellect seems to be the moving spirit, and there is little of the irrationalism and supernatural suggestiveness of the Romantic Movement. In this, the Göttingen poets are somewhat further removed than Klopstock from the direct emotionalism of the 'Sturm und Drang'. Hölty's 'An die Ruhe' (1771) is a good example:

> Tochter Edens, o Ruh, die du die Finsternis
> Stiller Haine bewohnst, unter der Dämmerung
> Mondversilberter Pappeln,
> Mit verschlungenen Armen weilst, . . .
>
> Endlich bietest du mir, Herzenserfreuerinn,
> Deinen goldenen Kelch, ach, und umarmest mich,
> Wie den flötenden Schäfer,
> Wie die tanzende Schäferinn.
>
> Überirrdisch Gefühl zittert durch meine Brust,
> Durch mein innerstes Mark. . . .[1]

That there is an undercurrent of this passive sentiment in some 'Sturm und Drang' writing has already been suggested, but it *is* an undercurrent. It is represented among the lyric poetry of Goethe in that period by a poem such as 'Felsweih-gesang. An Psyche', which was influenced by the poet's contact with the Sentimentalist circle at Darmstadt. The contrast between this poem and the fiery, dynamic tone of most of the others, is an excellent illustration of the relation between the two strands in Goethe's 'Sturm und Drang' writing. In the case of Schiller, the language and feeling of the 'Laura' poems of the 1782 *Anthologie* can be contrasted, to the same effect, with those of the early dramas.

Other points of difference between Sentimentalism and 'Sturm und Drang' will no doubt emerge later; for the moment it seems best to turn to the direct presentation of the former. We shall return to the seventies in due course, but will begin with the beginnings, before 1750, and use as our example Gellert's novel *Leben der schwedischen Gräfin von G.*, which was published more or less contemporaneously with the first three Cantos of Klopstock's *Der Messias*. This novel still has a strong admixture of the 'adventurous' element – a plot with a great deal of movement, concentrating on exciting and often strange events – which characterizes a type of novel which was very popular in the early eighteenth century and is often called the 'Abenteuerroman'.[2]

The real centre of the book, however, lies in the moral-emotional sphere which was Gellert's most consistent pre-occupation. The Countess's mind and heart are so favourably constituted by nature and so well schooled that her 'Gelassen-heit' and 'Tugend' are proof against all the shocks to which she is subjected. The inner world of feeling is given more scope and freedom, but there is no discrepancy between Gellert's attitude and that of the 'Aufklärung' in general. Reason is tempered by sentiment, perhaps, but the two are in harmony. Gellert is quite explicit about the harmonization of heart and head. The 'cousin' who takes over the heroine's education at a crucial juncture is an ideal pedagogue. He 'lent me his intellectual powers to put my heart [which was 'by nature good'] properly in order . . . he taught me religion in a rational way and convinced me of the great advantages of virtue . . . I believe that religion, thoroughly and rationally taught, can enlighten our understanding as excellently as it improves our hearts'.[3] Virtue, in fact, becomes second nature to her, 'not a cumbersome burden, but a pleasant companion'.

In certain circumstances, however, one does notice a certain self-indulgence and freedom of mood in the presentation of sentiment which is at least strong enough to suspend – for a short time – the authority of the reason. The emotion must be made morally and philosophically safe before this can happen. Such moments occur only when the emotions involved are not destructive or in any way consuming. If it is love which is dealt with, it is often a love which is in some way not *full* love (e.g. unrequited or lost love) and certainly not *immediate* experience: the loved one is almost always imagined rather than present and the emotion is usually indistinct and enjoyed in contemplation rather than dynamically poured out.

Friendship is a frequent Sentimentalist theme, and typically, gives rise to very much the same moods. In the *Schwedische Gräfin*, the love between man and woman partakes, when it is envisaged positively, more of the nature of friendship than of passion and the passages which show the greatest emotional engagement of all are in fact those which deal with the relationship between the Count and his friend Steeley. The reunion between the two is a set-piece and illustrates both the self-conscious, intellectually calculating aspect of this trend, and the way in which it introduces an element of freedom which, for the pure Rationalist, could be called at least potentially dangerous:

> Der Graf zitterte, dass er kaum von dem Sessel aufstehen konnte, und wir sahen ihren Umarmungen mit einem freudigen Schauer lange zu. 'Nun', schrie endlich Steeley, 'nun sind wir für alle unser Elend belohnet' und riss sich von dem Grafen los, und ich eilte ihm mit offenen Armen entgegen. . . . O was ist das Vergnügen der Freundschaft für eine Wollust, und wie wallen empfindliche[4] Herzen einander in so glücklichen Augenblicken entgegen! . . . etc.[5]

Gellert cuts the scene off fairly quickly after this, as if he himself is aware of the dangers of over-indulgence in this kind of sentiment. The key expression, which gives the clue to this danger for any 'Aufklärer', is the word 'Wollust': not simply pleasure, but a pleasure of a particularly seductive, voluptuous kind which is less easily reconciled with rational virtue than is 'Vergnügen'. That is evident in Gellert's own use of the word in describing the Countess's grief at the Count's death. He himself feels that this 'proof of her tender love, is great 'to the point of excess' and clearly does not entirely approve of the fact that the Countess 'found such delight ['Wollust'] in her tears that the thought of calm did not enter her head for many weeks', and that she preferred the siren voice of melancholy, in fact, to that of rational consolation.[6] Like Elinor Dashwood in Jane Austen's *Sense and Sensibility*, when her mother and sister succumb to grief over Mr Dashwood's death, Gellert views this 'excess of sensibility', with 'concern'. In the case of the Countess, as with Mrs Dashwood and Marianne, one feels that the 'agony of grief was voluntarily renewed, was sought for . . .'

Sentimentalism, then, prizes the capacity for tender feeling and seeks out occasions for cultivating it, but keeps it under control. Gellert, indeed, does not give the impulse to freedom as much scope as he might. Sophie von Laroche brings it more into the forefront in her *Geschichte des Fräuleins von Sternheim*. On the whole, her heroine shows the same harmony between inclination and the dictates of reason and virtue that was noted in the case of the Swedish Countess, but Frau von Laroche has conveyed a stronger impression of individuality in that inclination. The greater strength of the impulse towards freedom here is reflected in the fact that Wieland, in his preface to the first edition, cannot give Sophie von Sternheim his whole-hearted approval. He calls her a 'Grillenfängerin' – the word he used for the two philosophers in *Musarion* whose ideals may not have been despicable, but whose thinking was distorted by irrational exaggeration.

But she is no irrationalist, she is indeed 'a lover of understanding and knowledge', in the words of the seducer, Lord Derby.[7] Nor is there any real extravagance in her love for Seymour, or in her emotions in general. The freedom allowed to the heart by Sentimentalism is still relatively restricted. She is a person of strong character who has independent opinions and a sense of her own worth which makes her resent an injustice done her and express this resentment with some force.[8] Under severe provocation she agrees to an elopement, but, like that of Lessing's Sara Sampson, this is but a momentary fall from grace and is not typical of her. 'Self-love and sensibility', she says, have led her 'so far away from her own true self' as to make her embark on a course of action from which she would have 'shrunk back in horror' had she been in a calm ('gelassen') state of mind. She is not a rebel: 'I will not quarrel with my fate . . .' she writes to her friend Emilia 'I have been humbled in the dust . . . and I pray only that God will preserve me long enough for me to be able to enjoy the comfort of knowing that you see the innocence of my heart and weep a sympathetic tear over me.'[9]

The acceptance of, even liking for restriction which characterizes the 'Aufklärung' as a whole, still obtains in Sentimentalism and makes it quite distinct from another emotionalistic current in eighteenth-century German cultural life, Pietism. While there are some points at which the two overlap, Pietism is less inclined to accept limitations on its freedom. Politically, it is unrebellious, but it cultivates a more individualistic and (in the eighteenth-century sense) 'enthusiastic' emotional life. It is decidedly anti-rational in tendency and often retains a degree of mysticism.

The extent to which these elements remained strong in those writers who had some measure of contact with Pietism naturally varies from case to case. But they generally stand aside from Sentimentalism. There is Lichtenberg, for example, that curious mixture of scientific rationalism and irrational emotion, whose Pietistic side is well brought out by Paul Requadt.[10] One thinks of the (secularized) religious substratum in Lichtenberg, his liking for caricature and paradox, his tendency to melancholia, to 'aterrima cura'.[11] Or later in the century there is Karl Philipp Moritz, who shows a measure of detachment in his portrayal of the introverted mentality in his autobiographical *Anton Reiser*, but whose mature outlook still has a certain mystical and inward inclination.

This shows most strongly in the fragmentary *Andreas Hartknopf*, the book which so influenced Jean Paul. The insight which is rendered in the phrase 'the all in the moment' and which the author says is Hartknopf's most precious gift to him,[12] is hardly a purely rational one. Certainly, the phrase would not have seemed meaningful to any stratum of the 'Aufklärung'. And, significantly, Hartknopf has no time for the mere enjoyment of an inactive, indeterminate mood. He is described as 'certainly not one of your sentimental night-walkers who become so absorbed in the contemplation of the moon that they neglect their daily work'.[13] He is able to strike up a friendly relationship with the narrator because 'he saw that my soul was sincere and that I had not come out in order to arrange a solemn scene between myself and nature'.[14] There is an energy in this character which one does not find among the vast majority of Sentimentalist writers but which does occur, albeit in an erratic and sometimes misdirected form, in another writer who was close to Pietism and to 'Sturm und Drang', J. K. Lavater. It is significant that it was the 'Sturm und Drang' Goethe who took an interest in Pietism and the later 'Classical' novelist who embodied this, though in a detached style, in Book VI of *Wilhelm Meisters Lehrjahre*, whereas the Sentimentalist Klopstock, for all his deep religious feeling, shows little real trace of its direct influence.

It took a man of very considerable sensitivity and creative poetic ability to realize the positive contribution which, for all its limitations, Sentimentalism was capable of making, especially to poetry. The only writer of such calibre to appear was Klopstock.

We shall find in Klopstock the balance of two sides which we noticed in Gellert, Sophie von Laroche and others, but with a relatively strong bias towards freedom. Feeling now meets thought on more or less equal terms: at times, indeed, it can be described as 'victorious' ('siegend'), in the phrase of 'Der Zürchersee'. But it is never uncontrolled. Certainly, it does not usurp the role of thought; rather, in the highest (i.e. religious) forms of thinking, it becomes the crown of the whole process.[15] It must be made clear that in all things, the religious plane took precedence for Klopstock, and was always the ultimate goal of his thought and effort. This highest level of literary activity demanded a specially exalted quality of feeling and language. The poet must dedicate all his faculties to it, and the intellectual ones have their part to play. But without feeling, nothing can be achieved. He has to feel himself into the proper state of mind before he can have thoughts of God. Klopstock's first wife, Meta, describes him at work on his *Messias*: 'with the most nobly dignified ('würdigst') expression of devotion, pale with emotion and with tears in his eyes.'[16] The intellect alone cannot give man the knowledge he needs in this sphere. Klopstock embodies his thoughts on the inadequacy of the unaided intellect in his drama *Salomo* (1764), in which he describes the arid despair to which Solomon reduces himself through a philosophy without faith:

> Er treibt in seinen dürren Wüsten um
> Und gräbt sich Brunnen, die kein Wasser geben. [17]

While allowing the primacy of emotional experience, however, we should not fall into the error of identifying the final emotional product with the whole man. Meta, who had formed from his writings an image of a man who was a disembodied spirit, found, on meeting him, that he took an unexpectedly lively interest in her *décolleté*[18], just as the puritanical patriarch Bodmer had been shocked by his interest in physical as well as spiritual things in Zurich. This is the Klopstock whom we find later enjoying and hymning the delights of the open air, especially of skating, writing positively of the value of 'Der Frohsinn' and even showing touches of humour where the context allows it, as for example in 'Der Kamin'. None of this is meant to detract from his fundamental seriousness and spirituality, merely to guard against an excessively one-sided understanding of it.

That the right mood is to a large extent the result of conscious cultivation, and that the intellect plays its part in the process, is well illustrated by Klopstock's letter to Maria Sophia Schmidt, the 'Fanny' of his early love-lyrics, of 20 November 1750. Apropos of Richardson's *Clarissa*, which he had just finished reading, he wote:

> You were, I am sure, like me more moved by her (i.e. Clarissa's) death than by any other scene. It aroused many, a great many thoughts in me. How glad I would be to read any remarks ['Anmerkungen'] you might have on the subject.[19]

The poem 'Die tote Clarissa' (1751), which is in fact directed towards Meta Moller, to whom Klopstock was not yet engaged, might appear at first glance to be all mood and feeling. It is indeed a very delicately felt piece and a fine example of Klopstock's earlier lyric manner, yet there is a perceptible intellectual strand in it, not only in the carefully worked-out metaphor of the flower cut off by the storm – a favourite of Klopstock's – but also in smaller details which have their origin in 'wit', for example the idea that those left behind will still admire the beautiful girl, 'but through our tears' or that, with the cypress-branches which Cidli has gathered, the poet will weave 'wreaths of the leaves of mourning' ('des Trauerlaubes Kränz': stanza eight). This blend of intellect and emotion recalls the way in which, in 'Die frühen Gräber', the moon functions at the same time as a creator of atmosphere, and as a stimulant to thought (as a 'Gedankenfreund'). The feeling is the stronger element, but it is coloured, and to some extent controlled, by thought. The poem aims to 'set the soul in motion',[20] but assuredly not to free it from all rational controls. It makes a straightforward statement and works to a definite plan, drawing together in its third stanza the threads of moon (stanza one) and dawn (stanza two). The use of metaphor and allegory gives a decidedly intellectualistic tone to the whole.

Klopstock's song does flow 'full of feeling and blessed simplicity'[21] up to a point, but when we think of the more radical simplicity and directness of later 'Sturm und Drang' and Romantic poetry, especially that which was influenced by folk-song (which had no influence at all on Klopstock), we must qualify this. Klopstock's emotionalism is never free from rational consciousness and control. One of the most deliberately and intensively 'sentimental' episodes in Klopstock's whole *oeuvre*, that concerning the tender, yet hopeless love between Cidli and Semida, the 'youth of Nain' in Canto Four of *Der Messias*, is presented with analytical self-consciousness, even a certain pious *galanterie*. Semida asks his soul why, when he sees Cidli or thinks of her:

Warum *fühl'* ich alsdann im überwallenden Herzen
Neue *Gedanken*, von denen mir vormals keiner *gedacht* war?
Bebende, ganz *in Liebe zerfliessende*, grosse *Gedanken*!
Warum weckt von der Lippe Cidli's die silberne Stimme,
Warum vom Aug' ihr Blick voll Seele mein schlagendes Herz mir
Zu *Empfindungen* auf, die mit dieser Stärke mich *rühren*?[22]

The poet, as it were, feels his *thoughts about* feeling. The effect is considerably more emotive than any to be found in other 'Aufklärer': Klopstock has greater poetic power, of course; he can find more effective combinations of words and handle the hexameter with a sureness and flexibility unparalleled in German poetry before Goethe. But in view of the degree of calculation in this presentation of his young lover one cannot say that he looks likely to break the moulds of order and set passion truly free.

While wit has not entirely relaxed its hold on emotion in Klopstock's poetry, its effect is less inhibiting than it was in the case of Lessing, or even of Wieland. 'Ihr Schlummer' (1752) is a fair example. It is a calculated piece, which needs careful reading, especially when Klopstock refers to 'the peace of love and virtue' as 'the Grace of thy Olympus' ('Grazie deines Olymps': i.e. its function for the Christian is equated with that of the Graces in Greek mythology). At the same time, the poem is very successful in communicating the delicate and protective feeling of the lover.

It was probably as a poet of the cosmic and spectacular that Klopstock had most appeal for the 'Stürmer und Dränger'. Here, the thrill of freedom, of one's own independent strength and vigour, could most easily be felt. It is a thunderstorm and its aftermath, we remember, which calls Klopstock to mind in Goethe's *Werther*, the exact reference being to the fine hymn 'Die Frühlingsfeier'. Greatness – especially the greatness of God – was not in itself an uncongenial theme of the 'Aufklärer'. But there is a limit beyond which he will not allow himself to be overwhelmed and beyond which he must not overwhelm his readers if the rational taste is not to be offended. Whether Klopstock actually infringed this limit was a matter of dispute at the time. Certainly, if he in fact probably remained within it, he went closer to overstepping the mark than any other 'Aufklärer', and his effect on the young generation is quite understandable.

Some of the more conservative and cautious among the Rationalists of the 'Aufklärung' found that Klopstock went too far, as witness, for example, the frequent attacks on him by critics of the Gottsched school. On the whole, while he writes with more daring and energy than any other author before the 'Sturm und Drang', the situation in this sphere is similar to that discussed in connection with the more personal lyrics. In the *Messias*, for example, there are many passages of rhetoric, sweeping gestures and inventions, passages in which a spirit of dynamism seems to be beginning to make itself felt. But while the element of movement on the whole outweighs the purely static, one would be hard put to it to find evidence of positive irrationalism, and in fact, much of the movement and emotional language is contained in passages of reflection and contemplation, considerably reducing the impact. This epic is indeed one of contemplation rather than action and it is noteworthy, from the point of view of the tenor of its emotion, how much of the feeling is generated by passive, martyr-like suffering, even apart from the central event itself. References to other martyrs and to martyrdom in general are frequent; 'dulden' and 'leiden' are key verbs.

In many of his odes and hymns Klopstock sets out to scale the heights, and his concept of poetry demands that his spectacular object should be described in terms which are themselves spectacular. God, who is the ultimate goal of all these contemplations, cannot be 'thought', except through the emotions. The distinction between subject and object is not removed, and the object is still thought, but the thinker himself is inwardly in a state of motion. Thus, mere powerful rhetoric is not enough; that may be found, after all, in Albrecht von Haller, the potential dynamism of whose thought and emotion is always contained within a Rationalistic framework.[23] Klopstock allows the dynamic elements more scope. From his earliest attempts, he broke away from the strict form of the so-called alexandrine line, indeed from Germanic prosody as a whole as practised at that time, which relied on the repetition of simple, unvarying patterns of stressed and unstressed syllables, with no hint of the rich variety and subtlety which was later to be achieved by Goethe. Klopstock's handling of the ancient classical lyric and epic metres shows progressively more freedom and sensitivity to shifts of mood as he goes forward, and eventually he takes the further step to free rhythms. Structurally too, he moves away from the ultra-clear planning of most of his contemporaries to a form in which the element of planning subsists, but is more strongly influenced by feeling.

This picture of statics and dynamics holds good also of Klopstock's thought, a subject which can be studied best in those poems where he attempts to scale the metaphysical and

cosmic heights. Dizziness is often expressed, indeed it is deliberately sought. The fact that these great themes transcend the
powers of the mind is itself a stock theme with Klopstock. The
solution to this problematic situation is a religious and emotional
one, expressed in great bursts of exaltation (as in 'Die Glückseligkeit Aller') or of powerful imagery (e.g. the thunderstorm-
passage in 'Die Frühlingsfeier' or the cosmic review of 'Die
Gestirne'). The approach to the dilemma, however, is intellectual and philosophical: Klopstock makes no attempt to dethrone
the reason and substitute emotion. He does not reject thought
as a form for contemplation of these high themes, but rather
attempts to retain its basic pattern and expand it so as to contain the emotional element which, to him, is essential if certain
subjects are to be grasped at all. Themes which a Rationalist like
Haller would have to leave untreated, or at least could only
describe from the outside, are tackled head-on, but still with the
relatively disciplined approach of the 'philosophical' poem. It
is not the personal approach through inner individual experience of the 'Sturm und Drang' or the unformed and undisciplined 'Fülle des Herzens' which Stolberg praises so
highly.[24] Klopstock, in thought as in poetry in general, assigns,
as we saw, a high place to feeling, but does not free it from
discipline. He wants greater freedom within a disciplined form
rather than the vague meandering which tends to be what
Stolberg's 'following of nature' amounts to:

> ... es fleusst mein Gesang in schlängelnder Krümmung.
> Leiten kann ich ihn nicht.

We thus find Klopstock going much further than Haller
would have dared or Lessing would have considered admissible. 'Die Glückseligkeit Aller' is possibly the best example.
Here, Klopstock is considering the mystery of death and
resurrection, a theme which the 'Aufklärer', on the whole,
found unsuitable for philosophical treatment. The poem is, in
fact, one of Klopstock's most emotional and most difficult to
grasp. It has a less satisfactory structure, or perhaps one should
say a more decidedly dynamic one than most of the other great
hymns. Nevertheless, the thread of thought still runs through it,
in spite of the poet's simultaneous consciousness of the limitations of the intellect. Rational speculation takes the poet to the

steep side of the 'abyss' on which he can 'feel dizziness', but can see nothing in the depths (Stanza 21). But one notes that even when the impotence of the reason is being discussed, the form of the discussion is still that of rational thought and that there is no attempt to seek an irrationalist or mystical solution in the abyss of mystery.

This interaction between feeling and intellect is apparent in all Klopstock's presentation of thought – and a large proportion of his poetry is in fact presentation of thought. Klopstock treats ideas, not usually very intricate ones, but often quite profound in their implications, and makes coherent statements. Sometimes his technique obscures these a little, but it is rarely difficult to see what he means. The statement gives a clear and rationally appreciable framework. Within this, the handling of language, images and rhythm often gives considerable scope to feeling and there can be a kind of tension between the two sides. This is well contained and certainly not disruptive of order, though it does give the whole that dynamic and not exclusively rationalistic flavour which is Klopstock's most striking trademark.

So much has been written on the freer tendencies in Klopstock's style[25] that no more than a brief outline need be added here. His constant concern for strong expression is well brought out by F. G. Jünger when he says that the poet is so intent on saying as much as possible that he often sets out to express more than language can contain.[26] This often leads to a certain strain, a sense of repeated probes and leaps, like a salmon at a high obstacle. It often brings Klopstock to the point where statement gives way to mere exclamation. He will use words, especially nouns and adjectives, in a way which deviates radically from the accepted grammatical norm: the comparative form of the adjective, for example, to render, not a true comparative, but a certain vague enhancement of the quality, or the plural forms of nouns, particularly feminine abstracts derived from verbs and indicating a state, which strictly speaking cannot have a plural. Examples are 'Entzückungen' (e.g. Der Messias, xiii, 853) or 'Umschattungen' ('Der Zürchersee', Stanza 17). The cultivation of states and moods, of a certain indistinctness, is characteristic of him: the moon-mood of the opening of 'Die frühen Gräber' is a fine example of how far he will go and where he will stop in this 'musical' style of writing. In poetic vocabulary, he sought to increase and ennoble the range of expression of German poetic language and one sees the effects of this in the young Goethe, for example. Words like 'Schauer' and compounds like 'sternhell' have a familiar Goethean resonance.

To sum up, the situation with regard to Klopstock and the majority of those who admired and, to a greater or lesser extent, followed him, is that the impulse to freedom, whether in political and social thinking, or in literary themes or techniques, is still not strong enough to take control. It remains contained within a more or less orderly framework and while it causes a certain loosening, a more dynamic nature in the literature concerned, the liberating phrases are not meant *fully*. The forces of order, when they are evoked, have a positive attraction. This is perhaps easier to see in the Göttingen writers and others who stand on the periphery of the 'Sturm und Drang' than in Klopstock himself, who after all had poetic genius of a high order. Klopstock sometimes cultivates a mood which is 'youthfully impetuous' ('Auf meine Freunde'), Stolberg speaks of 'this raging in my breast' ('Der Genius'), Leisewitz's Guido sometimes speaks in tones which would not disgrace Karl Moor himself. These are not insincere moments, but in the wholes to which they belong they are balanced and contained by the forces of order. It is the interaction between the two sides which makes the literature of 'Empfindsamkeit' such a fascinating study.

Part 3

Freedom

8

'Sturm und Drang': the Struggle for Freedom

Our task in this part of our study is simpler than it was in the preceding one. In the 'Aufklärung', the problem of containment of the urge towards freedom, which was channelled in various ways, produced a complex pattern. Without being entirely simple in nature, the trend which we call 'Sturm und Drang' is more vigorous and unified, and the flow is much more in a single direction.

The 'Stürmer und Dränger' hated restriction much more than they feared disorder. They sometimes seem to cultivate disorder deliberately, nowhere more strikingly than in the approach and method of their literary theory, which seems to be symbolized in Hamann's provocative subtitle for his *Aesthetica in Nuce*: 'a rhapsody in cabbalistic prose.' They were much less willing than the Sentimentalists had been to submit their feelings to the authority of reason or conventional 'virtue'. Herder, awaking to a realization of the emotional self-mutilation often practised in the name of virtue, addresses a woman he once knew in Riga: 'You have been virtuous; show me your virtue. It is a tissue of renunciations, a grand total of zeros.'[1] Nature, for the 'Aufklärer', prescribes rules and restrictions; for Heinse, 'all compulsion inhibits and constricts nature.'[2] While an inherent balance normally prevents total and overt endorsement of criminality, there is in the period a significant proportion of not unsympathetic treatment of characters who infringe the commandments of morality and the law, including even the sixth commandment. One thinks of Guelfo in Klinger's *Die Zwillinge*, Golo in Müller's *Golo und Genoveva*, and above all of Karl Moor in Schiller's *Die Räuber*.

Whatever the exact reasons – and it seems too facile to refer simply to political and social conditions, for there is no startling change in these at this time and the French Revolution is still a decade away – leading German writers quite suddenly began to feel an intolerable constriction in what previously had been acceptable. 'Freedom! Freedom!', the final cry of Goethe's Götz von Berlichingen, became the war-cry of the whole generation.

It is a vague, but extremely strong feeling and its expression is often violent. Images of a violent, often destructive nature are common, whether in the 'quieter' realm of inner feelings or in the more active and heroic context. One of the finest is that of the chariot-race in Goethe's poem 'Wandrers Sturmlied', which is associated with Pindar and with a thunderstorm. This, and not the idyllic world of Theocritus or the light-hearted one of Anacreon which had been the haunt of Gessner and Gleim, is the medium which Goethe's mood demands. The thunderstorm reference reminds us of the enthusiasm shown for Klopstock's 'Frühlingsfeier' in *Werther*. But whereas the earlier poet, for all his emotional involvement, still uses the image as a link in a definite train of thought, one suspects that Goethe's response is less specific and intellectual and that it is the inherent expressive force of the image, its fitness as an outlet for a mood rather than its metaphorical potential, which interests him. There is, in other words, a strong constructive and orderly element in Klopstock's use of it which is not necessarily present in Goethe's understanding of it.

The restoration of a certain degree of order to a landscape fundamentally disrupted by the great outburst of the 'Sturm und Drang' is a central factor in the process of Goethe's development into a 'Classicist'. That he, and Schiller and Herder, were able to ride through this storm and effect such a restoration without reverting to the more negative, restrictionist attitude of the 'Aufklärung' is a measure of the stability and flexibility of their characters. It was certainly no easy victory. Goethe, in later years, always felt a deep unease when returning, spiritually, to the landscape of the 'Sturm und Drang', particularly to *Werther*, the work in which he experienced the inherent destructiveness of that mood to its full extent.

The dangers which go together with the exhilaration of the 'Sturm und Drang' attitudes are best illustrated by the case of J. M. R. Lenz, a gifted, but unstable, and not entirely welcome disciple of Goethe's. Writing apropos of *Götz von Berlichingen*, he lays exclusive stress on the theme of freedom:

We learn [from all this] that the active power within us does not rest, does not cease to work, to move, to rage in us until it has procured freedom all around, room in which to act . . . and even if it were a Chaos that thou [i.e. God] hadst created, desert and empty, if only freedom resided there and we could brood over it in imitation of thee until something came out of it – what a blissful, blissful, divine feeling that would be![3]

This kind of language, which is not more passionate, but more extravagant and vague than Goethe's, gives a clear warning light.

After we have read Lenz in this vein, we can see why not all those 'Stürmer und Dränger' who cultivated sentiment so assiduously, escaped unscathed. Lenz himself was destroyed mentally and G. A. Bürger at least materially. It is not at all surprising that the mature Goethe and Schiller looked somewhat askance at the confusions of the younger generation, even of a Hölderlin or Heinrich von Kleist. They would have called too vividly to mind the often unhealthy extravagances of days not too far gone by. Goethe, for example, had had experience at first hand of the instability of Lenz and of the embarrassing *démarches* of Lavater, who, 'seized by the freedom- and nature-spirit of the time', in the words of *Dichtung und Wahrheit*,[4] could control neither his emotions nor his prosyletizing zeal. And there had been even more dubious figures who had enjoyed a vogue and had taken in even the great, including Goethe himself. The most famous of these was Lavater's compatriot Christoph Kaufmann. This man, who is described as having had an imposing presence, was half charlatan, half Rousseauistic prophet and gave himself out to be a kind of divine emissary, seeking out the elect. Jakob Minor describes him, in the *Allgemeine Deutsche Biographie* as travelling about 'mounted on a white horse, his jerkin open and his hair flowing freely down' – no doubt an impressive sight![5] Schiller, when he attacked the extravagances of others, may well have had at the back of his mind a memory of the excessive emotings of his own youthful poetry, or of his youthful friendships, which are reflected in letters such as those to Scharffenstein and Boigeol of 1776.

Freedom

'The only thing the Kraftgenies [i.e. 'Stürmer und Dränger'] could not learn was restraint,' says Bruford.[6] There is irritation in this comment, and on occasion, when confronted by an example of self-indulgent adolescent iconoclasm, one is inclined to sympathize with it. 'Sturm und Drang' could be a mere manner, like any other style, and there is little that is more tiresome than conventional unconventionality. But the 'Stürmer und Dränger' usually act from positive principle, even if it is only hazily realized in terms of conscious thought. Their throwing-off of restraint was not merely a negative gesture; it was itself an expression of something positive, and the positive ideals were nearly enough and often enough realized to make the aberrations and wildnesses not too high a price to pay.

If there is a central point in the superficially rather confused mass of positive ideals and ideas of the period, it lies in the liberation of the Self. Society, theological and philosophical orthodoxy, poetic theory, conventional morality and many other orders within which men lived and which originated outside the individual, imposed on him restraints of various kinds. Previously, the impulse to individual self-expression and self-assertion had certainly existed, but had always been contained. At some stage, the discipline of an outside authority had been accepted. Now, these restraints were rejected along the whole front. This included the rejection of 'reason', as conceived by the 'Aufklärung', since in this form it is a kind of general, unvarying essence, extraneous to the individual and attempting to exert authority over him from without: a person's feelings, however inchoate, lacking in intellectual value, even 'immoral', could be seen as having more validity.

If we focus on the central position of the individual Self, we are also better able to understand the primacy of feeling as such in the scheme of things of the 'Sturm und Drang'. Lenz writes:

> Lieben, hassen, fürchten, zittern,
> Hoffen, zagen bis ins Mark,
> Kann das Leben zwar verbittern;
> Aber ohne sie wär's Quark.[7]

He says this in a poem addressed 'to the heart', the organ for which the generation of the 'Stürmer und Dränger' had most

respect. Knowledge, a thing acquired from outside, was infinitely inferior in value to the riches of the heart. 'What I
know,' says Werther, 'anyone can know. My heart belongs to
me alone' (letter dated 9 May in Book II). The heart is not, like
the 'reason' of the 'Aufklärer', a universal norm: it embodies the
principle of individuality. Thus Lenz, in his 'Versuch über
das erste Prinzipium der Moral', resists the tendency of the
rationalistic thinker to reduce everything to one principle. He
rejects the reason as chief guide and substitutes the heart,
which will produce harmony, but not uniformity, in human
activity.[8]

No one who has any acquaintance with the literature of this
period will have failed to be struck by its dynamism. It is
dominated by the language and imagery of power. There is
something approaching a cult of 'Kraft' (power, energy), hence
the common title of 'Kraftgenie' for this generation. The great
hero of the 'Sturm und Drang' is the man, like Götz von Berlichingen, who has innate strength and power and leads a life of
freedom in which these qualities can be expressed. This freedom
for individual action explains the enthusiasm of sophisticated
eighteenth-century Germans for the 'Faustrecht' (right of
private justice) of the sixteenth-century knights, as for more
'primitive' ages in general (Homer, Ossian, the Patriarchs). The
concept of genius is their most effective practical embodiment
of the ideal. Here, some kind of fulfilment was possible, some
satisfaction for the 'sweet impulse to create', as Müller calls it in
the dedication of *Fausts Leben*.[9]

The Storm and Stress generation felt almost suffocated in the
atmosphere which surrounded them. They felt within themselves the 'great and warm heart' which the young Schiller says
is 'all a man needs for bliss',[10] and yet that heart could not find
sufficient scope or sustenance:

> Nein, ich schreie – Vater! Retter!
> Dieses Herz will ausgefüllt
> Will gesättigt sein. Zerschmetter
> Lieber sonst dein Ebenbild.[11]

Ironically, the 'Sturm und Drang', in which the religious urge
was considerably stronger than in the 'Aufklärung', was more
likely to come into collision with orthodoxy. However much he

disliked the specific structure, the 'Aufklärer' would dislike even more the destruction of the order which it represented. In the form in which it appeared in the eighteenth century, however, orthodoxy offered little nourishment for the heart and little scope for the Self to feel and fulfil itself. Both the positive and the negative poles of the religious consciousness of the young Goethe, as represented by the poems 'Ganymed' and 'Prometheus' respectively, lead us back to a common origin – what in the latter is called the 'heilig glühend Herz' ('heart glowing with holy warmth'). God, for the 'Stürmer und Dränger', lived in the individual heart or conversely, the heart became God. There was an oscillation – reminiscent of the Renaissance – between the mystically oriented position of the founding father of the 'Sturm und Drang', Hamann, and that represented, for example, by Faust, especially as conceived by Müller, or by Heinse in *Ardinghello*. The latter work is set, significantly, in sixteenth-century Italy, and the hero proclaims the self-sufficiency of the individual in correspondingly bold terms: 'I believe that every man has a daimon in him which tells him what he should do . . . in every man there dwells a god and he who has sufficiently purified his inner feelings can perceive the oracles of that god without words or signs.'[12]

'Nature' is another watchword of the movement, and here again one comes back ultimately to the inner Self as the fountain-head. The nature now admired and sought was not, as in the 'Aufklärung', the truth deducible by the reason from the general run of things, but rather those things themselves, in their own individuality, before the intellect could detach them from their roots and reduce them to a characterless common denominator. Civilization was conceived, following Rousseau, as the enemy of nature: civilization, that is, in its generalizing, intellectualizing function. Goethe, reviewing a 'Characterization of the most prominent European nations' in the *Frankfurter Gelehrte Anzeigen* denies all true character to a 'polished' (i.e. sophisticated) nation:

As soon as a nation becomes polished it has acquired conventional ways of thinking, acting and feeling, it has ceased to have a character . . . What, then, is the 'character' of a polished nation? What can it be, other than . . . drapery, the most one can say of which is how well it suits a nation.[13]

Goethe seems sceptical as to the possibility of any kind of harmonious relationship between 'Politur' and the 'Naturstoff' underneath it. Later, Classicism was to attempt a reconciliation of the two. For the time being, it is the latter which needs to assert itself. The aggressive tone in which the 'Stürmer und Dränger' asserted their 'German-ness' is one reflection of this, and it was for this purpose that the ordinary people were particularly dear to them and were so affectionately portrayed by them, as, for example, in the figure of the coachman Walz in Wagner's *Die Reue nach der Tat*. All these things reflect the importance attached to natural, individual 'character', just as Goethe uses the word 'characteristic' to epitomize his new ideal of an art which, whether it originates from a primitive or a civilized source, should arise organically, and be shaped by a single, unified emotion into a 'characteristic whole'.[14]

The shift of taste in gardens from the formal lay-out which appeals to the intellect to one which, like that at Wörlitz[15] which so impressed Goethe, or Werther's favourite haunt (Book I, letter of 4 May), has more to offer to 'the feeling heart', is another feature of this same phenomenon. It leads to a consideration of the special relationship in which Goethe, particularly, felt himself to stand to the world of what we call inanimate nature which seems to have been more truly alive for him than sophisticated human society. Even if he asserts that Lili Schönemann carries 'Natur' with her wherever she goes, the antipathy he feels to the 'Lichter' and 'unerträgliche Gesichter' of the brilliant society into which she leads him is unmistakable.[16] That world is clearly *not* nature for him, and it is a world in which he cannot feel free and be himself.

Among the trees and meadows, on the other hand, Goethe seems to be enjoying a personal relationship, and he is free:

> Und frische Nahrung, neues Blut
> Saug ich aus freier Welt,
> Wie ist Natur so hold und gut
> Die mich am Busen hält![17]

There is an intimate, indefinable relationship between the personal feelings of the individual and the surrounding natural world. The great poem 'Mailied' is the supreme expression of this, together with several key passages in *Werther*, but even within the consciously artificial context of the pastoral 'Singspiel', it emerges quite distinctly. In *Erwin und Elmire*, Valerio speaks of the way in which 'all around, a spring-like weather rises out of our full souls'.[18]

Nature is rarely there for its own sake in 'Sturm und Drang' writing. If the nature-poetry of the time carries conviction, it is because the perspective is so completely given by the 'Ich', the Self which over and over again turns out to be the central point from which the sometimes quite complicatedly ramified growth takes its origin.

The assertion of the Self, its realization (this is the purpose for which freedom is sought), does not mean simply the reinstatement of feeling to the exclusion of the other faculties. The ideal is the complete man, which includes the mind; but the system of the 'Aufklärung', which chose the intellectual faculties as the centre and therefore subjected the individual to the general, naturally evoked a strong reaction which tended to overestimate the importance of feeling. Subconsciously at least, the 'Stürmer und Dränger' did not mean the primacy of the heart to imply mindlessness, and it could be argued that the word 'heart', as it was then understood, was a more fitting one to represent the unity and interaction of all man's spiritual faculties than was 'head'.

The writings of the new generation are not, in fact, antiintellectual. Theoretical discussion still bulks large in their production, and art, philosophy and other such subjects continue to be discussed at a sophisticated level, if not always in a sophisticated spirit. The spirit, rather than the substance of the popular is what interests them in such things as the 'Volkslied', and this is because it represents a state in which the unity of the individual's spiritual life has not been lost. They do not want to go 'back to nature' in any literal sense. Herder disclaims any idea of reverting to 'walking on all fours'[19] and Goethe expresses impatience with the intellectual limitation of the Pietists of Strassburg.[20]

It would have been an inconsistency for the 'Sturm und Drang' to have substituted one-sided emphasis on a single aspect of human nature for the different one-sidedness of the 'Aufklärung', for they were imbued with a longing for wholeness and universality. 'All', and 'ganz' (whole) are keywords of the movement. The appeal of figures like Faust is at least in part a result of this impulse. Both Goethe's hero and Müller's react against restraints on their self-fulfilment in this way. 'O, sie müssen noch alle hervor, all die Götter, die in mir verstummen . . .'[21] says Müller's Faust, and the idea of completeness is implicit here. Goethe has a more definite vision. His Faust desires knowledge of the ultimate in cognition ('Was die Welt Im innersten zusammenhält'), and the ultimate in experience. The great ideal of the movement, the demi-god hero, is not only free, but complete and creative.

The artistic variant of this ideal, the genius, shows this in a particularly clear form. He obeys no rules that one can codify, he confines himself within no plan that one can see clearly. 'His plans,' says Goethe of the great embodiment of the 'Genie'-concept, Shakespeare, 'are in the ordinary sense, no plans at all.'[22] Herder, in his characterization, constantly stresses Shakespeare's infinite variety and tangled disorder: he does so, indeed, to the point of distortion. An 'ocean of events,'[23] without shore or shape, is what he sees. 'Drunkenness and disorder' seem to characterize the creator of this dramatic world. But this is not meant to be understood merely negatively. All these jumbled pieces are 'symbols towards . . . a Theodicy of God': the particular chaos is the direct result of a universal vision. Herder's description of *King Lear* as a 'father-and-children-and king-and-fool- and beggar-and-wretchedness-*whole*',[24] sums up the tendency of the critique.

The literary theory of the 'Sturm und Drang' cultivates a deliberate disorder. Hamann, the first theorist to write in a consistently 'Sturm und Drang' spirit, gives his *Aesthetica in Nuce* the provocative sub-title: 'A rhapsody in cabbalistic prose' and always glories in his 'non-philosophical' (i.e. non-rationalistic) approach. Philosophy, as practised by the 'Aufklärung', is for him the enemy of nature: 'your lying philosophy has swept nature aside'.[25] The hostility to rationalism which — in spite of denials by some critics[26] — pervades the literary theory and practice of this generation is not, therefore, a totally negative thing. The *merely* rationalistic philosophy must be destroyed, if nature is to be restored. Poetry, the direct and sensuous 'mother-tongue of the human race', in Hamann's famous phrase,[27] has been overlaid by the language of the intellect, and needs to be set free.

There is primitivism of a kind in the 'Sturm und Drang', but it is neither negative nor truly unsophisticated. The wide range of learning deployed by Hamann, Herder and others, is sufficient evidence of this. G. A. Bürger, who even wanted to elevate 'popularity' to the status of canon for all poetry, by no means departs entirely from the concept of poetry for the educated. He advocates a poetry which is 'by educated people [literally, scholars] but not for educated people *as such*'. The ruling concept should be that of 'Volk', which is understood as meaning 'those characteristics in which approximately all, or at least the most reputable classes, agree'.[28] The most important of the 'Stürmer und Dränger' were, indeed, harder to understand than their predecessors. Only relatively peripheral and minor figures like Schubart or Bürger himself were really 'popular', even in Bürger's sense.[29]

The enthusiasm of this generation for folk-poetry, and the role which it plays in literary theory, especially that of Herder, is a symptom of a more wide-ranging attitude. The qualities of this literature appeal because they help the writer to throw off the restrictions on the feelings which are most important to him. Folk-poetry is precious because it is alive; because it is sensuous and immediate in expression and sets no restrictions on feeling, imagination or 'Kraft' (the inner energy which was always seeking an outlet); because it has 'character' and individuality and because it is a natural, organic growth.

Art should be the direct and complete expression of individual experience.

The idea of the norm is inconsistent with the outlook of the 'Stürmer und Dränger': his mirror reflects the complete panorama of nature, in all its diversity. As Hamann puts it in his reply to critics of the *Sokratische Denkwürdigkeiten*:

. . . our muse is suckled at the many breasts of the fruitful, shapelessly sprawling mother [i.e., presumably, nature], a pupil of that swarm of bees in the lion's carcass, where food came forth out of the Devourer and sweetness out of the Strong One.[30]

In the vision of the untrammelled creativity of genius, as in that of art as an organic and individual growth, the 'Sturm und

Drang' expresses its fundamental requirement that the Self should be free, and able to fulfil itself. The subjectivity of some of the 'Stürmer und Dränger' is extreme. Schiller shows an insight into this when he writes to Reinwald (14 April, 1783): 'In the last analysis, it would seem that all the creations of our imagination are no more than – ourselves.'[31]

The most important passage in Goethe's essay on the Strassburg minster is the one in which he talks about the crude artistic endeavours of the savage. He is able to find in this a particularly clear example of art that is, as he puts it, 'characteristic'; art, that is, in which a personal experience grows, or seems to grow naturally into a product which is an acceptable artistic whole ('Ganzes'), but is so without loss of individuality: 'a single feeling formed it into a characteristic whole.'[32] Then, in a sentence which comes as close as any written in this period to putting the artistic credo of the movement in a nutshell, Goethe continues:

When it [i.e. art] produces out of a heartfelt, unique feeling, a feeling which is independent and belongs to the one artist alone, unconcerned about, indeed ignorant of everything alien to it, then it matters not whether it is born of crude savagery or of cultured sensibility, it is whole and alive.

This 'characteristic' art (which, as we see, is not necessarily unsophisticated) is the art of the free Self, and according to Goethe it is 'the only true art'.

The negative aspects of the 'Sturm und Drang', though their effects are often spectacular, are not there for their own sake. The willingness to accept disorder and the undeniable hostility of the movement to the rationalism of the 'Aufklärung' are caused, at least in the truly important 'Stürmer und Dränger', by the fact that the order and the rationalism with which they found themselves confronted were a barrier to the complete and organic growth which they demanded. It was when social conventions had this effect that they became a stumbling-block to the young generation. Differences as such were not particularly objectionable. As far as the social structure was concerned, it would seem to have been not inequality, but the domination of the centralized system, the swallowing-up of the individual by his rank or office so that men no longer related to one another as individual men, that they hated most. 'Aufklärer' and 'Stürmer und Dränger' alike detested the *tyranny* of despots, but the former could appreciate the rational orderliness of the centralized despotic system as it had culminated in the eighteenth century, whereas the 'Stürmer und Dränger' hankered after a kind of 'family' structure, where there was authority, but also more organic, personal relationships.[33]

Just as the individualism of outlook discussed above tends to seek integration in a greater whole, there is in the 'Sturm und Drang' concept of art a premonition of a greater form and order towards which their apparent formlessness is the first important step. Freedom does not mean the denial of form. It is 'better to produce a confused piece than a cold one', says Goethe. But there is an 'inner form', one which cannot be intellectually arrived at, but must be 'felt'. The work must take the form which the artist intuitively feels in the material and which, as it were, emerges from within it. This form is much less unnatural than the rationalistic norm of the 'Aufklärung', but it is still form; it still, as Goethe admits, has something 'untrue' about it.[34] Complete lawlessness, the kind of freedom which is in fact licence, is no part of the 'Stürmer und Dränger's' basic desire. There is such a thing as beauty; a greater order within which the individual belongs and to whose heights he can aspire. Unless his genius and his heart are functioning without let or hindrance, he has no chance of making contact with the higher order at all. The freedom of the individual is an essential precondition, but there are gradations in the artistic feeling for beauty and hence there must be an objective measure for it, even if its inner secrets are accessible only to intuitive feeling. Goethe continues the section of 'Von deutscher Baukunst' from which we have just quoted:

In nations and in individual men, you will see innumerable gradations. The more the soul raises itself towards a feeling of those proportions which alone are beautiful and eternal, whose chief chords can be shown but whose secrets can only be felt, and in which alone the life of the godlike genius rolls round in blissful melodies, the more this beauty penetrates into the being of a spirit so that it seems to have originated with him . . . the more deeply we bow and adore the anointed of God.[35]

Goethe in fact employs the word 'beautiful' in two senses: that in which it is used by 'Aufklärer' like Sulzer, and that of the higher beauty of the passage just quoted. The former is restrictive and is rejected when Goethe assigns the formative ('bildend') element priority over the 'beautiful' ('schön') in art.[36] The second sense is in harmony with the full expression of the individual and is the true end of the forming process.

That Herder did not appreciate disorder for its own sake is evident from his prize essay of 1773, 'Ursachen des gesunkenen Geschmacks bei den verschiedenen Völkern, da er geblühet'. The unpolished, natural force of genius must come first, if true taste is to develop at all. An historical development brings the crude forces into a state of 'order'; reason (though it is a more dynamic, creative reason than that of the 'Aufklärer') is a vital motive force in bringing about the desired result:

> Given that taste is nothing but order, the capacity of [man's] forces to achieve beauty, however quickly it operates and is felt, it can only operate through reason, judgement and due consideration, through which alone order comes about. Even the bee's cell (if I may compare genius with animal instinct, and perhaps they are at bottom the same), even that needs the most excellent bee-understanding ['Bienenverstand'] if it is to be brought to perfection, and the more noble a genius is, the more worthy the sphere towards which it strives and the more worthily it fulfils its striving, all the more does it need to show an apt and comprehensive reason, even in the most swift-flowing fiery river of activity and feeling.[37]

What is envisaged here is something more complex than the straightforward, methodically calculating ratiocinative process of the 'Aufklärung': rather, a synchronization of the rational and non-rational.

The emotional energy of this generation was so comprehensive that artistic creation was possibly the only practical activity in which it could have found fulfilment. A re-structuring of society, for example, would hardly have sufficed: it desired a rebirth. Its preoccupation with the inner life explains the stress it laid on receptivity as well as creativity. 'Ganymed' is a poem of great dynamism, but its central figure is blessed at least as much in receiving as in giving. He is 'umfangend umfangen' ('embracing, embraced'). The receptive and active sides of the 'Sturm und Drang' sometimes come out in dramatic dualisms (e.g. Weislingen-Adelheid in *Götz von Berlichingen* or Luise-Ferdinand in *Kabale und Liebe*), sometimes in uneasy oscillation between two poles of a single character, like Goethe's Clavigo. Ideally, they are complementary and intimately interrelated which is why, when all is said and done, the one complete work which can count as a successful epitome of the movement is *Die Leiden des jungen Werthers* which, for all its apparent limitation, manages, without loss of unity, to encompass the themes of love, religion, art, society and the human heart in general, in their full range.

We have reached the stage at which we must take up once again the theme of idealism in German literature. For all its surface 'realism', its concern for nature as it is in the individual instance rather than in rationally conceived general terms, the 'Sturm und Drang' in fact represents the first stage in the development of that idealism of outlook which is a continuous thread throughout the literature of the 'Goethezeit'. In so far as the writing of this time has the *quality of reality* (and it does not often have it to a marked degree), it is an incidental element. The 'Sturm und Drang' is *less* close to it, indeed, than Classicism. It enjoys the feel and smell of the details of real life for their individual nature, their immediacy, their non-intellectual and sensuous quality. When, in the *Anmerkungen übers Theater*, he advocates imitation of the nature that lies around us, Lenz stresses its sensuousness and its quality of being 'gegenwärtig'[38] (literally, 'present'). It is the distillation of a certain spirit out of reality rather than a careful, objective re-creation of it which seems to be the aim.

For a time, of course, these two lines can run parallel. In *Die Soldaten*, in particular, Lenz gives a convincing picture of the milieu in which the action takes place. But the actual world is not able to satisfy the demands of mind and spirit completely. Even in *Die Soldaten*, we find the Countess saying: 'What has life left to offer by way of appeal if our imagination does not introduce it?'[39] And Lenz expresses elsewhere the Faustian desire to know and experience everything immediately and totally, 'all bliss in one feeling'.[40] Reality has immediacy, but it lacks totality; at least, it did for the 'Goethezeit'.

The 'Stürmer und Dränger' had a sense of history which is much closer to the modern one than that of the 'Aufklärung'.

As Collingwood points out, historians like Hume and Voltaire wrote in a polemical and anti-historical spirit, measuring the past by the standards of the eighteenth century.[41] Writers like Herder and Möser write in conscious opposition to this trend, so that Herder's *Auch eine Philosophie der Geschichte*, the precursor of the more famous *Ideen*, is itself in large measure a polemical work. Criticism of the 'Aufklärung' is the strongest single thread. But it is more than just a criticism of Herder's own time. It is imbued with the idea, which is foreign to Montesquieu even, that each nation and age has its own character and should be understood in its own context. Against Montesquieu's 'esprit' and his attempt to reduce the tremendous mass of material to a small number of general principles, so that every age and nation should 'hang up all its belongings on three weak nails', Herder puts a sympathetic understanding of the individual character and validity of each unit in the 'Taumel aller Zeiten, Nationen und Sprachen'.[42]

But we are still a long way from the history of truly 'objective' realism, the kind which sets out, as did Ranke, to see 'how things in fact were'. The 'Stürmer and Dränger' have more interest than the 'Aufklärer' in the factual details in themselves, because they contain life, character and individuality. But the detail is a stepping-stone to something bigger. It is not so much the actuality which interests Herder and Möser, but the spirit ('Geist') which informs it, without being comprehended by it. Möser, for example, writing of 'Faustrecht' the twelfth and thirteenth centuries, says that this is the age in which 'our nation showed most feeling for honour, most physical virtue and a national greatness of its own.' The nation 'would do well to study that great period and become acquainted with the genius and the spirit which worked, not on stone and marble, but on human beings and ennobled their feelings and their strength in a way of which we can hardly have any conception today.'[43]

To a significant extent, then, if not quite so exclusively as with the Romantics of the nineteenth century, Möser's main interest is in the 'Geist' of the past. This is even truer of Herder, who is concerned with the spirit in which men lived rather than the day-to-day details of their lives and sees human history as a unified whole, as 'the progress of God through the nations',[44] the ultimate goal being a kind of millennium of humanity, an idea more composedly worked out in the *Ideen zu einer Philosophie der Geschichte* of his Classical phase.

But already, in the different atmosphere of the 'Sturm und Drang', Herder is thinking in strongly idealist terms. He urges his fellow men to work together towards 'a great future' and sees all noble and worthy acts, in whatever age, as seeds for 'the noblest plant of humanity'. Contemplated in this light, all these acts lose their incidental, merely actual qualities:

> All the merely corporeal and political [i.e. presumably, practical] aims involved fall away like the broken casing and dead body ['Scherb und Leichnam']; the soul, the spirit, the content relevant to humanity as a whole remains, and happy the man who has been able to drink deeply of this pure, unsulliable spring of life![45]

In the more specifically literary field, the great source from which authors were able, according to Herder, to imbibe the spirit of real, living, unstultified nature, was the poetry of the 'Volk'. This concept, which Herder was largely responsible for introducing into German cultural and political thought, and which later caused such unparalleled havoc when men of a very different character set out to apply it in practical life, represents a kind of ideal essence for Herder. It is not synonymous with 'nation', in a political sense, nor with 'people', in a social, class-sense. It represents a quality which the cultured man can and should strive to possess, but it is not the result of culture or education: in fact, civilization, with its increasing intellectualization of life and culture, has militated against it. It is rather like the immediacy, sensuous life and simplicity of the 'natural' character projected on to the national plane.

Herder certainly believes in the reality of a German national character, one which needs to be rediscovered and revitalized, having been overlaid with an intellectualistic pseudo-character of foreign origin. This idea of national character goes together with the wider and more important concept of 'Volk' as such, whose qualities are life, power, sensuous immediacy, individual being, rather than generalized and anonymous ratiocination – in a word, 'that rich Nature which everyone is capable of feeling', as he puts it in the Preface to Part Two of the *Volkslieder*.[46] The prime example given in that work is Homer; elsewhere, it is Ossian: both together fulfil this function in Goethe's *Werther*.

In both cases, it is the spirit which Herder is most concerned to stress.

'Volk', then, stands for a spirit which is, in the biblical sense of the word, 'lively', a way of being which is natural and organic rather than controlled by an intellectually calculated pattern, and in which individual character finds expression and fulfilment. A similar formulation would apply to life at the personal level. This is the spirit which informs the 'Sturm und Drang' call for freedom. It is a revolutionary spirit up to a point: order, when it acts in a constricting way, is anything but sacred to the 'Stürmer und Dränger'. But to use a political analogy, the revolution is more right- than left-wing in its approach to problems. The Self desires to be free to be, and to fulfil itself, and has a destructive urge to smash what prevents this. At the same time, it is more interested in the spirit, the way of being, than in the power to plan and organize life. It does have a longing for integration into a greater whole, a complementary, perhaps quasi-religious urge to surrender itself. Conscious of itself when it is constricted, it is not afraid of losing that consciousness by merging itself with something bigger, as does Goethe's Ganymede, for example. Conflict is an integral part of its experience, but resolution of conflict is a central part of its deepest desire. The impression which emerges from Herder's ideal of the Patriarch is of simple *being*, diverse, individual, but with a real streak of passivity:

Siehe diesen Mann voll Kraft und Gefühl Gottes, aber so innig und ruhig fühlend, als hier der Saft im Baum treibt, als der Instinkt, der, tausendartig dort unter Geschöpfe verteilt, der in jedem Geschöpfe einzeln so gewaltig treibet, als dieser in ihn gesammlete, stille, gesunde Naturtrieb nur wirken kann! . . . Langes Leben, Genuss sein selbst auf die unzergliederlichste Weise, Einteilung der Tage durch Ruhe und Ermattung, Lernen und Behalten – siehe, das war der Patriarch für sich allein. Aber was für sich allein? Der Segen Gottes durch die ganze Natur, wo war er inniger als im Bilde der Menschheit, wie es sich fortfühlt und fortbildet: im Weibe für ihn geschaffen, im Sohn seinem Bilde ähnlich, im Gottesgeschlecht, das ringsum und nach ihm die Erde fülle![47]

It is not surprising that this generation was not politically revolutionary. That it produced a literary revolution, on the other hand, there can be no doubt.

9
Freedom in Literature
(1): Goethe

The problem posed by the 'Sturm und Drang' was, of course, a tremendous one: no less than the problem of achieving complete freedom without falling into utter disorientation. No wonder that it often gave rise to the wildest rhetoric and was often in danger of losing itself in formless extravagance. The 'Sturm und Drang' concept of life and literature not only enthroned the genius in theory, it demanded genius if it was to be fulfilled. Greatness was the aim, but not at the expense of balance and ultimate harmony. Tragedy in the 'Sturm und Drang' is often the tragedy of failure to find fulfilment on these terms.

When the young Goethe came to Strassburg in 1770, where he was to meet Herder, he had already begun to develop into exactly the sort of person who could fulfil the latter's plans for German literature. He had grown up in a reasonably happy and comfortable home, had no serious money worries, a sound enough educational background, abundant talent and a fair amount of experience, particularly through his stormy love-affair with Kätchen Schönkopf in Leipzig, where he had attended the University. He was the budding genius and he impressed almost everyone he met in the period of his 'Sturm und Drang' works (roughly, 1770–5) as such. Heinse described him as 'genius and power from top to toe'.[1]

An assessment of him by the rather dry Kestner, the fiancé of Charlotte Buff and probable prototype of Albert, is of special interest. He found Goethe somewhat 'bizarre' and describes the 'Geniewesen' coolly and objectively, from the outside: 'He does what he likes, without worrying whether it is in accord with the behaviour of polite society ('Lebensart'). Any kind of compulsion is anathema to him.'[2] His capacity for strong passion, which Kestner also notes, made itself felt even before he left Leipzig, the bastion of that 'Lebensart'. He made his older friend E. W. Behrisch the confidant of the tribulations of his love-affair with Kätchen Schönkopf and the letters which he wrote to him are landmarks on the way to a new sensibility. It is not just that he feels strongly. No doubt Klopstock did so too. But if one compares Goethe's letters with his, one immediately hears a new note. There is no distance between the writer and his emotion. The passion itself seems to be the chief formal principle in the writing, dictating its abrupt and irregular rhythms, sudden changes of mood, and shifts of subject. There is no question of containing the emotion by mastering it intellectually. The writing is impelled by an almost physical desire for release. 'I wish I had chains on these hands' Goethe writes, 'then at least I would know what to bite into.'[3]

There is a consciousness of disorder, but the disorder is inside the writer. He cannot detach himself from it and his main hope of escape is that some outside agency will help him: 'If only I could achieve some kind of order, or if only order would come to me.'[4] The heart demands order too, but its very fullness and strength, once it is emancipated, makes that order very hard to achieve. A little later, in 1771, he wrote to J. D. Salzmann: '... dear order! ... Oh, my head is in the same state as my room; I can't even find a piece of paper, apart from this blue one.'[5]

At this time, indeed for some time after his move to Weimar in 1775, Goethe felt great restlessness and uncertainty as to the direction his life was taking. In the 'Sturm und Drang' phase proper, self-questioning alternated with self-assertion, the latter being the stronger. Yet the yearning for peace which was a central preoccupation of the transitional Weimar years was present even in *Götz von Berlichingen*, in the figure of Weislingen.

Of the completed dramas, *Götz* mirrors the 'Sturm und Drang' mood best. *Egmont*, though it still shows signs of the heroic concept of the 'Sturm und Drang' and is also a play of freedom, is, like Schiller's *Don Carlos*, a transitional piece, heavily influenced by a mood of developing Classicism.

Götz may not be as neatly put together as *Egmont* in absolute terms, but it is much closer, in ideal if not always in achievement, to the structural principles of the 'Sturm und Drang', to a form which arises from natural 'growth' rather than conscious planning. The aim is to create a great tapestry or 'fresco', such as Herder saw in Shakespeare, which would be immensely wide and varied in scope, but held together by orientation towards a central theme (i.e. freedom) and character. This kind of form, in which one character overshadows the others and forms the centre of the work, is common to most of Goethe's dramatic production. Some kinds of conflict he is happy to deal with, but not that of dramatic antagonist and protagonist. It is significant that the chief among the really substantial changes he made in this play from the 'Urgötz', which had incurred Herder's displeasure, was a radical reduction in the role of Adelheid, who had threatened to become a real antagonist for Götz,[6] a kind of evil mirror-image of his freedom and greatness.

Personal freedom, within an ultimate all-embracing order (represented here by 'God and the Emperor' on the social, and nature on the personal plane) is the ideal which Götz represents, and it is not so much a thing which is definable in political and social terms as a spiritual essence which is reflected in all the innumerable facets of a man's life and character. It is associated with a certain nexus of qualities: courage, power and strength ('Kraft'), 'greatness' of talent or heart and above all inner truth and honesty, the quality which is later to reappear, in a modified and spiritualized form, as the core of Iphigenie's 'pure humanity'. A series of polar relationships between various characters helps to build up the understanding of this central idea. It forms, in fact, a kind of network of parallels and contrasts which is not without subtlety, and for which Goethe is often not given enough credit.

Thus there is the direct contrast between Götz's 'brav' and faithful squire Georg and Weislingen's treacherous Franz, in which the relation of their masters to one another is mirrored. And there is the contrast between the lively, robust, 'natural' Georg and Götz's own son, who makes a bookish and namby-pamby impression. Georg lacks, however, his master's greatness and vision, which includes the ability to see events in a wider context, as in the conversation with Weislingen at Jaxthausen. Georg appears only in situations of action. Or one might take the three main female characters. Elisabeth, Götz's wife, is simple, brave and robust in character. Marie, his sister, is timid and tends towards the sentimental and melancholy. On the other hand, she is honest and true, whereas Adelheid, who, like Götz, does possess the qualities of fire and 'greatness',[7] and whose beauty is more elementally vital than hers, is the embodiment of self-seeking treachery. Götz is the only figure in the play who combines all the positive qualities mentioned, just as only he is fully and heroically free.

Events can be related to the centre by the criterion of honesty. A pattern of trust and betrayal runs through the play and it is significant that in the last scene Götz, who is about to be granted release from the 'prison' of this world and breathes already the 'heavenly' air of freedom, singles out 'Betrug' as the essence of the dark new age which is coming upon the earth.[8] The play covers the whole social spectrum, from the Emperor to the gypsies and peasant rebels, and however deliberately kaleidoscopic the effect of the succession of pictures which is flashed before our eyes, there is also a deliberate effort to maintain the unity which should arise out of the relation of all these disparate people and events to a common centre. Key-words like 'frei' and 'treu', together with their negative counterparts, are worked through the play's linguistic fabric; the guard, for example, who allows Götz to walk in the garden in Act V is thanked by Elisabeth for his 'Lieb und Treu' and the gypsies who give shelter to the fugitive Götz ('die wilden Kerls, starr und treu') are characterized by a 'Treue' which is consistently denied to Götz's adversaries, 'the princes'. Light and shade are thus distributed through the apparently jumbled picture. Minor characters and episodes, such as the appearance of Brother Martin in Act I, are thematically related to the centre and to one another. Repeated motifs, such as that of the monastery or the image of the wolf and the sheep,[9] also point to the unified central consciousness which strives to hold the work together.

This is not to say that Goethe is entirely successful. The closeness of texture and the poetic unity which distinguish the great 'Sturm und Drang' lyrics and *Werther* are not achieved in this case. The painting is executed in quick, bold, short strokes – brisk scenes, full of action, direct, unsophisticated, often rough language and so on – a technique which is no doubt itself an expression of the 'Sturm und Drang' mood but does not allow the central idea enough time or scope to establish itself with sufficient depth. At the 'real' dramatic level, such as is used in this play – clearly under the influence of Shakespeare – the achievement of such a unity demands more time, dramatic talent and experience than Goethe had at his command. In fact, one notes a considerable narrowing of the horizon in the other historical play in which Goethe attempted the theme of freedom, namely *Egmont*, and at the same time an increase in the use of techniques which one might call poetic rather than dramatic in a Shakespearean sense. The handling of the character of Klärchen, particularly of the scenes leading up to her death and the increasing poeticization of the hero in the last Act are the outstanding examples. The next step is the 'Seelendrama' of *Iphigenie* and *Tasso*, in which 'inwardness' and the avoidance of 'external' action are carried to an extreme.

Götz, then, probably cannot be said to succeed aesthetically in its aim of being simultaneously individual and universal. But it is the only one of Goethe's dramatic works, apart from *Fauts*, which attempts this and is therefore properly viewed as his most truly 'Sturm und Drang' play. It is at one and the same time a hymn of praise to the spirit of true freedom, as embodied in Götz, and an indictment of an age of un-freedom (i.e., vicariously, Goethe's own), and of an age in which it is difficult to be both free and good. This latter situation is the basis of the series of 'split', inwardly torn characters who appear in many 'Sturm und Drang' works. Clavigo and Weislingen are characteristic examples in Goethe. They can take neither the path of order nor that of freedom. They cannot stifle individual desires in favour of a rational convention, and it is not implied that they should. They are caught in the half-way house between the good freedom and the bad (e.g. that of Adelheid in *Götz*).

If one thing is clear about Weislingen, it is that he is *not* free. He is always seeking freedom, whether in diplomatic and political activity, or in the idyll of love with 'my gentle Marie', as he calls her. But the most he ever achieves is to glimpse a vision of such freedom, i.e. a situation in which there will be no disharmony in his heart, in which he will be rid of the feeling of constriction which plagues him. Momentarily, in Act I, after the betrothal with Marie, he feels that his heart 'expands' ('erweitert sich'), that he is 'as free as if I were in the clear air'. But the scenes of retired country bliss he imagines and the rather sentimental phrases he uses are reminiscent of the conventional, half-intellectual feelings of 'Empfindsamkeit', just as Marie herself has much of that atmosphere about her. It is significant that Götz, in this scene, notices a certain constraint about him.[10] He really desires to be set free from himself. He is, as he puts it to Adelheid in the sixth scene in Act II, 'so tortured by what I am that I don't care what people take me to be'.

Weislingen shares with others of Goethe's characters (and sometimes Goethe himself) the feeling of being ruled by a Fate, by forces beyond his control: 'Götz! Götz! – We men are not masters of our own lives; evil spirits have been given power over us . . .'[11] The 'Aufklärer', who has subjugated his heart to other conventional orders, does not feel this kind of constraint, this helplessness of the will which is there also in Clavigo and Fernando.[12] The ideal hero does not feel it because he has broken free from the narrower order which imprisoned his heart, but found a wider order – God, nature and so on – with which he can be in harmony. Weislingen has deliberately thrown away his birthright of freedom, cut himself off from the natural life of the free knight, and it is now too late for him to attempt to return to it. It is significant that only in the idyllic dream of life with Marie do we find him in contact with nature. Götz has a firm and uncomplicated faith in God and accepts his will,[13] but we seldom have the impression that Weislingen has any consciousness of him. Whereas Götz, when he dies, scents 'heavenly air', Weislingen can make no contact with God through prayer. His heart is 'closed' and in the 'fearful battle of life and death' he feels 'the torments of Hell'.[14] In *Werther*, we shall see a study of the process by which a heart which possesses wholeness, freedom and harmony (and contact with God and nature) can lose this greater freedom and take the path back into the prison of its own self. Werther combines the two characters, in that he is part victim and part his own executioner.

As with *Götz von Berlichingen*, the surest path to the centre of *Die Leiden des jungen Werthers* is through the main character, and as in *Götz*, though more consistently and intensively, the work is structured around that central figure. The emphasis laid by the 'Sturm und Drang' on the individual Self is reflected – in the first version particularly – in an almost extreme concentration on the inner spiritual and emotional life of the hero. So that what might at first glance appear to be a somewhat haphazard sequence of disparate episodes and reflections turns out on closer examination to have a texture as close-knit as that of any lyric poem.

Thomas Mann, with his fine eye for these things, speaks of the work as a 'mosaic' of emotional and psychological moments and details, wrought 'without a gap, with a wise, delicate and knowing hand.'[15] Mann himself, of course, often worked in a way similar to that described here, as for example in *Der Tod in Venedig*. The great difference between his technique and that of *Werther* lies in the much stronger element of detached intellectual calculation in the twentieth-century writer, at least as far as the impression made on the reader is concerned. Mann's work does in fact strike one as an immensely skilful assemblage of pieces, such as the word 'mosaic' suggests. In Goethe, the impression is more that of spontaneous growth and this impression is strengthened, paradoxically, by what appear superficially to be the most contrived elements in the structure: the way in which people and places which appear in happy, healthy colours in the first part of Book I (when Werther himself is in a state of relative harmony) reappear in the second Book sad and devastated, or in which, in Book II, Werther just happens to meet a man who has been driven mad by unrequited love for Lotte. Everything in the book flows so directly and entirely from Werther's 'Herz' that it seems entirely natural that the state of that heart should dictate not only what subjects are discussed, but even what events and encounters take place. Even the revised version, in which Goethe was at pains to strengthen the 'objective' side of the book,[16] is written so overwhelmingly from the one perspective that one can think of no adequate parallel in any other novelist of rank. Subjectivity is not only at the heart of the *matter* of this work, it seems to be its formal law as well. And while individual freedom is not so obviously or explicitly the issue as it is in *Götz*, it is woven deep into the fabric.

What, then, is the character of the hero? In a letter to G. F. E. Schönborn of 1 June 1774, Goethe describes him as 'a

young man who, gifted with deep, pure feeling and true pene-
tration, loses himself in phantastic dreams and undermines
himself by speculation until, ravaged by unhappy passions and
in particular an infinite[17] love, he shoots himself'. As not
infrequently happens in Goethe's comments on his own writings
(e.g. some of his comments to Eckermann), he tends to stay
fairly close to the surface and to understate. This description
almost gives the impression that this is the run-of-the-mill
story of a talented, but in no way extraordinary youth. There
is one word, however, which does not fit in with that impression, namely 'infinite', as applied to the hero's love. Goethe
was throughout his life capable of conceiving and experiencing
love as simultaneously an individual, 'real' and also a universal,
quasi-religious phenomenon. That is why he can equate it, in
the very late 'Marienbad Elegy' ('Was soll ich jetzt vom
Wiedersehen hoffen?'), with 'piety', the surrender of oneself
to a higher spiritual entity. Such love could and did expand to
encompass the whole of a person's universe and when it went
wrong the lover could say, with Gretchen in her famous
spinning-wheel song ('Meine Ruh ist hin') in Part One of
Faust, 'the whole world has turned to gall for me'. This is not to
say that all need for self-control and self-denial is swept away,
but it does mean that Werther's love is not simply to be equated
with a shallow adolescent passion.

Three main themes – nature, religious feeling and love – and
a number of sub-themes (e.g. social relationships, art and so on)
are intertwined in the book and they all meet at a common
centre: the heart to which Werther himself makes such constant reference. In this context, this should be taken to include
sentiments as well as sentiment. In the great discussion on
suicide (Book I, 12 August), Werther argues with just as much
intellectual incisiveness as Albert. But whereas his interlocutor
is cool and detached, and sees the problem in general terms,
Werther *feels* his arguments as well as thinking them, although
at this stage the discussion is purely academic for him. Albert's
rationality upsets him, because 'nothing discomposes me so
much as when someone comes along with an unimportant
commonplace when I am speaking completely from the heart.'
This heart, Werther's 'only pride', as he once calls it (Book II,
9 May), runs, in the course of the novel, through the whole

gamut from harmony and serenity, which is at its peak after his meeting Lotte, to emptiness and devastation, from a state of ease and freedom to one in which it feels itself so shut in ('eingekerkert', Book II, 12 December) that no other escape-route offers itself but the plunge into death.

The main motive force which impels Werther is a desire of the heart which bears some resemblance to Weislingen's searchings in *Götz*. It is a need for the 'striving, longing breast' (Book II, 9 May) to be 'filled and contented'. The Self seeks freedom within a universal order in which it can both fulfil itself and be filled. Thomas Mann sees the root of the character in its 'longing to leave the [world of the] limited and conditioned and enter into that of the infinite and limitless'.[18] In that this side of Werther is largely responsible for his downfall, there is some point in singling it out. But it does not lack a counterweight which, while it is not strong enough to save him, is evidence that his feelings and longings are not always the expression of an unhealthy, purely negative rejection of the limitations of order. True, he has the idealist's tendency to be satisfied with nothing less than the absolute. At times, he exhibits the dangerous extremes of this attitude, not in his social thinking, where he expressly accepts that limitations on the ideal are inevitable, but in the matter of his love, when it seems to be a question of what he calls an 'either/or'. He cannot accept that this is a valid way of posing the problem and tries 'to steal my way through between the either and the or' (Book I, 8 August).

There is still reason in this point of view: the difficulties raised by a person's emotions are not always amenable to the neat formulae of sweet and detached reason. But absolute love can lead to absolute demands, which infringe the rights of others. When his 'sickness', as he repeatedly describes his state of subjection to his emotions, is at an advanced stage, Werther exclaims: 'I often cannot understand how anyone else *can* love her, has the *right* to love her, when I love her so uniquely, so deep in my being, so fully' (Book II, 3 September).

Non-attainment of his ideal, together with the development of the potentially destructive element of self-indulgent introspection in his character, bring him to the point of contemplating the murder of others, condoning a *crime passionnel* and finally, carrying out murder on his own person. But that ideal itself is not irresponsible freedom, but freedom for the complete Self, in harmony with a wider order. There is a polar balance of forces in him which, while it is eventually tragically upset, nevertheless shows that a positive outcome might have been possible. His truly un-free part, the tendency to cut himself off and live in a private world inside himself, where 'everything swims before my senses and dreaming, I smile out into the world',[19] is at the root of the negative side of his feeling of 'Einschränkung' (constriction). This must be distinguished from its healthy counterpart, the side which rebels, for example, against the restraints placed on human relationships by social convention.

These two threads are both present in the letter (Book I, 22 May) from which we have just quoted, and which is one of Werther's most important reflections on the theme of limitation. Here, he exposes, with a perceptiveness which has not lost its relevance with the passage of time, the imprisoned nature of an existence consisting of activity whose sole purpose is to enable that same existence to continue on its unending circular path, deceiving itself into the belief that it is meaningful by 'painting many-coloured shapes and bright prospects on the walls of its prison'. The solution to this is not the retreat into dreamy intro-version with which Werther continues in this same letter, with its illusory 'sweet feeling of freedom'. Goethe, in fact, exposes the negative nature of this thinking by expressing it in a melan-choly, dreamy style, which entirely lacks 'Sturm und Drang' power (e.g. expressions like 'schwimmt' and 'träumend'), and by associating it with the idea of suicide. Werther concludes this letter with the thought that he can leave 'this dungeon' when-ever he wants to.

Werther's strong capacity for immediate feeling is accom-panied by a subsidiary, but not negligible streak of self-conscious, melancholy Sentimentalism. The latter, which becomes stronger as Werther's psychological state grows more precarious, and reaches its peak in the episode in which he reads to Lotte his translation of a gloomy Ossianic poem, is part of the negative strand in Werther, even if it is the aspect of him which appealed especially to many contemporary readers. Werther's attach-ment to the clothes in which he first danced with Lotte and his wish to be buried in them emanate from this source. After the poetic and powerfully expressive beginning of the final letter to

Lotte, the references to the clothes which 'you have touched and sanctified', to the pale red bow she gave him, which 'is to be buried with me', to the fact that 'my soul will hover over the coffin', and others, show a less impressive side. The spirit which hovers over this passage seems to be that of the cult of Klopstock,[20] who was still a fashionable literary idol in the seventies.

All this does not outweigh the positive side of Werther. The ideal of freedom and harmony, which is portrayed at length through Werther's thoughts and feelings, particularly in connection with nature, in the early stages of Book I, *is* capable of being realized in terms of a human relationship. Indeed, the fact that what Werther seeks is a real possibility is explicitly made clear in the reference (letter of 17 May) to the now dead woman who had been such a wise and valuable friend to him. In her company, he felt able to realize all the potentialities of his being. He feels happy at the beginning of the book, but it is not the complete ease and satisfaction which is described in this passage. Admittedly, he feels himself 'completely sunk in the feeling of peaceful existence' (strictly, 'existing' – 'Dasein')[21] and in direct communion with God, but there is a certain one-sided subjectivity in the language and the angle of presentation. There is a warning note in the first paragraph of the next letter, in which Werther says that he does not know whether the paradisiacal feeling he experiences in this region is the product of 'deceiving spirits' or 'the warm, heavenly fantasy in my heart'.

The prospect of Werther's enjoying all these feelings without becoming the prisoner of his own inner self is opened up only after he has come to know Lotte. The long letter in which he describes this first day with her (Book I, 16 June) really needs to be brought in evidence complete, as the 'leidige Abstraktionen' to which restricted space must limit us run counter to the method used here of conveying Lotte's quality through direct description of events, places and people and their dialogue. We can only reproduce the outline and stress that, as developed in the scenes showing Lotte with the children, or at the ball, the general phrases take on individual reality.

Werther begins his portrait by calling Lotte an 'angel' then, realizing how much of a cliché that is, simply refers (twice in fact) to her 'perfection': 'So much simplicity allied to so much intelligence, so much kindness allied to so much firmness.' And then he continues with the most important aspect, the 'peace of soul combined with true life and activity'. Like Weislingen, Werther lacks this true peace of soul, he is a seeker, a 'wanderer' (Book II, 16 June), a man described in an editorial footnote as 'unstet' (unstable).[22] Lotte, with her apparently perfect harmony of feeling and intelligence, of the physical and spiritual, becomes the embodiment of the ideal for Werther and the desire for her, which is desire in the full sense of the word, becomes bound up with that for the ideal. His religious feelings are projected on to her rather than nature. True, we become progressively more aware of the potential imbalance in his attitude. Goethe expresses both her harmony and Werther's imbalance in her warning to him (Book I, 1 July) that he involves himself too deeply in everything with his emotions and that this could destroy him, but with that harmony in mind we can understand, even when his 'sickness' is manifesting itself very clearly, why he feels (Book II, 29 July) that to possess her would be a kind of religious fulfilment which would make his life 'one continuous prayer'.

It is thus understandable how he can come, apparently, both to reject limitation and to desire it. The letter of 21 June in Book I is the nearest we have in the novel to a realization of the complete harmony of existence mentioned earlier. It hardly mentions Lotte, but it springs directly from the fulfilling experience of Werther's love for her: the foregoing letter closes with the ecstatic assertion that she has become the centre of the universe. After a brief reference to Lotte and to his happiness, Werther launches into a discussion of the two polar impulses in man: to move outwards, explore and rove freely, and then to return willingly to limitation. The desire to wander is rendered with great poetic force and followed with an equally effective portrayal of the polar desire for home. One is reminded of the nostalgia for the 'Hütte' (cottage) in 'Der Wandrer'.

Werther ends the letter with a description of the 'patriarchal' simplicity and harmony of his present existence in Wahlheim. We have not met it in such a pure form before and it is soon to be gnawed away by the canker within, but now, it is real, and its loss must be rather like expulsion from a Garden of Eden. The strategic placing of this letter, which both echoes and contrasts with that of 22 May (i.e. before the meeting with Lotte) on the 'limitation' of man, is of course very shrewd. Only the experience represented by Lotte can bring Werther to the state of mind and heart needed for this fuller and more rounded treatment of the theme of freedom.

The whole technique of *Die Leiden des jungen Werthers* is that of a great poet. Handling of description, dialogue, characterization, structure, all depends on the lyric poet's capacity to assimilate and unite within himself an infinite variety of thoughts and perceptions and then find the language to fix his understanding of this unity on paper. Of the great 'Stürmer und Dränger', Goethe and Herder were particularly 'lyric' in their genius and showed, then and later, a correspondingly deep interest in the problems of expression and an individual and intuitive approach to aesthetics in general. Schiller, who had a very different spiritual constitution, and whose 'Sturm und Drang' poetry is of inferior quality, says little or nothing of real value on matters of aesthetic theory until the 'Classical' period, when the intellect reasserts itself to some extent. Artistic genius and expression formed a major theme in the writing of the young Goethe, not least in his poetry.[23]

Werther, as an artist, is no more than a dilettante (another finely judged detail of characterization), but he has interesting ideas on the subject and he several times expresses preoccupations which must have been Goethe's own. One of the most interesting of his remarks is one which, at the same time, shows Goethe's theoretical insight into the problem of expression and his ability to find the words to solve the problem, without tampering with the mystery of the process. The letter of 10 May is one of the high points in the first, pre-Lotte phase of Book I. It sets out to render the experience of nature in Spring and through this, the ecstatic, semi-mystical feeling of one-ness and harmony with the infinite, which seems literally to have entered into him. The comment at the end is perhaps as good a formulation as any of the challenge to the artist which this represents: 'Oh, if only you [i.e. he] could bring (literally, ex-press) this out again, if only you could breathe on to the paper what is so fully, so warmly alive within you, so that it became the mirror of your soul, as your soul is the mirror of God in His infinity!'[24]

The language in which Werther expresses himself is very varied; sometimes brisk and forceful, sometimes strongly reminiscent of the emotionalism of the Sentimentalists, as in his description of his first parting with Lotte (Book I, 10 September), sometimes rising clear of that level to a great and free poetic diction, as in the letter of 10 May in Book I. The theme is the marvellous serenity ('wunderbare Heiterkeit') which Werther feels, living amidst beautiful natural surroundings, free from inner conflict and disturbing speculation, and the impossibility of giving his feelings adequate expression. An idea from Lessing's *Emilia Galotti* is taken up in the remark that even though he is so full of feeling that he could not now paint a stroke, he has 'never been a greater painter than in these moments.'[25] But whereas Lessing does not go beyond this point, which is perhaps the furthest that the analytical intellect can reach in considering the process by which beauty is brought about, Goethe uses it as a starting-point from which he moves on to what one might call an intuitive or 'poetic' method, namely that of attempting to communicate the emotional state involved. From this point onward, the letter, if it recalls any predecessor at all, makes one think of Klopstock, who not infrequently tries to communicate his experience of the inexpressible by referring to his emotional state.

But Goethe has gone further even than Klopstock, in that he ignores the dividing-line between the observer and the thing observed and entirely submerges rational understanding, which is always present in Klopstock's consciousness, in the emotional experience. The crucial passage consists of a single sweeping period, based on the simple construction 'wenn . . . dann . . .' ('when . . . then . . .'). Pauses for breath are provided – marked by the semicolons – after which the writer gathers himself together, repeats his 'wenn', and launches into the next stage of his assault, which takes him progressively inwards and upwards: from description of the outside world, in which he eventually feels the presence of God, to a rendering of the quasi-mystical experiencing of that whole world within himself.

The structure of the passage is not concerned with presenting thought in logical stages, but with building up an emotional effect. The rhythms are dynamic and complex, affording some variation, but never allowing the intensity of the passage to drop below the level required to maintain its powerful forward movement, and so give the reader a chance to detach himself from, and reflect upon it. It is a description, but the choice and use of words make it simultaneously an outpouring of emotion. Words indicating warm personal feeling abound ('lieb', 'meines Waldes', 'inneres Heiligtum', 'näher an meinem Herzen', etc.), and one cannot but feel that the external details are far less important to the man who is ostensibly observing them than are his own feelings. The world centres on his heart and all the movement in this passage, in which he talks of the world around him, is directed inwards to that heart. The nature-description has little which is objective or visual: one of the very few such details, the haze rising from the valley, is rendered by the powerful verb 'dampft' (i.e. gives off steam, or a thick haze), which could be said to be as much a reflection of Werther's overwhelming feelings as an accurate rendering of what he sees. The use of language, which has been bold in the first half of the passage, becomes even more 'inward' in its orientation, and definitely irrational in the second.

The general tendencies illustrated in the passage just examined hold good, at varying levels of poetic intensity, for the style of the work as a whole. The range of vocabulary is greater, and more conditioned by feeling, than would be typical for an 'Aufklärer'. The variations of prose rhythm, sentence-structure and so on are treated with more freedom than his love of smooth flow and balanced, antithetical cleverness would allow. Only in the lyric poetry does the freedom of the heart have a greater effect on Goethe's use of language.

Goethe began to write seriously in the late sixties, in Leipzig, which was a stronghold of the Rococo. As with some of his works in dramatic form (e.g. *Erwin und Elmire*), his lyric poetry continues to show traces of this style even after 1770. 'Kleine Blumen, kleine Blätter'[26] is a case in point, not least in its insistence on smallness in the first line. The rest of the opening stanza continues this mood:

> . . . Streuen mir mit *leichter* Hand
> Gute junge *Frühlingsgötter*
> *Tändelnd* auf ein *luftig* Band. (*Luke*, p. 6)

Goethe goes on to imagine the conventional 'zephyr' carrying the ribbon to his beloved and draping it round her so that, as she steps before the mirror 'in all her cheerful gaiety' ('Munterkeit'), she may see herself surrounded by roses, 'herself young as a rose.' The orientation of the following lines is much more directly emotional and at the end, Goethe uses the 'Rosenband' to provide a contrast with the stronger bond of feeling which is to unite the two. That does not mean that the grace, gaiety and wit of the opening are set up merely so that they may be knocked down. The attraction of these qualities subsists, and Goethe sees no reason to forfeit the charm of Rococo material and manner merely because he is no longer circumscribed by the basic Rococo attitudes. At the same time, one could not mistake this and similar poems (e.g. 'Das Veilchen') for products of Wieland or Gleim. The strong dominance of the orderly intellect and 'wit' over the individual no longer applies.

Earlier poems, written in Leipzig, had shown flashes of free personal feeling in which the convention vanishes momentarily, as for example in 'Die Nacht' (later, 'Die schöne Nacht') where, after an impressive nature-description, the poet bursts out: 'Freude! Wollust! kaum zu fassen!' (Joy! pleasure! hardly to be grasped!) – not a reaction to appeal to an 'Aufklärer'. But here, as in the other Leipzig poems, this layer floats entirely separate from the standard Rococo element in which it is contained and which tends to neutralize it. Goethe continues:

> Und doch wollt' ich, Himmel, dir
> Tausend solcher Nächte geben,
> Gäb' mein Mädchen eine mir![27]

We are back in a controlled and organized world where nature is a backcloth, manipulated so as to provide a foil for the treatment of a 'theme', in this case that part of the Rococo convention which makes the depersonalized lover ever anxious to spend the night with his equally depersonalized 'girl'.

The situation is very different in 'Kleine Blumen, kleine Blätter'. Even before the poet brings his personal feeling to the forefront in the second half of the poem, the Rococo scene itself has been tinged with a personal colouring. A simple, almost naïve phrase like 'All in ihrer Munterkeit' (stanza two) does much to balance any hint of artificiality in the motifs used, but even more effective is the use of the simple adjective 'gut' to characterize the 'gods of spring'. This is a word which, when used without condescending irony, has a warmly affectionate tenor and associations of natural simplicity and honesty which do not suit those swarms of little winged *putti* which inhabit genuinely 'Anacreontic' Rococo verse in the guise of Amors or spirits of play. It is not a word favoured by the Rococo writers and the exceptions tend to prove the rule. When Wieland describes the hero and heroine of his *Sixt und Klärchen* as 'fromm und gut', this is in fact one of the traits which make the tale, to some extent, a deviation from the pure Rococo style and which contrast with the bantering tone in which it began. And these two are – unusually for Wieland – identified as 'German', as being pious and good 'nach deutscher Art'.[28]

Goethe, then, assimilates the Rococo elements he uses into a different, more personal, freer style, shaking off the artificial trappings of the Anacreontic pastoral convention, infusing a degree of seriousness which is without deadly earnestness, but also without the self-possessed and intellectualistic levity of the Rococo. He finds freedom in his lyric poetry in many different ways, both thematic and technical, but the lynch-pin of the whole is the freedom of the Self. This 'Ich' dominates whatever ostensibly 'external' material is being treated and is the main-spring behind the words, images and rhythms used. As we have seen in the case of *Werther*, there were built-in safeguards in Goethe which prevented this subjectivity from becoming truly pathological or from reaching a state in which definite and coherent communication is threatened (as can be said to have happened in some of the rhapsodizings of men like Lavater and Lenz). Nevertheless, the feeling that the Self was in fact the centre of the universe was very strong at that time and while it gave him freedom, it also gave rise to a confusion in him – about his true identity, his place and purpose in life and so on – which went with him to Weimar and was only gradually resolved in his first stay there and – finally – in Italy.

This trend towards extreme subjectivity is present, as has been indicated, in almost all Goethe's 'Sturm und Drang' lyric poetry but there is one poem which is a key-work in this regard, namely 'Wandrers Sturmlied'. Whereas in other poems (with the possible exception of the almost equally 'difficult' 'Künstlers Morgenlied') there is some 'other', external factor in the equation, which absorbs and channels some of the intense energy radiated from the 'Ich', the 'Sturmlied' has no such 'other'. The poet's own emotional and intellectual consciousness is both medium and message. It is the 'centre-point' to which he appeals at one stage, his 'inner warmth'.

The 'Sturmlied' is a product of the period spent by Goethe in Frankfurt after his experiences in Strassburg and Wetzlar. The basis, as for so many of Goethe's works, is the material of his own life. During this period, he often undertook long walks, in all kinds of weather. The raw material for this poem is such a walk, made in stormy weather, the rain and cold on his body, the mud through which he wades, the objects he sees. But these do not constitute the thread which binds the whole together. The wanderer is primarily concerned with himself and these 'objective' elements hardly enter into the poem at all, except as they appear after having been assimilated into his train of thought. The 'god-like' power and strength of the individual genius is the speaker's main preoccupation and so the mud becomes inextricably mingled with the legendary mud of Deucalion's flood. With the other inconveniences and hindrances, and the polar images of fire and warmth, these physical factors are merged into the thought, in which they exist as an undercurrent, suggesting a theme here and there, as when the rain brings to mind Jupiter Pluvius and the Castalian spring.

The actual form of the poem is a kind of 'stream-of-consciousness' technique. Elements from various levels of experience, from the actual skylark he sees to his knowledge of Greek literature and mythology, come unsifted, in the kind of sequence and associative interrelation in which they might have occurred to the poet as he walked along. The freedom of the 'Ich' to say what it feels as it feels it, with no thought of the reader's difficulties, is well illustrated by the abrupt leap in the final stanza. Thinking of the 'storm-breathing' divinity which visits and strengthens the true genius (here represented by Pindar), Goethe writes:

> Wenn die Räder rasselten
> Rad an Rad, rasch ums Ziel weg
> Hoch flog
> Siegdurchglühter
> Jünglinge Peitschenknall,
> Und sich Staub wälzt'

> Wie vom Gebürg herab
> Kieselwetter ins Tal,
> Glühte deine Seel' Gefahren, Pindar,
> Mut. – Glühte –
> Armes Herz –
> Dort auf dem Hügel,
> Himmlische Macht,
> Nur so viel Glut,
> Dort meine Hütte,
> Dorthin zu waten.[29]

It is not entirely surprising that the older Goethe called this 'half-nonsense', but he neither suppressed it, nor did he attempt to water down its difficulties. It does put great strain on the reader, but it is not meaningless bombast, nor is it nonsense. It does 'work', if one allows the principle of more or less untrammelled subjectivity to operate. While it is not the best of Goethe's 'Sturm und Drang' poems, it is possibly the most revealing and it casts light on some of the more integrated products of the same period.

The extreme freedoms which the poem takes in matters of structure and the communication of meaning are paralleled in its handling of language and form. In the extract just quoted, for example, 'glühen' (to glow) is used as a transitive verb, taking 'Mut' (courage) as object, and directing this courage towards the dative plural 'Gefahren' (dangers). Other examples include the epithets which render the character of those poets whom Jupiter has scorned, Anacreon ('Tändelnden ihn, blumenglücklichen') and

> Den bienensingenden
> Honiglallenden
> Freundlichwinkenden
> Theokrit.[30]

The use of free rhythm, which is often rather violent in its effects in the 'Sturmlied', is well illustrated by 'Mahometsgesang', a poem which is thematically related to it by virtue of its concern with greatness and creative power, but which is constructed in a less extremely subjective way. Here the thought is presented through an image – that of the river – which is consistently maintained throughout. The rhythm is shaped, to a large extent, by the context. When the mountain-stream is being described, there is a concentration of short lines which convey youth and vitality:

> Seht den Felsenquell
> Freudehell,
> Wie ein Sternenblick!
> Über Wolken
> Nährten seine Jugend
> Gute Geister
> Zwischen Klippen im Gebüsch ... (*Luke*, p. 19)

Even here, one notes a certain regular pattern of alternating short and very short lines. When the river enters the plain, the rhythm immediately becomes much more regular. There is still a great deal of force in the trochaic lines which are now used, but they are less abrupt in their effect.

While this poem is less totally subjective than the 'Sturmlied', and presents thought in a more ordered manner, it is certainly not a systematically 'philosophical' nature-poem of the type which became popular later. Goethe himself indulged in philosophical nature-poetry of a kind in his later years. Here, however, and to a very large extent still in the early Weimar period, before the journey to Italy – one thinks of 'An den Mond' – his nature poetry is highly personalized. The layer of physical reality is, on the whole, overshadowed by the subjective content in the verbs and adjectives, so that one is not surprised to see the river personified, indeed endowed with feet, when Goethe refers, without any explicit drawing of parallels to ease the transition, to its 'Führertritt' and 'Fusstritt' in stanzas three and four.

Personification of nature in the spirit of an individual's experience of it is one of the most immediately striking aspects of many 'Sturm und Drang' lyrics, notably 'Willkommen und Abschied' (*Luke*, pp. 9–10), which embodies the sights and feelings of Goethe's excursions on horseback to Sesenheim during his love-affair with Friederike Brion. He sets the ride in the late evening and sees the natural objects around him mainly as threats and hindrances to an impetuous, almost heroic love. But a far more surprising turn in the treatment of nature occurs in the third stanza, when these personifications have been left behind. Previous to this point, the 'Ich' who is narrating was alone, riding through the gathering gloom. At the beginning of the third stanza, he sees his beloved, and as his emotional state changes, everything changes with it. The abrupt turn brought about by the meeting is marked by the strongly accented word 'Dich' which begins the stanza, contrasting with the weakly accented syllables which have begun every line up to this point. The format remains that of apparently objective description, but the mood is completely changed. The rhythm sheds the dynamism and unevenness of the night ride. The vocabulary adapts itself to the new situation (*'milde* Freude . . . *floss* von dem *süssen* Blick . . .').

And nature itself goes through a similar change at the behest of the lover's feeling. Now, in the stanza of gentle joy and tenderness, the lighting is the 'roseate light of Spring'. It is difficult to see how this can rationalistically be fitted in, in the sequence of the stanzas. We have just been imagining dark night, with its 'thousand monsters', and the following stanza will begin with the rising of the morning sun. No doubt there were moments of meeting when the light was like this, but to an objective and cool observer, the description as it appears must seem odd. The point is, of course, that it is not conceived from this point of view, and the presentation is so convincing poetically that we see the scene through the medium of the lover's feelings and feel no need of a 'natural' explanation.

As has been said, the 'Sturm und Drang' ideal of freedom was not necessarily negative and destructive. Totality and integration were its eventual goals and it was in the lyrical genres, where the opposition and inadequacy of the outside world were less able to inhibit, that it was most likely to be achieved. Goethe was capable, in the *Urfaust*, of expressing the desire, but only in much later stages of the work (such as the 'Wald und Höhle' scene of Part One, and above all in Part Two) could he find an objective image for its fulfilment. A dramatic work needs such objectivity, but the lyric is less dependent on it, and at least two of Goethe's great 'Sturm und Drang' poems, 'Ganymed' and 'Mailied', manage to render the ideal.

'Ganymed' expresses both the desire for union with the 'All', and its fulfilment, in terms of a state of being, though hardly of a precise role and meaning in life. It is a highly subjective work, and full of the dynamic impulse of the 'Sturm und Drang'. It speaks the language of personal and passionate love, and everything in it is deeply felt. If it were not, the poem would look very silly indeed, as it no doubt did to the 'Aufklärer'. To call Spring a 'beloved' would have seemed to him a dangerous absurdity, and the idea that it could be 'embraced in this arm' would have been the last straw.

But subjective as the poem is, its movement is not all outward, from within the speaker. There is a corresponding impulse towards him from the world outside. Nowhere else in this period is the potential of the positive idea of 'polarity', which was such an important element in Goethe's mature philosophy, more apparent than here. The calm and certainty of the mature years is not yet attained, but the incessant and intense movement in this poem prefigures it in its own form. At this stage, it can only take the form of an ecstatic, quasi-mystical vision, with its attendant vagueness and subjective feeling for nature.

With all its vivid consciousness of the divine reality and its dynamic relationship with it, 'Ganymed' expresses the moment of achievement of the state of oneness rather than the enjoyment of the state itself. This latter is what distinguishes 'Mailied' (*Luke*, pp. 7–8). With that in mind, we are less likely to be surprised by its combination of profundity with directness and simplicity. 'Ganymed' is full of daring phrases, as in the opening: 'Wie im Morgenglanze Du rings mich anglühst, Frühling, Geliebter!'[31] How much simpler is the opening of 'Mailied': 'Wie herrlich leuchtet Mir die Natur!' The statement is direct, uncluttered and seemingly not in need of any kind of interpretation by the intellect, whereas the almost identical statement in 'Ganymed' (as far as content is concerned) treats the question of the relationship between the observer and surrounding nature in a more complicated way.

Each poem continues as it began, 'Ganymed' moving to and fro between the internal and external in a style one must describe as 'difficult', the 'Mailied' continuing to state its message in a straightforward, syntactically and rhythmically simple way, which quite justifies the description 'song' which Goethe gave it in his final version (the first was entitled 'Maifest').

The quality of simplicity, which is undeniable and is no doubt not unconnected with the interest of the 'Sturm und

Drang' in nature and the folk-song, is not, however, the result of any kind of watering-down of the poem's thought-content, but rather of integrity at a higher level. The Self and the world around it are harmonized to such a degree that the former can express itself simultaneously at a number of different levels. Goethe's own feelings of joy in living, of love, of the beauty of the natural world around him, are all parts of one organic whole, so that the poem itself makes the impression of a process of organic growth taking place before our eyes. Nor is the divine element entirely overlooked, though much more assimilated into the personal here. The elevated language (e.g. 'herrlich', 'segnest') and the strong sense of the energy and creative force at work in nature (in the early stanzas particularly, and with the greatest economy in the boldly simple formulation 'die volle Welt' – literally, 'the full world') make us aware that this is certainly a love- and nature-lyric, but something above and including that at the same time.

The 'simple' words, on re-examination, often turn out to be extremely complex. A very good way of making oneself aware of this is to try to translate them. The opening itself is a fair example. 'With what glorious radiance nature shines (glows?) to me (for me?).' The radiance is understandable, though it savours less of the objective description of the sunshine than of the transference to the outside world of the radiance of the poet's own feelings. The dative 'mir' is most easily understood as an ethic dative (i.e. 'for me', 'for my benefit') and is so understood by Professor Forster.[32] One is tempted to use the more unusual 'to me', not from any desire for strangeness for its own sake, but because this phrasing seems to convey a little more of the energy of the activity described, and of the way in which it is all centred on, and flows into and out of the 'Ich', whose exclamations in fact make up the whole poem.

From this point on it is impossible to draw a line between what is felt and what is seen. The sun 'glitters', the fields 'laugh', the blossoms 'thrust themselves forth' from every twig. The inner feeling merges the life of nature and love into one unified activity: 'O earth, O sun, O happiness, O delight, O love . . .' (the peak of this ascending scale, beautifully marked by both rhythm and sound). Love is then described, as the poem hovers for a brief period on the height just reached, as being like the sunlit morning clouds, 'golden in its beauty'. It is linked, then, with the world of nature, just as Goethe shows it irradiating nature in his essay 'Über Falconet und nach Falconet': 'who has not, in the presence of his sweetheart, felt the whole world to be golden?'[33] We are not at all put out, therefore, as perhaps from a rationalistic point of view we should be, to find Goethe saying that love 'blesses the fresh field gloriously'. The poet then turns to the girl (though without detaching himself from nature) and hymns their mutual love.

This is, then, a poem of complete subjectivity and freedom, without a hint of limitation or constraint, but also none of introversion, isolation, or conflict with the surrounding world. It is entirely of the 'Sturm und Drang', both in its linguistic and rhythmical dynamism and in the personal nature, the inwardness of its integration, which rests in the inner state of the individual and subordinates everything else to that. It achieves a harmony, though the way to a more surely based harmony led eventually along more objective and 'social' paths and one feels that it is not possible to remain on this particular height for long. Even so, though we recognize the dangers involved in thus giving the heart its head, it is undeniable that here the 'Sturm und Drang' justifies itself, aesthetically at least, by producing poetry which is head and shoulders above anything one could possibly conceive of as emerging from the 'Aufklärung'.

Freedom in Literature (II): Schiller and Lenz

If conflict is not the central phenomenon in the experience and writing of the young Goethe, it certainly is in the case of Schiller. The reason lies partly in circumstances, partly in character. Schiller was less well placed than Goethe. Economic factors bore more heavily upon him and the ducal academy where he was educated, was an institution of stern, well-nigh military discipline: even allowing for the exaggeration which was endemic in the younger Schiller, we can agree that 'an inclination to poetry ran counter to its laws'.[1]

Schiller is thinking here of the conditions under which *Die Räuber*,[2] the greatest achievement of his youth, was produced. He goes on to call it a product of 'the unnatural copulation of subordination with genius'. To some extent, of course, Schiller has an eye to the public and the powerful, on whose favour he depended economically. Even today, *Die Räuber* has not entirely lost the power to shock. The sheer force of its conception and its language is not paralleled in very many plays, even of our era. Its impact in the eighteenth century can only be approximately imagined. But Schiller had not only shocked his contemporaries, he had genuinely shocked himself. This work continued to preoccupy him for several years and over and over again he comes back to the central issue of the 'sublime criminal', the intertwining of the abominable and the admirable, especially in Karl, but also in the villain Franz Moor, which he himself clearly felt.

Neither the force and universal scope, nor the complexity of Schiller's experience of the conflict between 'greatness' and restriction, between freedom and order, is discernible in any of the other treatments of the theme of rebellious and warring children which was so popular at this time. However wild the language, however violent the action, neither Klinger's *Die Zwillinge* nor Leisewitz's *Julius von Tarent* nor any of the others can live with *Die Räuber*. Even in its absurdities, its lapses from good taste and good sense, it has a kind of extravagant grandeur which seems to demand that it be appreciated at a metaphysical rather than a 'realistic' level. Perhaps a subconscious realization of this fact was the main reason which prompted Schiller to say that he had written 'a novel in dramatic form and not a drama for the theatre'.[3]

There are passages in *Kabale und Liebe* which make one uneasy when one imagines them played straightforwardly on a stage – especially an English stage! – but they pale into insignificance beside the episode in *Die Räuber* in which Franz employs an accomplice, disguised as a war-comrade of Karl's, to convince his father that Karl is dead and Amalia that she should transfer her affections from Karl to him. The agent, Hermann, produces a sword purporting to be Karl's. Suddenly, Franz exclaims:

What do I see? What is that there on the sword? written in blood – Amalia!

AMALIA. By him?

FRANZ. Do I see aright, or am I dreaming? Look there, written in a bloody hand: 'Franz, do not abandon my Amalia!' Look, look! and on the other side: 'Amalia! all-powerful Death has broken your oath! – Do you see, do you see? He wrote it as his hand grew stiff with death, wrote it with the warm blood of his heart, wrote it on the solemn edge of eternity! His fleeting spirit tarried to bind Franz and Amalia together.

AMALIA. Holy God, it is his hand....

At this point, surely, melodrama trembles on the brink of farce. But it is the kind of mistake that is made – under strain – by a writer of significant imaginative and emotional power.

Reading some passages in a mood of cool objectivity, we feel almost embarrassed. But the point is that this play cannot be read in such a mood. The author's intense feeling and the grandiose sweep of his conception make it possible for Herbert Cysarz to say with justice that its scene is not an obscure corner of Franconia, but the whole universe, with Man and God as the principal actors.[4] A not very interesting story from Schubart's

Schwäbisches Magazin[5] has been transformed, partly through influences from Plutarch, Milton, Shakespeare and others – Schiller's experience at that time was largely literary – but mainly through an intensification of the characters' emotions and attitudes which derives from Schiller's own inner resources, into a vehicle for the eternal battle between Light and Dark, God and the Devil. The heat generated is such that it does not seem inappropriate for Karl to compare himself with the repentant fallen angel Abbadona (from Klopstock's *Messias*) in Act III, Scene 2 and with the Prodigal Son on a number of occasions. Schiller's first instinct, in fact, was to entitle the play *Der verlorene Sohn*.

As Cysarz puts it, not outside objects but inner tensions form the basis of Schiller's experience in his early years,[6] and these tensions – between the religious and ethical extremes, between integration in a universal harmony, such as is glimpsed by Karl in Act III, Scene 2 and is linked (as in the 'Ode to Joy') with the father–son relationship, and total freedom amounting to anarchy or a crass materialistic nihilism – existed within him. The depth to which he felt these impulses made him capable of spinning out of his own interior the characters of Karl and Franz. Both are rebels and each achieves his own kind of freedom.

Karl champs at the bit imposed on genius and youthful 'Thatendrang' by circumstances and convention, both social and moral (cf. particularly Act I, Scene 2). The constricting forces are brought together in the single bogey of the law. At this stage, however, Karl still has hopes of being reconciled to his father. Only when he feels himself cast out, not only of his own family but of the whole human family, does he embrace the ideas of murder and robbery and link them with his desire for fulfilment of 'Kraft' in action and with his hatred for the restraint of law. In the end, he stands horrified at the fact that, while thinking to redress the disharmony of the universe, he has in fact been sinning against harmony, against 'the whole structure of the moral world' (Act V, Scene 2). Rejecting the idea of suicide, because the 'harmony of the world' would not be advanced by such a 'godless discord' (one notes how overtly metaphysical the language of the play has become), he decides to give himself up but – reacting against the pride and thirst for greatness which was an initial motivating impulse in his rebellion – in such a way as to avoid all éclat and admiration. None of his criticisms of society and convention, of the immediate and specific restraints and obstacles placed in the way of the fiery youthful spirit by 'this ink-slinging century' (Act I, Scene 2) are invalidated, but if the freedom of the individual spirit is endorsed, so too is the wider principle of order.

This is also true, though not shown on the same sweepingly metaphysical scale, of Schiller's other 'Sturm und Drang' plays. In *Fiesco*, he describes a republican revolution, but the differing conceptions of the hero – reflected in diametrically opposed versions of the ending – show his inability to decide between the authoritarian and the democratic model. Even in those versions with a republican solution, the ones in which Fiesco is killed, the ending is in each case muted. In *Kabale und Liebe*, the young aristocratic rebel, Ferdinand, is finally reconciled with his father in death, and the middle-class heroine, Luise, is herself an upholder of the principle of social and moral order.

In Karl Moor, Schiller shows the dangers of self-emancipation, even – perhaps especially – in a character of greatness. He challenges society, he challenges God and tries to be his own heaven and hell, but he finds himself more and more a prisoner, 'fettered to vice with iron bands', as he puts it in the second scene of Act III. The desire to find integration remains as strong as ever to the end, but it has no hope of fulfilment. When Karl does go home, in Act IV, the memory of the 'golden May' of his boyhood, with its 'cloudless serenity', only makes him the more keenly aware that he is a prisoner.[7] But the same force which prevented him from finding total emancipation as an outlaw, his religious and moral consciousness, also prevents him from becoming totally the prisoner of vice. Through his own free death, he is able to break free and reintegrate himself, in a moral sense at least.

Not so his brother Franz, who is as 'great' in amoral evil as is Karl in moral nobility and who rounds out this study of the metaphysical nature of freedom and unfreedom, and of the strong and subtle link between the two. Franz is a monster of heroic proportions.[8] He represents certain currents in eighteenth-century freethinking taken to their logical conclusion in terms of practical human action, a thing no 'Aufklärer' would ever have been capable of realizing with conviction. The radical nature of Schiller's portrayal consists not only in the fire and conviction of the language, but also in the absence of safeguards which can make the *frisson* aroused by this kind of character capable of being contained, even enjoyed: the humanizing realism, even humour of Iago,[9] for example.

Franz is quite incredibly ugly. Nature has 'thrown the most horrible parts of all human types into a pile and cooked me out of them'.[10] He is devoid of all humour and nobility. He has cut himself off from the moral consciousness by utterly denying it and living out his denial. The rather trite phrase, 'the man who fears nothing is no less powerful than the man whom everyone fears',[11] becomes frightening when someone takes it literally and sets himself free from all inhibiting moral conventions, as Franz does in his first monologue. Schiller presents the character (alternately with the contrasting and parallel one of Karl) in a series of evil decisions and actions, punctuated by long and, in their way, impressive monologues in which the metaphysical basis of the character becomes apparent. The one in which his twisted grandeur is most conveniently studied is probably that in Act IV (scene 2), in which he cuts himself loose from all ties of blood and conscience and decides on the murder of his brother. Schiller arrives on a rising tide of rhetoric at a formulation of Franz's concept of the meaninglessness of the cycle of existence which is as radical, at least, as Macbeth's description of life as a 'tale told by an idiot':

> . . . der Mensch entstehet aus Morast, und watet eine Weile im Morast, und macht Morast, und gährt wieder zusammen in Morast, bis er zuletzt an den Schuhsohlen seines Enkels unflätig anklebt.[12]

This kind of non-naturalistic, but very-much-alive embodiment of an ideological attitude has few literary parallels, certainly very few outside Germany. Even Schiller himself soon modified his technique into something which was probably better suited to stage-performance and certainly less able to convey completely the metaphysical preoccupations of the author. Questions of order, and personal freedom in its strength and weakness, are no less central to *Fiesco* and *Kabale und Liebe*, but the greater concern which these plays show for closeness to actual life does tend to reduce the impact of the ideas. Later, when the unbridled subjectivism of the 'Sturm und Drang' phase had been brought under control, the trend towards ideality reasserted itself in Schiller, and his last completed play, *Wilhelm Tell*, is perhaps the closest of all, in this respect, to *Die Räuber*.

Like Dostoyevsky's Stavrogin, Franz has 'liberated' himself by shutting himself in a cage. His end is devoid of freedom and dignity. Outfaced by Pastor Moser, he is left writhing in rage and terror. His soul is 'so barren, so dried up' that his desperate attempt at repentance fails and when Daniel will not run him through from behind, he has not the courage to fall on his sword like an antique hero. At the last moment, he throttles himself with the cord from his own hat. His death has the sordidness, if not quite the meanness, of Stavrogin's and Schiller lays stress on this in the robbers' comments on the corpse. Franz is likened to a dead cat and the verb used ('verreckt') indicates a sordid death indeed.

Sheer force of conception and execution make *Die Räuber* a masterpiece, albeit a grievously flawed one. It is marred by a plot which often strains credibility to breaking-point and an extravagant, self-indulgent rhetoric and emotionalism which, when they fail, fail catastrophically. Some of the characters (e.g. Amalia) and dialogue must give acute embarrassment to actors. Its structure gives less thought than do Schiller's other plays to the requirements of stage performance. This is not merely the usual 'Sturm und Drang' contempt for regularity. The structural integrity of this play is undramatic, rather like that of *Götz von Berlichingen*. As in many novels, a sprawling mass of characters and events is held together by a common relation to a central theme, in this case, the problem of freedom and its morality.

The more one reflects on this work, the more one is inclined to accept Schiller's definition of it as a 'dramatischer Roman', and a rather better one, in fact, than *Götz von Berlichingen*. At the same time, it cannot be said that this only partly conscious process of unification is successfully operative at all times. Its sheer length, and the variety and mass of the material it contains, must make it a considerable strain on the theatregoer, given the kind of structure we have been discussing. At times, we cannot but accuse Schiller of self-indulgence, whether in the coarseness which is quite abundant in this play, or in a kind of overstrained heroic sentimentality in the Amalia-action. This element of self-indulgence is there in the other 'Sturm und Drang' plays of Schiller, as indeed also in *Don Carlos*, but it is less inclined there to get out of hand.

These negative elements, self-indulgence, strain, lack of control and so on, are the darker side of the freedom of that time. One has only to read Schiller's letters of those days, or some of the poetry he wrote then, to see them in full flower. The poem 'Eine Leichenphantasie' (Funereal Phantasy), written in 1780 on the death of a friend's brother, is a good example of this kind of mentality. Sincere or not, the sentiment gives the impression in this raw, unshaped and uncontrolled aesthetic form, of hollowness and strain:

> Zitternd an der Krücke,
> Wer mit düsterm, rückgesunknem Blicke,
> Ausgegossen in ein heulend Ach,
> Schwer geneckt vom eisernen Geschicke,
> Schwankt dem stummgetragnen Sarge nach?
> Floss es "*Vater*" von des Jünglings Lippe?
> Nasse Schauer schauern fürchterlich
> Durch sein gramgeschmolzenes Gerippe,
> Seine Silberhaare bäumen sich ... etc.[13]

This comes perilously close to bathos. Some of it hardly makes sense in the original and looks even worse in English, as for example the phrase 'damp shivers shiver fearsomely through his bones, dissolved in grief.' One imagines how the Jane Austen who wrote *Northanger Abbey* might have amused herself in parodying it!

But this is, of course, only the obverse of a really great achievement. When one remembers Schiller's situation in those early years, isolated and restricted in a grim, totally uncongenial environment, then a fugitive, ridden with unpayable debts and already suffering from ill-health, searching sometimes in real desperation for a firm footing in life, one is impressed by his victory over himself and his surroundings. It was no mean feat to find, as he did, the path to a sound artistic achievement and, eventually, to a settled existence, without compromising his idealism or his art, even if he did – quite voluntarily – make some concessions to reality.

This achievement was beyond the resources of one of the most tragic and at the same time one of the most irritating figures in the history of eighteenth-century German literature, Jakob Michael Reinhold Lenz, who, from his beginnings as son of a German Pastor in the Russian-administered territory of Livonia and university study in Königsberg, travelled as the companion of some noblemen to Strassburg, came to know Goethe and to belong to the circle of the 'Stürmer und Dränger', but could give no firm shape either to his personal or his artistic life and eventually, after a vagabond existence punctuated by fits of mental unbalance, died miserably in Moscow in 1792. Among his areas of experience are the life of a private tutor, the military life and a number of unhappy love-affairs, in which passion and imagination seem to have played an equal part. All of these things, and other material from his own life, figure prominently in his literary works, which are almost all autobiographical, and autobiographical in a much more literal sense than is the case with Goethe.

In those days of an un-free and un-ideal social reality, it was particularly important to be able to draw the line between art and life. They must be related, certainly, but just as everyday life in Germany was not a suitable vehicle for high ideals, so one could not freely live from day to day through one's ideal or artistic personality. Schiller, more than anyone, was acutely conscious of the gap between the two sides, but he was able to find a solution, both in art and life. Lenz, a very talented, extremely sensitive character, could not do so. He often acted, or imagined himself into a situation where he found himself involved in a hopeless love, as in the case of Cleophe Fibich, the daughter of a Strassburg jeweller. A friend of his was strongly attached to Cleophe, but had to go away for a time and Lenz seems to have determined to act the part of lover to her in order to protect her against the possible attentions of others, involving himself in the process in a relationship which was half-real, half assumed, but definitely emotional and painful. This is described, in a form which is half-way between autobiography and fiction, in the *Tagebuch*, which was published some time after his death.[14] Goethe's comments on this episode (in Book 14 of *Dichtung und Wahrheit*) are of interest. Being himself of a different disposition and well able to distinguish reality from imagination, he does not, perhaps, fully realize the pain of the situation for Lenz, but he sees very clearly how Lenz projects his 'ideal' on to the actual person and how, in a sense, the whole relationship is 'play' for him as well. Goethe goes on to tell us that he suggested to Lenz that he should give these 'Kreuz- und Quer-g bewegungen' artistic form in a short novel and sums up the reasons for his failure to do so in the acute observation: 'but that was not his *métier*. He could only feel at ease in losing himself in the limitless sea of detail and spinning himself out [i.e. presumably his mental and emotional energies] without purpose on an endless thread.'[15]

Lenz was certainly a devotee of freedom as against the orderly rationalism of the 'Aufklärung'. Activity and feeling were the stuff of life for him and he could not have kept his imagination in check even if he had wanted to. He was full of ideas and plans. But he needed a controlling element at the centre, something to hold all this together and give it some degree of organization, and this seems to have been lacking, in his social and his literary life. Whereas the young Goethe, for example, could keep the expression of his exuberance and his emancipation from philistine pedantry within the bounds of what was tolerable, Lenz was continually going too far during his stay in Weimar. He had to be treated, according to Goethe, 'like a sick child',[16] and eventually his presence there became too much for everyone and he had to leave. What strikes one most of all in his lyrics is not just the very intense inner life, but also its restlessness, its lack of clear purpose and direction, by contrast with which even the most tortured of the younger Goethe's self-questionings show a sure basis. This state of affairs is mirrored even in many of Lenz's titles and subtitles, such as 'Ausfluss des Herzens' ('Eine esoterische Ode') or 'Nachtschwärmerei'.

His habit of introducing undigested fragments from real life (such as the person of Goethe in 'Freundin aus der Wolke' or 'Nachtschwärmerei') is also a symptom of lack of calm and of mastery of the material on which his sensibility is constantly working. Many of the dramatic fragments (particularly

Catharina von Siena) and even ostensibly 'finished' works like
Der Engländer ('Eine dramatische Phantasei') or *Der neue
Menoza* are characterized not only by swift movement and
change, to which we have become accustomed after Büchner
and the Expressionists, but also by a wilfulness and lack of focus
which these works do not possess. We can see it as legitimate
that Lenz should seek to present the world as he experienced it,
rather than in a tidy, falsified form, but his subjective view itself
has no true inner coherence and the abruptnesses, oddnesses
and inconsistencies of which these works are full are reflections
of himself rather than controlled literary devices employed to
an aesthetic effect.

Lenz was aware of his own problem of lack of control and of
contact with reality. He portrays it, for example in his 'dramatische Phantasei', *Der Engländer*, where the hero, Robert Hot, is
consumed by a passion for a Princess whom he has hardly even
seen, makes himself a laughing-stock, like Herz in the novel-
fragment *Der Waldbruder*, by pursuing this ideal and eventually,
in a very Lenzian ending, kills himself by stabbing himself in the
throat with a pair of scissors. As in *Der Waldbruder*, Lenz makes
it clear from the comments of all the surrounding figures, that
he is aware of the unbalanced nature of his hero, and yet at the
same time he throws the main weight of his sympathy behind
Robert. Partly, one can see here the assertion of individual freedom to be oneself in one's own way, but one doubts whether any
of the other 'Stürmer und Dränger' could have taken it to this
length. Both Goethe (especially in *Werther*) and Schiller (in *Die
Räuber*, or the figure of Ferdinand in *Kabale und Liebe*) showed an
awareness of the dangers in unrestrained individualism which
did not have an inbuilt balance; Lenz seems to say, with Prince
Tandi in *Der Neue Menoza*, 'these caprices are sacred to me,
more sacred than anything else'.[17]

It is extremely significant that in 1797, the now composed and
classical Schiller should have used the word 'pathological' to
describe the spirit of certain 'Lenziana' (including *Der Waldbruder*) which he was considering for publication in *Die Horen*.[18]
It is certainly true that the social environment imposed strains,
especially on a sensitive person like him. But the evidence of
other men who were not exactly insensitive, like Karl Philipp
Moritz, for example, indicates a special disorientation in Lenz.

Likewise it can be pointed out that his writing, for all its flashes of brilliance and acute observation, never achieves the overall integrity of even lesser talents like Klinger.

Lenz's best play, *Der Hofmeister*, is a succession of Acts and scenes strung on what is dramatically a rather slender thread, the institution of private tutoring, both as a means of educating the young, and as a profession. The tutor Läuffer (literally, 'runner'), leads a miserable existence as a kind of genteel servant in Major von Berg's house, seduces his employer's daughter Gustchen, takes refuge with the robust, rather cranky village schoolmaster Wenzeslaus, castrates himself – to free himself from servitude to the passions – and finally marries a simple country girl. The drama alternates between this action and the events involving the Major's nephew Fritz, who loves Gustchen and eventually marries her. He has not been educated by a tutor and is frank, open and perhaps a little wild, but though his incaution leads him into some trouble as a student, his healthy and upright character saves him from involvement in real vice and he ends with the prospect of a happy and fruitful life ahead of him. He determines that Gustchen's child, whom he accepts as his own, will not be educated by a tutor. The whole is presented with a large number of alarums, excursions and diversions, which are often amusing or shrewdly observed (especially in their dialogue) but which do not make the play easy to follow.

There is, certainly, a wider underlying theme, which might be formulated as the search for the secret of a good life, for mental and moral health, which is connected with the idea of individual freedom and natural simplicity. It is brought out from time to time, but allowed to sink well into the background in the intervening periods, which are taken up with colour and detail, at which Lenz often excels. The escapades of Fritz's scapegrace friend Pätus, for example, are presented with great immediacy and humour, and Frau Blitzer, with her salty speech, has no rival in classical German literature as a portrait of a landlady. But although the Pätus-action is part of the pattern of right and wrong values to which we have referred, the colour, life and comedy obscure the message. It is not until Fritz lectures his friend in Act IV, scene 6, that the theme is stated, and the general effect of the character is of only a very loose connection between the detail and the general theme. A similar pattern can be traced in the handling of other characters, including Läuffer, but space does not permit of an analysis here.

Our main purpose in studying these examples has been to show that Lenz, while he shares many preoccupations with Goethe and Schiller, lacks the measure of integration which they are able to achieve. It is not simply a matter of the disregard of rules and of carefully planned and dovetailed structure, for the other great 'Stürmer und Dränger' show these features also. But if they rejected one discipline, they had an adequate substitute in the integrated inner consciousness which linked the apparently heterogeneous fragments of their experience. Lenz's preference for colourful, flesh-and-blood 'reality', his penchant (especially in *Der Hofmeister*) for the coarsely expressive detail, his desire to be all-embracing and always dynamic, and many other traits, can all be paralleled in Goethe, Schiller and Herder. But with him, there seems to be no sure control at the centre. The various impulses, all valid, perhaps, in themselves, never settle into a workable relationship, so that he is a writer of excellent scenes and fragments rather than finished works. He has no very clear philosophy of life, but the most likely rationale of his activity would seem to be that he could not settle for any kind of view which involved a more or less fixed perspective. A flux, in which everything could be included without the need for clear arrangement, something closer, perhaps, to the radical emancipation of the Self of the Romantic Movement (with its correspondingly open and amorphous form) might have corresponded to his mentality.

But even the Romantics had a more definite philosophy than Lenz: their religious views, for example, were surer than his. Their dual concept of reality robbed the practical, concrete things of their separate identity and validity, to unite and in some cases transfigure them in the reality of the spirit, as it worked in and was apprehended by the individual consciousness. They could develop an amphibious capacity for living at different times at the practical and spiritual levels and it is noteworthy how many of them, in spite of the strains and stresses in their personal and artistic lives, managed to function efficiently at both levels. These possibilities of orientation do not seem to have existed for Lenz, who was convinced of the validity of the practical world on the one hand, yet at the same time so almost wilfully individualistic that though several tried, no one was able to help him to a firm footing in life. His work fits no exact pattern and has none. It may be that it is possible to detect, as Walter Hinck claims to do in *Der neue Menoza*, a kind of 'trellis-work of correspondences'[19] (though this is by no means indisputable), but even allowing this, there is a lack of control which must be accounted dangerous, given the conventional and formalized world in which Lenz lived and which was bound to bear down upon him and condition him. The 'Stürmer und Dränger' were not 'Aufklärer', but neither were they Romantics, in spite of a number of points which they had in common with the latter. They could not, for example, have accepted the pure dreamy fantasy which the Romantics cultivated; for them, this would have been 'romantic' in the critical understanding of the term which the 'Stürmer und Dränger' mainly shared with the other trends of the eighteenth century. Even Lenz uses it to point out the excessively introverted nature of Herz in *Der Waldbruder*.

Yet it should also be remembered that Lenz is not unequivocally critical of this character, in whom after all he embodies one of his own love-relationships. He had, as Pascal for example points out,[20] a greater Romantic potential in him than the other important 'Stürmer und Dränger'. Under less favourable conditions than theirs and in a situation in which German literature and philosophy provided less in the way of sure achievement and insight to act as a springboard for the individual seeking to make his own way, Lenz was in greater danger than they. The sentimental climate of the seventies had a tendency to be overheated, and melancholia and thoughts of suicide were part of the landscape, which was not yet brightened by such things as the playful and spiritual Romantic Irony of Schlegel and the others. In the main, the central core of the 'Sturm und Drang' and its cult of freedom was healthy enough, but there were dangers to which, in its very freedom, it exposed itself and which those who had surmounted them in Classicism might well have seen recurring in the new movement of the nineties. Schiller, after all, in the letter discussing Lenz from which we quoted earlier, referred also to a recrudescence of the same tendencies in what must be a reference to the Romantics. And Goethe could well have been influenced by his memories of the seventies when he made his famous remark to Eckermann: '. . . das Romantische [nenne ich] das Kranke'.[21]

Part 4

Synthesis

The Classical Ideal: Freedom with Order

The other half of the remark by Goethe which was quoted at the end of the foregoing chapter, is, of course, 'Das Klassische nenne ich das Gesunde.' What Goethe meant by 'healthy', as indeed by a number of other simple adjectives which he was fond of using during his Classical period and afterwards, is a more complex matter than at first appears. Classicism is characterized by simplicity, but it is the simplicity of mastery, and means the reverse of a simplistic approach to the problems of life and thought. A convincing impression is given, for example, of the strains and uncertainties to which the 'pure humanity' of Goethe's Iphigenie is subjected. Only *Tasso*, in fact, outdoes this one among Goethe's plays in psychological subtlety and depth. Yet the character also maintains throughout a special sureness and integrity which makes us concur with other characters who associate with her the simple word 'rein' (pure). Firstly in potential and then in fact, she has the moral mastery which places her on a level quite separate from that of the older and more experienced people who surround her, and we feel that her goodness is a positive quality. The ideal of wisdom of the 'Aufklärung' contains a great deal of negative limitation. When the Classicist talks of virtue, or of renunciation (as he will), he means something more positive and he is much less immediately inclined than the 'Aufklärer' to seek 'Ruhe'.

Goethe's understanding of the dualism of healthy and sick is well illustrated by his use of the words in one of the *Xenien*, 'Der Chinese in Rom'. In this epigram, Goethe directly refers to Jean Paul as a 'Schwärmer' who is 'krank'. A brief examination of this author, whom, as we saw in Chapter Three, Schiller also found wanting, will be of considerable use to us in defining the Classical position.

Jean Paul, who was on the brink of the breakthrough to fame and popularity, had a certain amount in common with Goethe and Schiller. Like them, he believed in the reality of spiritual values which transcended the everyday, and in the ability of 'higher men' to live in the world of these values without entirely forsaking that of ordinary reality. At the same time, there is less inner harmony in him, as is evident, for example, from his mannered and often capricious style, his oddnesses of conception and structure and his stronger consciousness of opposition between real and ideal. He was more open than they to subjective indulgence in fantasy and emotion. He was no pure Romantic, but it is certainly true that however much he sought balance, his mood and approach favoured spiritual withdrawal from the world of practical and outward-looking activity more than would have met with the approval of the Classical Goethe and Schiller. Although his novels describe that world, and the many and various objects in it, in greater detail than is to be found in *Wilhelm Meisters Lehrjahre*, there is a sense in which they are less realistic than that work.

For in Jean Paul, there is very often a tendency to bathe this 'objective' world in the light of a free-playing, humorous, essentially subjective imagination which robs it of that equality of status with the subjective which Goethe and Schiller strove to attain. Freedom, in a word, is less well balanced by order in him. No wonder his work was particularly highly regarded by the Romantic critic Friedrich Schlegel.[1] To label it as 'sick' is unfair, for it does not give complete licence to passive, self-indulgent dreaming. There is a clear undercurrent of criticism, for example, in *Schulmeisterlein Wuz*. At the same time, Jean Paul's portrayal of the little schoolmaster shows a responsiveness to that character's subjective sensibility which indicates that that same sensibility is deeply ingrained in him.

Something similar could be said of Karl Philipp Moritz. There was, in fact, quite a bond of sympathy between the two men. Moritz's *Hartknopf*, in particular, had influenced Jean Paul[2] and Moritz himself was more appreciative of the latter's work than Goethe showed himself to be. On the other hand, he had, in his own *Anton Reiser*, recognized the dangers inherent in indulgence of the imagination. In describing Anton, a hyper-sensitive youth who uses the world of his imagination as an escape from the grey, pinched existence he is forced to lead, Moritz emphasizes the tendency to melancholia, even to a suicidal state of mind and in general, our impression of the character is well summed up in the phrase 'romanhaft und überspannt'.[3] This latter word may well have recalled to the reader's mind Schiller's use of it in commenting on a number of what he regarded as spoiled talents, including Jean Paul. We shall take up that thread a little later: for the moment we must retain contact with Goethe.

In 'Der Chinese in Rom', Goethe uses the contrast between the substantial simplicity and grandeur of the architecture of Rome and the flimsiness, heterogeneity and liking for superficial ornament, as he sees it, of the Chinese taste to symbolize the opposition of healthy and sick. The word he uses to characterize the 'healthy' attitude further, the German word 'solid', is of special interest. It leads us back to one of the great changes in Goethe's life, the rebirth, as he himself calls it in his *Italienische Reise*, which happened during his stay in Italy (1786–8), and of which he was immediately aware on arrival in Rome. On 7 November 1786, he wrote to Frau von Stein:

... anyone who looks seriously around himself here and who has eyes to see must become *solid*; he must acquire a concept of solidity more lively than he ever had before. I at least feel that I have never had such a correct appreciation of the things of this world as I have here.

Solidity, then, means a firm, sound, clear judgement, an eye which sees things as they are. And Goethe's writings about this phase in his life are informed by a consciousness of ease, clarity and incipient mastery. Both the *Italienische Reise* and the *Römische Elegien* convey, not so much the impact of new ideas, as the attainment of a new state of mind. In the years in Weimar preceding the Italian journey, he had felt increasingly the need for more objectivity and self-control, but inwardness had still been very much to the fore: the Classicist had been struggling to get out. Now, the Self is definitely capable of attaining order and control. It is not the negative control of mere restriction, which is firmly rejected, for example, in *Torquato Tasso*, but it no longer gives scope to self-indulgent individualism, which is also rejected in that play.

Synthesis

From the outset, the letters of this period, while they do not lack sensitivity, are written in a calmer style – certainly without the violent changes of pace and direction of the youthful ones to Behrisch – and they contain a great deal of clear description. The 'Augenmensch' in Goethe is coming into his own. Over and over again, one is impressed, in the various records of Goethe's experiences in Italy, with the quality of his visual perception, which is not unreflective or impersonal but certainly clear and three-dimensional and totally devoid of the propensity to see anything but what is objectively *there*. We remember how the impressions of the outside world were swallowed up in the internal vision in 'Wandrers Sturmlied'. This tendency had not entirely disappeared in the pre-Italian years in Weimar. The 'Harzreise im Winter', in which Goethe distances himself analytically from the introversion of Plessing[4] is still only a half-way-house on the road to Classicism. The fragments of external reality, which are often quite objectively described, nevertheless have little coherence until related together by the inner unity deriving from the poet's inner Self. In Italy, the validity of external things in themselves is much more strongly appreciated.

The control to which he subjected his personal feelings and desires at that time is implicit in a remark in an early letter to the Herders: 'As long as I am here, I intend to open my eyes, see with modesty and await whatever developments take place within me.'[5] The concept of 'seeing' (Goethe uses 'sehen' here) or of what one might call 'creative looking' ('anschauen', Goethe's favourite expression, implying objective observation with mental activity) became, from this time forth, a common one with Goethe when the search for truth was concerned. His scientific studies, which took on a new lease of life in this period and remained a major preoccupation afterwards, have a great deal to do with this, but are hardly the first cause. It is more likely that they took such a firm grip on his imagination precisely because he could feel here in a vivid form the sense of knowing nature and God through 'Anschauen'. It is, for him, at once a subjective and an objective activity, and even if the former element was curbed to some extent during Goethe's Classical phase, it never ceased to be a strong force. As Goethe wrote to Wilhelm von Humboldt (3 December 1795), apropos of a philosophical essay by F. A. Weisshuhn:

> It is very pleasant for people like us, who operate through human good sense, when pure speculation is brought so close to us that we can use it for our own domestic purposes. Since it is absolutely vital in my studies in physics and natural history to purify my contemplation of things through the senses ['sinnliches Anschauen'] of all personal opinions, any teaching which points in that direction is very welcome and all the more so since creative looking, insofar as it deserves to be so called (for it is right that it should be clearly distinguished from simply looking at ['Ansehen'] a thing) is itself subjective and exposed to many dangers.

There is nothing lifeless about this experience or its effects in Goethe. In the *Italienische Reise*, the letters from Italy, and the *Römische Elegien* one is constantly aware of the joy and happiness he feels. 'Froh' (glad) is a key-word, especially in the *Elegies*.[6] He is full of the sense of having found himself, of going through an epoch-making educational and formative process such as he was to portray later in the 'Bildungsroman' *Wilhelm Meisters Lehrjahre*, of having been 'cured' of 'an enormous passion and sickness'.[7] A personal process of self-training and self-discipline went on in the case of both Goethe and Schiller, shaped and furthered by external catalysts: Italy and the study of nature for Goethe, rigorous study of philosophy and the friendship with Goethe in the case of Schiller. The latter could also say with justice that he had achieved a more or less harmonious balance without forfeiting the valuable part of the fire of his youth. He had refined away the excessive subjectivism. In his letter to Goethe of 5 January 1798, in which he talks of his *Wallenstein*, he claims that the 'calm control' ('Besonnenheit') which is the fruit of 'a later epoch' in his life has not robbed him of the 'fire of an earlier one'. It is not a dead and negative calm which he celebrates, but the harmony which results from bringing subjectivity and objectivity, freedom and order into a fruitful balance, a kind of synthesis.

For all the Classicists, the symbol of this harmony was Greece. But this Greece could not be obtained from outside sources. It was necessary, as Schiller put it, to 'give birth to a Greece from inside oneself',[8] i.e. to attain the harmonious balance in inner, personal terms. This involved a certain acceptance of limitation and self-control, and of the fact that reality would not always correspond to all the legitimate demands of the inner Self. It did not mean that one should give up striving for the ideal. But to fall into a negative and destructive rage if the world deviated from the inner ideal is the way of the torn and overstrained mentality whose excessive subjectivism Schiller criticized in the letters to Goethe already referred to. These people maintain their absolute freedom, perhaps, but it is at the expense of their 'health', as Goethe and Schiller would see it. It will be recalled that along with Schmid and Jean Paul, Schiller made mention of Hölderlin.

Hölderlin was a lover of the Greek ideal, like Goethe and Schiller, but was certainly much more severely bruised by life than they. He achieved enough inner order to produce a large body of poetry of extreme beauty and great philosophical depth. At the same time, he does not have the clarity or ease of the pure Classicists; his structure and syntax are often involved, his meaning hard to grasp, his mood unsettled and unhappy. None of this, of course, makes him necessarily any the worse as a poet, but it makes him un-Greek in the Classicists' sense of the word. And though he had a decided need for order, he was also probably more definitely committed to freedom, emotionally, than Goethe or Schiller. His enthusiasm for the French Revolution as a student, his continued veneration for Rousseau and the sympathy with which he portrays a revolutionary struggle in *Hyperion* all point in this direction. Certainly, he distances himself, in his portrayal of Alabanda, from the ultimate, destructive violence, but the mood of the whole is not exactly calm.

A more spiritually collected personality than Lenz, Hölderlin did often achieve a mastery of poetic form and expression which can rival Goethe's. But it is not security or peace that he conveys. Even his great re-creation of Greece in 'Der Archipelagus' is a lament for the lost and unattainable. The combination of formal beauty and balance with extreme emotional intensity and fragility in the poem 'Hälfte des Lebens' (*Hamburger*, p. 242) in which Hölderlin seems to sense the approach of madness, is a fair example of his precarious position. Like most of his important work, it was written later than the letter in which Schiller dismisses his prospects so cavalierly, but one feels that the older man would still have reacted unfavourably to the (from his point of view) over-subjective mentality which is reflected in it:

> Mit gelben Birnen hänget
> Und voll mit wilden Rosen
> Das Land in den See,
> Ihr holden Schwäne,
> Und trunken von Küssen
> Tunkt ihr das Haupt
> Ins heilignüchterne Wasser.
>
> Weh mir, wo nehm ich, wenn
> Es Winter ist, die Blumen, und wo
> Den Sonnenschein,
> Und Schatten der Erde?
> Die Mauern stehn
> Sprachlos und kalt, im Winde
> Klirren die Fahnen

Hölderlin was not one of those who welcomed darkness and the dissolution of fixed form, as one could say Novalis, for example, did. He strives towards the clear light which he associates with Greece. His plan for a 'humanistic journal', to be called *Iduna*, and whose aim was to have been to reconcile warring opposites, '. . . the sciences with life . . . the real with the ideal' (cf. *Hamburger*, pp. xiv-xv), shows how close he was to the Classicists in many respects. But night, the Romantics' element, and confusion are so much part of his experience that he cannot attain a consistent Classical serenity and some of his sweetest songs tell of loneliness, disharmony and near-despair. In his rendering of the night-mood at the beginning of the legy 'Brod und Wein' (*Hamburger*, p. 104), a passage whiche particularly impressed the Romantic poet Brentano at a time when few others recognized his talents, Hölderlin does not sink the mind so entirely in the atmosphere as might be the case with a Romantic proper, but he shows himself deeply infected by it and while the poem does not suffer aesthetically from this, it demonstrably does not have the firmness of mood and the clarity of outline which one associates with Classicism and which remained with Goethe as part of its legacy even after the death of Schiller. Goethe's very late night-poem 'Dämmrung

senkte sich von oben' (in *Chinesisch-deutsche Tages- und Jahreszeiten*, 1830) is firmer in tone and more objective in description
than Hölderlin's.

The later work of Goethe, from *Die Wahlverwandtschaften*
onwards, does move forward from the Classical position in that
it cultivates a form with more movement and a style with more
deliberate cloudiness in it than was previously the case, and
allows more scope in general to mystery and individual emotion.
But it never becomes languorous or narcotic, and if its content
is often complex, it is never deliberately confused. Among the
same nineteenth-century political, social and cultural developments which surrounded Hölderlin – though admittedly, not
under the same extreme pressure – Goethe preserves, sometimes
in a modified form, essential attitudes of the Classical era.
Nowhere, not even in the 'Marienbad Elegy', do we see his
control wavering as does Hölderlin's in 'Hälfte des Lebens'. The
vision of winter in that poem reminds one of Hyperion 'spinning
himself in (i.e. into a protective inner cocoon) because it is
winter everywhere'. *Hyperion* is a particularly passionate and
subjective early work, but even so, the anguished, if not quite
despairing attitude of its hero in the face of an 'incurably' bleak
reality, and his pronounced subjectivity, are only extreme forms
of attitudes which run through this author's work.

To the near-despair of Hölderlin, as to what another great
'spoiled' Classicist, Heinrich von Kleist, called the 'gebrechliche
Einrichtung' of this world,[9] Goethe would have opposed Faust's
phrase: 'Dem Tüchtigen ist diese Welt nicht stumm'. The
inability of men such as this to reconcile themselves to the
gap between their ideals and the possibilities in reality would
have strengthened him in his continued belief in the importance
of the Classical virtues of self-control, the ability to renounce
('entsagen') and so forth. In *Wilhelm Meisters Wanderjahre*
(1829), which is subtitled, incidentally, 'Die Entsagenden', we
find this reflection:

The least of men can be complete [i.e. balanced, in harmony] if
he moves within the limits of his abilities and capacities; but even
fine talents are darkened, suspended and destroyed if that absolutely
essential quality of proportion is lacking. This unhappy state of
affairs will appear more frequently in this modern age, for who will
be able to satisfy the demands of a present which has been under-

going the most total development [i.e. which is 'durchaus gesteigert'] and is continuing to move with the greatest rapidity?[10]

Goethe's own experience of the instability which lurks as a potential in subjectivity made him, if anything, exaggeratedly suspicious of this trait in others. In spite of his genuine appreciation of musical talent – he thought very highly, for example, of *Die Zauberflöte* – he was wary of the great musicians of his day. Even Beethoven, whose music is certainly not devoid, for all its emotional intensity, of 'Classical' qualities of control and shape, was never really *persona grata* with him. Beethoven, of course, was of a more radical political persuasion and Goethe reacted unfavourably to the 'sansculottisch' mentality whenever he met it, not because he was a hidebound reactionary but because of its lack of 'solidity' and control. His comment on Beethoven, in a letter to Zelter (2 September 1812), is revealing:

I was astounded by his talent; unfortunately, his personality is entirely undisciplined. True, he is not wrong in finding the world detestable, but he doesn't make it more enjoyable thereby, for himself, or for anyone else.

Goethe does not deny, it should be noted, that the world is far from perfect. He simply rejects the self-indulgence, as he sees it, of a person who makes not only himself, but others miserable in consequence. It seems, sadly enough, that he would not have been ready to grant even Beethoven a completely 'clean' bill of spiritual health. And is it too heretical to suggest that, if Goethe in his later years may have erred on the side of stiffness and lack of sympathy in some relationships, Beethoven was sometimes guilty of a more destructive, self-indulgent emotionalism? This emotionalism is, of course, magnificently harnessed and contained in the music and the experience of tension and release which it generates are thrilling and exhilarating to the listener in the safety of the concert-hall. It is another thing to imagine these cosmic storms taking place inside a man, without the softening effect of artistic form. Goethe knew all too well how harrowing they could be and while he neither could nor would close himself to them, he came to see them as hostile and to wish to keep them at arm's length. When life itself involved him in such disruptive experiences he did not baulk at the issues, but followed his policy of working them out in artistic form, and he did this quite consciously, as the ending of *Torquato Tasso* and the last section of the *Trilogie der Leidenschaft* clearly show.

The strictly 'Classical' period (i.e. approximately 1786–1805) is the one in which Goethe enjoyed the greatest clarity and serenity, but even this time was not devoid of tragic moments. Passion of a very personal, often rending kind plays a major part in some of the works of this period, notably *Torquato Tasso*, and it is portrayed with great force. Nor does Goethe arrange things so as to give an easy victory to the forces of light. He allows the dark and destructive forces to reappear at the very end of Tasso's final monologue (lines 3448 ff.).

His view of these things is not the uncompromisingly tragic, absolutely subjective one which echoes in the catastrophe and conclusion of *Werther*. But the conciliatory element which is always present in the endings of works like *Tasso* is not the only, or even the chief sign of the Classical mentality. This lies much more in the marriage to the dynamic, 'free' impulse of a balancing element of stability and order. The two are distinguishable; in terms of character or outlook they are sometimes shown in opposition, at least temporarily. But there is never an absolute disharmony between them. They are not so much in conflict as in a state of interaction, and in terms of the overall effect of the work of art they often come together in a synthesis in which there is no question of one side giving in to the other.

The most important agent of the Classical synthesis, however, on the aesthetic level at any rate, is not this more philosophical element but the all-pervasive effect of more or less strict form. This was felt to embody control, rational clarity and objectivity, without cramping feeling and imagination. In the practical sphere on the part of Goethe, and in both the practical and theoretical ones on that of Schiller, questions of form assumed an entirely new significance for the Classicists. Goethe, who before and, to a considerable extent, after this period, relied much more on his native poetic instinct and accumulated experience, became concerned with the technical principles of things like versification and even sought and followed 'expert' advice. This was not mere pedantry. In Italy, as he says in his *Italienische Reise*, he had come, for the first time, really to appreciate the value of 'das Handwerk einer Sache' (the technical side of an activity) and to find positive pleasure in it.[11] Its intrinsic qualities of law and discipline would have appealed to him at this time, just as, in the scientific sphere, he derived so much joy from the discovery of Law in nature that he called it a 'beautiful concept'.[12]

The Classicists have no intention of simplifying the multifarious individual reality of the world of nature down to the point at which it will fit into a scheme, however ingenious, devised by the intellect alone. Rather, they think of form as representing the workings of the independent rational and spiritual capacity of man (his God-given 'prerogative') – which is *in* the world of nature merely, whereas the passions are *of* it – upon the unorganized and heterogeneous 'Stoff' (material, matter) provided by the world around him. It is an emanation of the true ideal of man which is a spiritual reality, and whose importance is not confined to the field of the arts by any means. Not so much what a person or agency does, as the way in which it is done is expressive of the inner spiritual constitution.

The two are, of course, intimately linked, but they are distinguishable and need to be distinguished. Thus Schiller's *Über naïve und sentimentalische Dichtung*, expounding his concept of the naïve (our experience of 'nature', as it manifests itself in things or in people), in which we must always think of nature as admirable and right, has to distinguish between the undifferentiated mass of natural objects and actions (which can, of course, be nasty and brutish) and the inner, ideal nature of nature, its universal ways of operating, its 'form as a moral quantity'.[13] 'Nature' in the world outside man means wholeness, self-sufficiency, calm and above all, necessity; in man, it would appear to be something very much like the practical workings of the spiritual ideal of 'Humanität', in which pure morality and a pure heart as well as intellect are involved.

The Classicists revere the reason, but in its form as 'Vernunft', that is, as a harmonious whole, formed by an equal partnership between the understanding, the heart and the will imbued with right moral principles. The 'Aufklärer' had tended to use the word 'Vernunft' in a way which was more or less synonymous with 'Verstand', i.e. the faculty which knows theoretically and intellectually and which, at the non-philosophical level, is 'gesunder Menschenverstand', sound common sense. The

Classicists did not deny the validity of this faculty, but were not content to remain within its confines. They defined reason more widely, to mean something very like the conscious centre-point of man's innate, if often only potential Humanity, the prerogative which marked him off as 'free' by contrast to other creatures who were totally circumscribed by nature, as having been created, however this was understood, in God's image. Herder, indeed, equates 'Humanität' with the essence of true religion.[14] To return to our main point in the present discussion, it is not surprising that Goethe, many years after Schiller's death, should see in the latter's skull the 'form', the 'God-thought trace',[15] of the divine part of his friend.

Form, then, is not something totally external, to which the active agent conforms, but something that works from within, something personal. It is not conceived restrictively: anything in nature, human or inanimate, can, in theory at least, be admitted and justified in the Classical world-view and artistic outlook, as long as it is capable of being brought in some way under the wing of the 'true' nature to which man's Humanity gives him access. Whereas the 'Aufklärer' had always been at great pains to avoid any material with the potential to disrupt order, the Classicist regards much less as being of itself unclean. Even such things as prostitution (Goethe's 'Der Gott und die Bajadere') or sickening cruelty (e.g. the blinding of Melchthal's father in Schiller's *Wilhelm Tell*) can be rendered more or less directly. Certainly these things are not described for their own sake. In rejecting the letter of propriety, the 'Sturm und Drang' had often also rejected its spirit. The Classicist aims to preserve what is good in the principle while freeing himself from its restrictive tendencies, by enshrining it in the aesthetic form in which the material is presented. An ugly or deeply disturbing subject can be treated in a way which is not itself ugly or disturbed.

Nor does Classicism feel the need to reduce human nature and experience to a series of common denominators. Like the 'Aufklärung', it is interested in general truths, but it has no need or desire to achieve them at the expense of individuality. Its conception of form as something both universal (a manifestation of 'Vernunft') and personal, a way of being rather than an abstract external standard, is perhaps the key to this. Without leaving nature, the individual man can also experience as Man. The gods can speak to us, as they do to Iphigenie, 'through our hearts'. Such harmony is not achieved easily. Mere limitation will not bring it about, and there are no simple rules to follow, as Iphigenie herself discovers.

As far as literary theory in the strict sense was concerned, the Classicists were largely content to consolidate and perhaps modify where necessary. While they were out of sympathy with what they regarded as the excessive subjectivism of the preceding era, they had no desire to return to restrictionist rationalism and accepted as more or less self-evident the great 'Sturm und Drang' insights into the nature of poetry as the expression of the individual's inner experience. They were not particularly interested in questions which had fascinated previous generations, like those of the three unities or of pity and fear in tragedy. Schiller's most strictly theoretical essay, in this sense, on tragedy, namely 'Über die tragische Kunst', is one of his least 'engaged' works.

As to another problem which exercised their predecessors greatly, that of the relation in which literature should stand to morality, they did not regard it as a problem at all and only discussed it in reply to attacks made on them on this ground by the residual 'Aufklärung', or by others who were of a particular ideological persuasion and lacked the objectivity necessary to appreciate beauty apart from content. Herder had achieved a lesser degree of balanced objectivity than had Goethe and Schiller. He genuinely shared the Classical ethos, but it went rather less deep in him, so that, in his discussion of German literature in the eighth volume of the *Humanitätsbriefe*, he could show what Goethe felt to be a 'prejudiced enthusiasm'[16] which prompts the younger man, in his letter to the Swiss painter and art-historian J. H. Meyer of 20 June 1796, to clarify his own standpoint. He criticizes the unevenness and one-sidedness of Herder's treatment, his readiness to tolerate the mediocre and his lack of sympathy for 'that which is alive and striving' (i.e. striving for the highest values). Goethe continues:

. . . and so the old, half-true philistine tune drones through the whole thing: the arts are to recognize the moral law and subject themselves to it. The first of these they have always done and must do, since their laws originate in the reason [i.e. the Classical 'Vernunft'] just as much as does the moral law. If they were to do the second thing, they would be lost and it were better that a millstone were hung round their neck and they were cast into the sea rather than that they should be made to sink gradually down to the level of utilitarian flatness.[17]

The essential thing was, not to obey certain rules or follow specific moral aims, so much as to become imbued with the spirit of 'the true, the good, the beautiful', one unitary spirit which manifested itself in closely related ways in the philosophical, moral and aesthetic spheres. Schiller renders it in *Über naive und sentimentalische Dichtung* as 'schöne Natur', or 'wahre menschliche Natur', an orientation towards nature (in a higher sense) being what distinguishes the poet from other beings. Anything in human life can, in theory at least, be poetically admissible, even what might otherwise offend against accepted morality, provided it is seen in the right way. Goethe's frankness about sexual aspects of love in the *Römische Elegien* is defensible because it does not isolate this aspect of human nature but presents it in the context of man's *whole* humanity. Not just the physical side, but 'all the realities of humanity' must be expressed in such portrayals.[18] The concept of poetry (as indeed of all the arts) is 'to give humanity the most complete expression possible',[19] and this would naturally include the aesthetic impulse, the 'play-urge' ('Spieltrieb') which, as Schiller expounds it in his *Ästhetische Erziehung des Menschen*, complements and can hold the balance between the rational (intellectual and moral) and the sensuous impulses which make up man's psychological constitution. Any one-sided insistence on single aspects would be rejected: it would militate against the harmonious free play of the faculties which was the Classical ideal, in both life and art.

And in both life and art, the Greeks represented this ideal in concrete form. True to the tradition of Winckelmann, Goethe finds it easiest to discuss the aesthetic ideal in relation to the plastic arts. The primacy of Greek culture is affirmed with great forcefulness in the fourth paragraph of the *Einleitung in die Propyläen* (1798). In a later passage in this essay, Goethe talks of the principal characteristics of the art he admires: its quality of complete self-sufficiency and its ability to satisfy both the senses and the spirit.[20] Restfulness and the harmonious balance of apparently opposed forces, then, are important features of the aesthetic ideal. In another essay in the *Propyläen*, Goethe develops his concept of Classical harmony through the example of the famous Laocoon statue, which had first become an object of interest through Winckelmann and continued to occupy the minds of German writers.[21] Goethe sees a violent and emotive subject so handled and arranged that it becomes 'a model of [the combination of] the symmetrical with the manifold, of restfulness with movement, of contrast with gradation', appealing to both senses and spirit and softening 'the storm of suffering and passions' through grace and beauty.[22]

Harmony, achieved not through elimination of multiplicity but through a balanced interplay, is a recurring concept in Goethe's Classical writings on art. In *Der Sammler und die Seinigen*, he discusses the opposition of 'seriousness' and 'play', seen as one-sided approaches: the one taking things too sternly and seriously, the other too lightly and loosely. Only a proper combination of the two sides brings 'development into the general style, artistic truth, beauty and perfection'.[23] Passion, moral earnestness and so on have full validity as parts in a properly harmonized whole. The same is true of the free fancy: it was the Classical Goethe, after all, who really laid the foundations of the genre of the 'Kunstmärchen'.

As in other fields, this Classical attitude continued to be an important factor in Goethe's artistic outlook after the death of Schiller. The important essay *Myrons Kuh* (1812) reconstructs a piece of statuary as a varied but perfectly integrated group, characterized by 'the balance of the unidentical, the contrast of the similar and the harmony of the dissimilar',[24] and the perfectly balanced Makarie in *Wilhelm Meisters Wanderjahre* expresses the wish that 'the study of Greek and Roman literature may remain the basis of higher culture' and, in an echo of 'Der Chinese in Rom', dismisses Chinese, Indian and Roman antiquities as 'Kuriositäten'.[25] We know, of course, that the taste of the later Goethe, who wrote, among other things, the *West-östlicher Divan* and the *Chinesisch-Deutsche Tages- und Jahreszeiten*, cannot be circumscribed by this formulation, but it does show the continued strength of the Classical element in him, the element which expresses itself in Faust's rejection of modern taste as 'bad'.[26]

Synthesis

The path to the achievement of the Classical ideal lay in self-development and self-perfection, the 'Bildung' which the Classicists were so fond of extolling, from the artist's mastery of the technical aspects of his medium to the crown of 'Humanität': to the achievement of the state which Goethe sees embodied in the Greeks, and in which 'all qualities are united in equal proportions', with no self-conscious sense of imbalance or division.[27]

The main theoretical problem arising out of this basic demand on the artist was one which we touched on in an earlier chapter,[28] namely that of the treatment of reality. The Classicists, as we might expect, set out to reconcile the ideal with the real as much as possible. Just as a kind of synthesis between the two 'psychological types' of realist and idealist seems to be the logical conclusion of Schiller's *Über naive und sentimentalische Dichtung*, so his presentation of the two main trends in literature, the 'naive' writer who is characterized by the qualities of nature itself and expresses natural reality objectively and without reflection, and his 'sentimentalisch', reflective counterpart, reveals a certain incompleteness in each. The 'sentimental' poet is oriented towards the ideal and runs the risk of losing touch with the real world altogether and becoming a 'Phantast', while the naive poet is in danger, if the reality on which he depends lacks the higher, ideal nature which is the kernel of all poetry, of ceasing to be a poet in order to remain naive. Each attitude, it would seem, needs a certain injection of the other to maintain the balance.

Goethe, of course, being much less troubled by a feeling of disparity between real and ideal and much better able to gain stimulus from the world around him, did not have such an inner struggle. He does show a certain theoretical awareness of the problem, particularly in his keen sense of the special nature of art. 'Nature is separated from art by an enormous gulf,' he writes in the *Einleitung in die Propyläen*.[29] The artist must certainly study natural reality, but he must see it in such a way that he can, not copy nature, but emulate it, in shaping out of it a product which has the formal beauty and spiritual validity, the 'general' content, as Goethe often called it, which is latent but not always immediately apparent in the specific. It must be 'simultaneously natural and super-natural'. We are reminded of the discovery of a 'symbolic' potential in reality in the letters between Goethe and Schiller quoted in Part I of this book,[30] and once again of the continuity which leads on from the Classical to the late Goethe. In the Classical phase, true symbolism is still more of a potential than an achievement. Goethe's observation is by no means devoid of feeling or imagination, but it lacks the extra flexibility, the direct emotional appeal, and the quality of mystery in comprehensibility which distinguishes the later work (e.g. the *West-östlicher Divan* or *Faust*, Part II), where there is a greater willingness to accept a clouding of the intellectual side and to indulge the personal impulses. At the same time, there is no obvious break in continuity between the Classical position and the definition of symbolism, in the section of the *Maximen und Reflexionen* headed 'Art and Artists':

> True symbolism exists where the particular represents the more general, not as a dream and shadow, but as a revelation of the unfathomable which is living and belongs to the [present] moment.[31]

That both order and freedom are of central importance in the Classical ideal is more or less self-evident from a reading of the philosophical and literary works and letters of the main personalities involved. There is some degree of variation between them: Kant, for example, shows a stronger streak of pure rationalism and a sterner moral rigorism than even his devoted admirer Schiller can agree to. Just as he lacked the organ for true appreciation of sensuous and imaginative beauty, so he was too deeply convinced of the inherent sinfulness of human nature to be able to concede the degree of freedom to the individual heart which is present in Schiller's concept of the 'beautiful soul', i.e. the person whose inner goodness is such that desire and duty coincide. In him, the impulse towards order rather tended to outweigh that towards freedom, though his preoccupation with the latter is evident from all his works. His insistence on excluding any kind of 'empirical' element, anything but pure abstract reasoning from the working-out of the principle of morality, his belief that virtue, 'stripped of all admixture of sensuous things and of every spurious adornment of reward or self-love', vastly eclipses all that charms our senses,[32] would hardly have commanded the assent of Goethe. Herder, whose development had followed the same general lines as Goethe's but who had retained more of the subjective and emotional element, actually set out to combat the Kantian philosophy in some of his later works.[33]

But with due allowance for these personal variations, we can still state confidently that freedom and order were accepted as twin pillars of the Classical outlook and that no real conflict was felt between them. If, in many a 'Sturm und Drang' work, some kind of peace between the two could only be achieved through the sacrifice of the individual, Goethe can now write that limitation and mastery go hand in hand and that 'only Law can give us freedom'. And though the title of the sonnet from which these words are taken is 'Natur und Kunst', this does not restrict their meaning to the aesthetic field. 'Kunst' as the counter-pole of 'Natur', had the much wider social and cultural connotation of the artificial in general and the works of civilization in particular.

The opposition between civilization as it was and nature as it was thought to have been, had by this time become part of the conventional wisdom of the eighteenth century. The Classicists took a much less strongly Rousseau-istic line towards it, however, than did the 'Sturm und Drang'. They recognized that contemporary civilized society and its spirit were imperfect, and had moments of nostalgia for 'natural' wholeness and harmony. The opening stages of Schiller's *Über die Ästhetische Erziehung des Menschen* are particularly redolent of this feeling. But nostalgia is a beginning rather than a final mood. There is no thought of going back to a state of nature through smashing convention; rather, the way leads forward through 'Kunst' to a restoration of harmony which is embodied, in Schiller's thought, in concepts like the aesthetic state (society as a whole), the beautiful soul (personal morality) or the 'sentimental idyll' (in poetry itself).

For the more intellectually inclined Classical thinkers (like Schiller and Kant), who tended to think in terms of dualism, the pattern is one of opposed categories, which need to be clarified and then reconciled, or at least balanced. For those in whom speculative cognition played a less dominant part and inner experience a correspondingly greater one, the sense of opposition is much weaker, once the inner development from 'Sturm und Drang' to a modified way of thinking and feeling has been completed. Thus Herder, who sees the history of the world in terms of a progression towards concrete realization of the ideal of Humanity, makes the tendency to 'art', presumably in the wide sense, an essential part of man's nature: 'everything for which the potential capacity lies within him can and must become, with time, an art.'[34]

Goethe, after Italy, seems to find no serious difficulty in combining the controlled formality of this spirit of 'art' with true nature, e.g. in the form of deep personal passion. The tortures of jealousy, for example, are in no way glossed over, or treated simplistically, in the elegy 'Alexis und Dora'. They are rendered as 'this great and violent fire which rages through my breast'. But in the poetic form in which it appears, this formulation is not rough or rending. The young man's plea to the gods to moderate this fire falls into the second half (the 'pentameter') of the distich:

> . . . mässiget, Götter,
> Diesen gewaltigen Brand, der mir den Busen durchtobt!

The pentameter in the elegiac distich has an element of rest in it by its very nature, with its two decided pauses, in the middle and at the end. Allied to this in the present case is the regularity of the line, which is precisely and evenly stressed. The phrasing too has a certain objectivity: it is expressive, certainly, but precisely put and seems to presuppose a measure of detachment and clear observation. It does not seem to be distorted in its form by the inner confusions and stabs of pain which Alexis must be feeling. Especially when we take this moment in the context of the whole poem, we may say that Schiller's dictum: 'life is serious, but art is serene'[35] is well exemplified.

This means, of course, not that one side of the dualism is suppressed in favour of the other, but that both are present in harmony. It is because art can free man from domination by one side of his nature without driving him completely over to the other, because it can satisfy that reconciling and liberating urge in man (the 'Spieltrieb') which, without frivolity, aims at the free play of all the faculties, sensuous and spiritual, that art is so important to Schiller. That is why he sees it, in fact, as the educative element which offers man's only hope of one day returning to the state of harmony which, together with the other Classicists, he found in the practical reality as well as in the art of ancient Greece. Over and over again, in Classical German literature and thought, one comes, in one context or another, on the theme of reconciliation of opposing demands not by a compromise which satisfies neither side but by a solution which can satisfy the positive principles of both. Thus we have the vast scheme of Herder's *Ideen zu einer Philosophie der Geschichte*, with its full recognition of the identity of various ages and peoples and at the same time its unifying theme of Humanity, and Goethe showing general, social humanity *in* the individual in *Wilhelm Meisters Lehrjahre*.

In this work the self-oriented hero's quest for fulfilment, in a kind of Faustian 'dark impulsion' ('dunkler Drang'), leads him, along a twisting and very individual path, to realization in the status of a 'Bürger', as part of a general order, in fact. His self-indulgent imagination and indiscipline of mind have been refined into a more disciplined form but there is no violation of his true personality, for this is what he has been unconsciously seeking all the time.[36]

Reconciliation of the individual and the general in a way which avoids anarchy but preserves as much as possible of individual freedom is the aim of Classicism, and the philosophical and artistic achievement in this field is often very high. The trend towards something more than a mechanical balance, towards a genuine synthesis, is there, and whether or not one agrees that this difficult ideal is always achieved, the result is often such as to demand this word or another (which we do not possess) which is very like it. Wilhelm von Humboldt's concept of a state which gives full freedom to individuality within order,[37] with its reduction of state intervention to a minimum, may well look like a prescription for nineteenth-century laissez-faire, but one has to view it against the background of the stultifying effect of eighteenth-century despotism and the impossibility of combining with this the ideal of the development of man to wholeness, which is the basis of Humboldt's thinking. Man must not be robbed of the opportunity and stimulus for activity,[38] his true purpose in life is 'the highest and the most proportioned development of his powers to a [harmonious] whole',[39] for which freedom is essential, and the function of the state should be to guarantee him this freedom, and the maximum of opportunity and stimulus, within the sole limitations of his powers and his rights.[40]

In many other spheres, too, this apparently paradoxical combination of form and flexibility, order and freedom, is apparent. Kant, for all that he was less optimistic than many as to the goodness of human nature, nevertheless enshrines the principle of individuality in his moral philosophy, in his insistence on each man's freedom and responsibility and most strikingly in the categorical imperative, which marries the individual action to the idea of universal moral law. Schiller, in his Classical dramas, creates characters and situations which are entirely individual, yet at the same time, and without a discernible break in the texture, clearly representative of the working of abstract laws. Goethe, who embodies the desired synthesis in himself to a much greater degree, also, naturally enough, gives it the best expression. This usually occurs in an indirect rather than a conscious theoretical form, but as he said to Schiller,[41] contact with the latter's more reflective mind had increased his appreciation of this mode of perception and he did make some attempts at general formulation of laws in this period, most notably in the scientific field. In an exchange of letters centring on his work on optics, he accepts Schiller's phrase 'rational empiricism' (i.e. a balance of theoretical and purely 'objective' observation) as an accurate formulation of his aims.[42] His own finest statement of this attitude (later to culminate in the *Farbenlehre*) in our period is the passage from the 'Metamorphose der Tiere' which has already been alluded to:

Dieser schöne Begriff von Macht und Schranken, von Willkür
Und Gesetz, von Freiheit und Mass, von beweglicher Ordnung,
Vorzug und Mangel erfreue dich hoch![43]

This insight arises out of observation of the way in which, according to Goethe, animals evolve in a polar interaction of inner forces and outer influences but as he goes on to point out, the concept is by no means limited to the non-human animal kingdom. Rather, it represents the highest wisdom for man in all his doings, which explains the blend of solemnity and exhilaration with which it is proclaimed. 'Mobility in [literally,

Synthesis

'moving'] order' was the secret of Goethe's own success in maintaining stability with unabated freshness of life until the end. It did not spare him difficulty or pain, but it did preserve him from self-loss in confusion on the one hand and petrification on the other in a period riddled with uncertainty and change. The late summary of his life's wisdom, the poem 'Urworte. Orphisch' (1817) is in many ways an application to his own life of the formula just quoted and shows how the older Goethe, very much an alert citizen of the nineteenth century, was still the child of the eighteenth. He was, after all, already fifty-one in 1800.

Synthesis in Literature (I): Goethe

The vast majority of Goethe's finished works of this time are concerned with or express directly the synthesis of which we have spoken. Among the dramas, *Iphigenie auf Tauris* can be related to our general theme without much difficulty. In *Torquato Tasso*, which was produced at very much the same time, the situation may not seem so favourable at first glance. The central figure is one who has a certain amount in common with Werther. The achievement of a balance within the individual, which enables him to endure in life without denying himself, is presented as a task whose accomplishment is an urgent necessity but by no means a foregone conclusion. The hero's undisciplined individualistic freedom brings him to the brink of destruction, and the ready-made order into which the others have tried to integrate him is clearly inadequate to his needs. The theme of a 'bewegliche Ordung', one which will enable him to survive *as himself*, is implicit in the play and the ending makes it clear that he must find it within himself.

Tasso's artistic sensitivity of mind and soul certainly makes it specially difficult for him to relate to a world in which the poetic is, at best, diluted. But this play is more than simply 'the tragedy of the poet', as it has been called.[1] Tasso cannot bring the demands of his inner self into balance with the state of the real world in which he has to live and indeed wants to live. Like Werther, he has the capacity to create a dream-world from within himself, but he cannot wrap himself in this dream as completely and contentedly as Werther was able to do. The portrait of him painted by Leonore Sanvitale (Act I, lines 159 ff.) as a man who lives more or less entirely in the world of the spirit is, like almost everything this character says, at best a half-truth. The Princess (lines 173 ff.) sees deeper and recognizes a preoccupation with 'das Wirkliche'.

When, in the important third scene of the first Act, in which he is crowned by the Princess with a laurel wreath, Tasso indulges briefly in a dream-vision of harmony between 'hero and poet' (lines 527 ff.), it is, as he replies when Leonore bids him return to the present, 'the present which has lifted me up'. He 'only seems to be absent'. For a moment, the alienation which he feels so acutely in present reality seems to have been suspended. But the extreme reluctance with which he wears the crown points to an awareness that the harmony between poetic and practical which he longs for, and which it might be thought of as symbolizing, is only a dream, as he himself calls it (line 519). He wants it as a reality and this recognition as a poet only is only half a loaf. When he is brought into a state of exaltation by the friendly words of the Princess in the first scene of Act II, he glimpses the Golden Age restored in reality and immediately acts as if this were so, disregarding all the barriers of social convention, age, experience and temperament in his behaviour towards Antonio – with the catastrophic results which one might expect.

It is not, then, a lack of *desire* to play a part in the practical world which makes Tasso an isolated person, nor a lack of desire to relate to others which makes him incapable, as the Princess puts it (Act II, lines 922–3), of finding a friend with whom he can be in harmony 'even after many years'. Alfonso is his Lord, Antonio's cradle was not blessed by the Graces, and with Leonore, however well disposed she is towards him within her lights, he feels, quite rightly, the absence of uncalculating sincerity in friendship: 'One feels the intention and it jars on one.'[2] He knows himself that this is not the Golden Age, but it seems as if he cannot live at peace unless the freedom of that age to be oneself and to relate to others without any kind of ulterior consideration is available to him. If he gives himself, he does it, as the Princess says to Leonore, 'completely' (Act III, Scene 2, line 1686), but with one possible exception, to which we shall come later, no one in the play can take him in this way. Even the Princess desires a limitation in their relationship. She wants it to go no further than the 'pure harmonies' of the spirit of which she speaks to Leonore (Act III, Scene 2, line 1868) and when she can no longer prevent him from offering his 'whole being' (Act V, Scene 4, line 3283), she rejects him.

This could seem to be a simple black-and-white matter of a fatally one-sided, subjectivistic view which demands the impossible and makes life intolerable for its possessor and for others. Certainly Tasso is 'ungebändigt', as Goethe later said Beethoven was, and Goethe would not have wished to set that up as an ideal. The ethos of the conventional courtly society has in it an element of positive self-discipline which would be very desirable for Tasso. Nor has Goethe glossed over the pathological side of his hero's attitude, his retreat into himself and his twisting of the words and actions of others into a totally imaginary conspiracy against him. For all that, Goethe's sympathies lie definitely on the side of Tasso.

In the conversation with Leonore in Act II, Scene 4, Antonio sees Tasso, quite fairly from his point of view, as a man who tends to sink into himself for long periods and then, in sudden outbursts, to be unable to control either tongue or heart. At such moments, he wants the moon:

> Dann will er alles fassen, alles halten,
> Dann soll geschehn, was er sich denken mag; . . .
> Die letzten Enden aller Dinge will
> Sein Geist zusammenfassen . . .[3]

Hardly a comfortable companion, and not one of whom Goethe himself approves – in this state. But Antonio's negative view-point makes him blind to the element which, like the 'striving' of Faust, is capable, after it has been tested and purified, of at least partly legitimizing, in retrospect, his wrong or silly actions. He needs to live with others, he certainly needs to achieve self-discipline. But he must not do so at the expense of what we might call his 'infinite' capacity (in Goethe's sense of 'unendlich', real but transcendent). This would admittedly be vitiated if channelled into an introverted dream-life, but such is not his real desire. He must find and wants to find a satisfactory relation to practical reality, but he must not simply conform to it. For whereas his vision of life is in need of discipline, it has a fullness which raises him above all the other characters. None of the others is a complete person. The Princess is closest to him spiritually, but her personal solution, to live *purely* through the spirit, is more resignation than positive renunciation. It gives a kind of fragile order to her life, but for Tasso to seek peace by this route would be as much a denial of his inner spark as to sink himself in purely wordly satisfactions.

Tasso is alone in this society of well-meaning people. He is both more highly endowed spiritually and less fitted for happiness in this world than they, and if there is to be any salvation for him without self-negation, it lies in finding in himself an inner standard, what Goethe elsewhere has called a 'law',[4] which enables a person to trace out for himself an individual path ('Bahn') in life without coming into tragic conflict with the people with whom he has to live. Whether Tasso has any prospect of finding this, is left an open question. He will certainly need a different kind of contact with other people than he is likely to find in Ferrara. So it is not entirely a hopeless prospect that lies before him at the end of the play, and it is appropriate that Antonio, the man whose life is largely spent in practical activity in the world outside, should be the one to provide, in the final scene, the most effective help he has so far received: firstly, by directing his attention to his own personal bedrock, his inalienable poetic ability, and then by giving him the first moment of full human contact he has enjoyed in the play.

Antonio's action in clasping Tasso's hand throws into relief his previous lack of contact with the others and helps him in his task of taking stock of his situation objectively and practically. He uses the traditional image of the rock in the sea, and while he is entirely the poet, as he exploits its various aspects (stability and instability, inflexibility and flexibility, salvation and danger) to render the complex situation, he is also more entirely objective than ever before. He ends (prompted, no doubt, by the handclasp) with the idea of the shipwrecked sailor 'clinging tight to the rock which it seemed was to be his destruction'. We know that he will never lose the 'Beweglichkeit' (mobility) which earlier made him liken himself to the water. Whether he will acquire enough of the firmness of the rock to enable him to survive is uncertain, but what does seem certain is that a continuation of the kind of existence he led previously would never have provided it.

Part of the Classical nature of this play, then, lies in the insight into what the sensitive, idealistic, inward-looking character needs to do to be saved. An equally important part is the flexible and expressive, yet clear and stable form in which the often un-Classical material is presented to us. A phrase from the later drama *Die natürliche Tochter* (1803), which is perhaps *too* reticent and calm, but which also aims at the Classical blend of freedom and order, formulates the ideal spirit which is rather better realized in *Tasso*:

> So hast du lange nicht, bewegtes Herz,
> Dich in gemessnen Worten ausgesprochen![5]

Some might argue that the spirit of orderliness has too great an influence in *Iphigenie* and that the result is a shade too static. It is worth reminding ourselves that it is difficult enough to formulate the ideal of perfect balance convincingly, but much more difficult to realize it with any consistency. But if we can admit that, in *Iphigenie*, we sometimes feel the guiding hand of which we should ideally be unaware, there can be no accusation that Goethe has restricted mobility in *Tasso*. In this case, we feel more the need to find evidence of the stabilizing factors which prevent us from being swept hither, thither and yon. Form plays a particularly important part in this process. It would be impossible to give each aspect the detailed discussion it deserves here. We can only point in general terms, for example, to the effect of the strict classicistic dramatic principles on which the play is constructed: the movement of the scene only within very strict limits, the observance of the other traditional unities, the paring-down of the cast to a symmetrical group of five, in which the concentration of attention on the central figure is more intense even than in *Iphigenie*. The iambic blank-verse form is not departed from (contrast, for example, *Iphigenie*, IV, 1369–81 and 1726–66) and is itself handled with greater regularity.

The firmness of the metre helps to balance and contain the fluid, often highly volatile emotional content, in conjunction with the even more important factors of imagery and language in general. In Tasso's final speech, for example, all the iambic pentameters are regular and there are no serious aberrations from the norm of even pace and accentuation. The image of water is certainly allowed its full emotional expressiveness (e.g. 'es ruhten die Gestirne An dieser Brust, die zärtlich sich bewegte'), but in combination with a precise and objective observation which gives a clarity that some earlier treatments of the image by Goethe (e.g. in 'An den Mond', or 'Der Fischer'), from the pre-Italian period, do not possess. In the latter of those poems, for instance, Goethe contents himself with a brief, if effective evocation:

Das Wasser rauscht', das Wasser schwoll

which is all he needs, since it is the psychological effect which the water has on the fisherman which interests him. In *Tasso*, Goethe is also interested in using the waves to reflect the emotional ebb and flow, but his description:

... die Welle flieht
Und schwankt und schwillt und beugt sich schäumend über.[6]

also etches the *object* clearly in our minds.

When, in Act I (scene 3, lines 532 ff.), Goethe uses the water of a spring as a bridge from reality to Tasso's dream-vision of the harmony of hero and poet, this 'Zauberspiegel' (magic mirror) is rendered in language which is carefully purified of all elements which might pain the sense with a drowsy Romantic numbness. Tasso himself undoubtedly has the tendency to sink himself emotionally into a subject, but Goethe's *portrayal* of him avoids even the indistinctness of a Keats, let alone that of the more radically 'inward' German Romantics. A certain departure from absolute objectivity is obviously required, and Tasso does describe himself as '*wunderbar* bekränzt' (wondrously garlanded), and the water as a 'Zauberspiegel'. But this is all, and the other descriptive elements, particularly the opening:

Und zeigt mir ungefähr ein *klarer* Brunnen
In seinem *reinen* Spiegel einen Mann . . .[7]

provide a more than adequate balance.

The Classical period in Goethe's life was also the period of the French Revolution. As has been said, he was out of sympathy with its violence and with the extreme nature of the social upheaval it represented, while admitting that it was not without justification and certainly a development from which there could be no going back. He detached himself from the actual events and personalities, but was by no means uninterested in the general phenomenon and treated it in a number of major and minor works. The most important are *Hermann und Dorothea* (which was mentioned in an earlier chapter) and *Die natürliche Tochter*. In both, as in more minor productions,[8] he tries to instil order into freedom, bring individual energy and fire into harmony with the general, as happens, in a non-political context, in *Wilhelm Meisters Lehrjahre*. The figure of Eugenie in *Die natürliche Tochter*, the girl of royal blood who lacks neither daring nor the taste for the commanding heights of society, but who, in a state of impending civil disintegration (cf. Act V, lines 2826 ff.), becomes the hope for the future through free and positive renunciation of her estate, is the best artistic embodiment of Goethe's political drift. The tone of the whole is perhaps too far removed from political practicalities to constitute a completely satisfactory solution of the problem it outlines. Yet, at the practical level, there seems to be little scope for a full development of the theme of order and freedom. The resolve of the Countess in *Die Aufgeregten*, to act with more 'Billigkeit' (justice and fairness) towards those of lower degree within the existing system, or the moral of *Der Bürgergeneral*, that each man should, in a general harmony, honestly fulfil the functions of his station, were probably as much as contemporary conditions offered by way of practical political morals, unless one was prepared to accept a major upheaval.

Formally, too, *Die Natürliche Tochter* offers a particularly interesting example for our purposes, in its tempering of energy by Classical metre and language. The play leans further towards the symbolic than does *Tasso*, both in its presentation of its heroine, who is recognizably an individual, but portrayed in less strongly personal terms, and in its use of words and images. The episode in which Eugenie examines the costly finery which she hopes to wear on her appearance at court allows us to study this latter aspect very conveniently. The vivid attraction of the royal estate is mirrored in the richness and fascination of fine clothes and jewels, which are at the same time objectively described. The almost demonic quality of their fascination is underlined by the 'Hofmeisterin' (who, like so many characters in this play, is not personally identified by a name), and comes out in the expressive description. But the choice and arrangement of words maintain an overall effect of measure and calm. The objectively observing eye, and the intellect which gives

form to its impressions, play an equal part with the excitement
aroused by the interplay of light from the silver and other colours on the undergarment:

> Das Unterkleid! wie reich und süss durchflimmert
> Sich rein des Silbers und der Farben Blitz.[9]

And the rendering of the pearls and jewels in the phrases 'der
Perlen sanftes Licht' and 'der Juwelen leuchtende Gewalt'[10] is
equally expressive and equally precise and controlled.

The strands of order and freedom are less tightly interwoven
in the great novel of Classicism, *Wilhelm Meisters Lehrjahre*, and
though there is a clear desire to interrelate and balance them, it
could be said that in this case the vital first and last impressions
are that the former tends to dominate. There is a certain dryness
in characterization and style, even some measure of the theoretical in the last two Books in particular, which seems to
inhibit the personal and poetic impulses so that they tend to
become inset (like Mignon and the Harper) rather than fully
integrated into the picture. The long period of concentrated
effort expended on this very substantial work, especially when
one recalls that it fell during the period of close collaboration
and exchange of ideas with Schiller, may be the principal
factor behind this situation. Some of their letters, particularly
those of Schiller to Goethe of 8 July 1796 and his reply of the
9th, in which he asks Schiller to continue to 'drive him beyond
his own boundaries', point in this direction.

However this may be, the novel, which is conceived as the
story of the hero's attainment of balance, through the natural
development of his innate characteristics in interplay with the
objective lessons of experience on the one hand, and rational
guidance from 'Turmgesellschaft' on the other, does seem to
stress the objective rather than the subjective side. Mignon, the
embodiment of the irrational and emotional, is ripe for death as
soon as Wilhelm comes into the circle of Therese and Natalie.
She cannot be separated from him simply by the appeal to sweet
reason. Goethe was never prepared to accept that a deep personal feeling could be overcome by such considerations, and he
gives it best when Mignon replies to Wilhelm's perfectly
'reasonable' arguments for a temporary parting in Book
Seven, Chapter Eight: 'Reason is cruel. The heart is better.'[11]

So she continues in sadness and eventually dies, adding a dark and emotional strand to the generally clear and calm texture of the last two Books. But she occupies the centre of the stage only for brief periods and is at best a subordinate factor in the overall pattern.

This novel is in more than one sense the classic example of the German 'Bildungsroman', a form whose popularity among the Germans could be said to constitute additional evidence for the supposition that their realism is, relatively speaking, skin-deep. Its basic assumption is that the real events and experiences in the hero's life may be seen as a process of development, or 'formation', which leads to the achievement of a certain ideal goal: reality itself is subject, to some extent, to the superior authority of the idea. Since this goal should, strictly, be both attainable in the real world and satisfying to the highest demands of the spirit, it is not entirely surprising that the Classical *Meister* is probably the only truly satisfactory example of the genre. Wilhelm's process of development takes him from a basically correct, but confused and one-sidedly subjective outlook at the beginning to a state of clarity of vision and balance of character which will not spare him difficulty and pain in life, but which will prevent him from being sucked, as his passion for the theatre threatened to do, into a 'false activity, into which fancy lures us'.[12]

Apart from the more obviously 'Romantic' figures and motifs, fancy plays a significant part in the novel through its influence on Wilhelm. He has a strong feeling that it is better to be led by one's inner impulses than to try to impose a calculated pattern on life, and tends to use the word 'Fate' to give this attitude some degree of superior sanction. There is some good in this. Wilhelm's rejection of the calculated approach of the commercial world which is his home background, its tendency to measure the worth of things by money alone, is a sign of health. Nor does Goethe wish to cry down the theatre itself, which is a carrier of high spiritual values; especially as represented by Shakespeare, who figures prominently in the theatrical discussions and performances in which Wilhelm becomes involved. But without a true vocation and a sure mind and character, a man could easily be spoiled by it. Its attraction for a person of a somewhat too imaginative and individualistic tendency, especially in the rather uncertain and unformed state in which it existed in eighteenth-century Germany, could be dangerous, as Moritz showed very well in *Anton Reiser*. Wilhelm is attracted to it only partially for the right reasons. As is made clear at a number of points throughout the book, he is seeking something, with no very clear idea of what it is. He is a man who 'strives', like Faust, and like him too, he is enabled, by the fact that his is, in Therese's words, 'a noble seeking and striving for what is better',[13] to reach the true light in the end, in spite of his wrong turnings.

While it becomes clear, as he pursues the chosen career of actor, that this is not Wilhelm's true *métier*, his nobility and seriousness mark him out as being on a higher spiritual plane, and closer to the real higher nature of theatrical art than many of the other players, including the charming Philine. However, it remains true that his personal enthusiasm has betrayed him into a false start. He needs to find his way out of this gradually, and the guidance and rational good advice which are always available cannot be fully effective until he has reached the right stage in his own inner development. Here again, Goethe preserves the individual element. Nevertheless, he shows Wilhelm in a largely critical light, if not unsympathetically, and the opposite point of view is usually articulated more convincingly than Wilhelm's, even if he is not affected by it directly. One of the clearest examples occurs in Book One, Chapter Seventeen, in the conversation with the stranger whom Wilhelm meets before he has embarked on the theatrical career proper, but who talks in a voice which we are to hear later – above all in the words of the Abbé. To Wilhelm's 'fatalistic' view of life he opposes a more Classical wisdom:

The web of this world is woven out of necessity and chance; the reason puts itself between these two and is able to command them . . . only in so far as it stands firm and unshakeable does man deserve to be called a god of this earth . . . [to see a kind of free volition in necessity and a kind of reason in chance], is that anything more than to renounce one's own understanding and give free rein to one's desires?[14]

There can be no serious doubt of the primacy of reason in the picture of man in his social and moral relationships, which is the heart of this work. There is a similar primacy of Man (in his general capacity), made in God's image (i.e. with 'Vernunft') and destined, if he is guided by this light, to inherit the earth,[15] over Nature, of general, positive social activity over the private, inward life. We may recall that the extreme importance of nature in the 'Sturm und Drang' Goethe was linked with the strength of the pull towards freedom and individualism. In *Wilhelm Meisters Lehrjahre*, more loving care is devoted to the description of buildings and interiors than to that of the natural landscape.

As an instructive contrast with the nature-passages in *Werther*, which, as we saw, are strongly affected by emotion, we could quote the description of the surroundings in which Wilhelm and the other members of Melina's troupe, pause for a midday rest on their journey to a new town:

> . . . Eine grosse, sanft abhängige Waldwiese lud zum Bleiben ein; eine eingefasste Quelle bot die lieblichste Erquickung dar, und es zeigte sich an der andern Seite durch Schluchten und Waldrücken eine ferne, schöne und hoffnungsvolle Aussicht. Da lagen Dörfer und Mühlen in den Gründen, Städtchen in der Ebene und neue, in der Ferne eintretende Berge machten die Aussicht noch hoffnungsvoller, indem sie nur wie eine sanfte Beschränkung hereintraten.[16]

This is not a description with strong colour or individuality. The intensity, down to the smallest detail, and the living quality of the valley as described by Werther in the passage quoted in Chapter Nine, give way to a description in general and fairly neutral terms. The view has little that is intimate about it: the broad lines are sketched in, with some emphasis on places of human habitation and activity. The description is by no means mere 'scenery', but it has a strong element of objectivity, both in its wide, general vision and clear structure, and in its direction of the observers' attention outwards, not in a vague mood such as might be generated by the Romantic motif of the far distance, but in a 'hopeful' feeling of future activity and achievement, presumably of a 'social', constructive kind.

Objectivity is a word which constantly springs to mind, and one is tempted to couple with it 'realism', by which is meant, not the specific, three-dimensional realism of a Tolstoy, which

grants more or less equal literary validity to all individual real
things or people and portrays them, as far as possible, as they
are, but a preoccupation in general terms with Man in the
practical relationships and activities of this world: 'Action'
and 'Knowledge of the actual', as Schiller defines this mentality
apropos of Wilhelm's development.[17] Certainly, the sense of the
higher spiritual values in the Classical concept of Humanity
remains and is expressed, but the ideal does not mingle easily
with the actual and the work falls between the two stools of
'real' colour and life and spiritual and poetic loftiness. Goethe is
determined not to stray too far from the sphere of the actual, of
objectivity (what he calls his 'realistic *tic*'[18] is particularly active
in this work), so that his attempts to bring out the ideal sub-
structure have a rather theoretical flavour.

The conception in *Wilhelm Meisters Lehrjahre* which attempts
to marry the ideal to reality – an inner group in society whose
Humanity is specially highly developed and who have certain
secrets and ceremonies of their own – remains comparatively
cold and lifeless, when measured against the function which it is
meant to fulfil, just as Freemasonry, on which it is clearly based,
has always seemed a little unsatisfactory if one regards it as a
substitute church. An aura of abstraction adheres, for example,
to the 'Saal der Vergangenheit', and in spite of the seriousness
of its intent and the poetry of its execution, the scene of the
'exequies' of Mignon (Book Eight, Chapter Eight) has an
abstract and at the same time almost operatic flavour. In keeping with the generally secular outlook of the whole novel,
Goethe has put his religious feeling on a tight rein, as he has his
whole emotional and imaginative side. It would be wrong to
say that the work promises us bread and gives only stones, but
the bread is a little dry.

Goethe wrote a great deal of fine poetry in this period which,
for want of a better term, we must call 'lyric poetry', but which
is, relatively speaking, considerably less 'lyrical' in nature than
that written earlier or later. By this is meant that, just as the
plays and prose-writing of this time are less overwhelmingly
concentrated on, and permeated by the one individual centre,
so the poetry has less of that quality of being the direct outflow-
ing of an inner emotional state, unshaped by the mind, which is
strong in the pre-Italian lyrics and returns in some measure in

the work from *Westöstlicher Divan* onwards. The subjective unity of the great 'Sturm und Drang' works gives way to something more redolent of conscious planning, the more atmospheric, delicately tuned, softer and more musical style of the first Weimar period to a clearer light and firmer texture. Conscious thought of a more general, if not quite abstract nature, which had begun to make itself felt in poems like 'Grenzen der Menschheit' and 'Ilmenau', now begins to occupy a more central position and it is even possible, for the first time, to talk of a Goethean 'Lehrgedicht', of which the *Metamorphosis* poems are the best example.

Certainly, all this is not accompanied by a loss of sensitivity, a hostility to the non-rational, in a word, the deliberate restriction of the 'Aufklärung'. But it is true that, in this period, what might be termed the freer end of the poetic spectrum gives some ground to the more orderly. The more exclusively personal song, the quicker, more fluid rhythms and less precise vocabulary, as they appear in a poem like 'Frühzeitiger Frühling' (1801) do not disappear entirely, but they are much less frequent or prominent and the only major poem of this time which could truly be called 'lyrical' is probably 'Dauer im Wechsel' (1803), a poem which in many ways anticipates the attitude and style of the later work.

The *Römische Elegien*, written soon after his return from Italy, when the fresh impressions of that experience blended with his uncomplicated and fulfilled love-life with Christiane Vulpius, give vigorous expression to his new consciousness and nowhere more than in the first ten lines of the seventh elegy, with their contrasting of the clear light, colours and outlines of Italy with the grey and obscure, misty atmosphere of the north, where 'I immersed myself in quiet contemplation of my own self, trying to spy out the gloomy paths of the unsatisfied spirit'. Not that the 'I' who speaks to us in this cycle is an assumed identity, or merely a pair of eyes. Every aspect of the theme of Rome – the city's present shape and ambience, antique culture and myth, and above all, love – is presented in terms of personal feeling and all these aspects are integrated together and felt more or less simultaneously. The effect is not *totally* different from the way in which, in 'Wandrers Sturmlied', we saw all the strands of experience crossing at a centre-point. Here, though, each is allowed a separate validity in its own right. The sense of the concrete present is never lost. Objects are real and solid, whether it be the stones and palaces of the city (I) or the hair and neck of the 'brown girl' in No. IV. Statements are not prosaic in nature and often show great poetic sensitivity in their choice of wording, but they are also precise, and they do not draw any kind of obscuring veil over the meaning, even when it is the question of the sex-act, as in the opening of the third Elegy.

The most justly famous of these Elegies, the fifth (*Luke*, pp. 95–6), stands out precisely for its achievement of a synthesis of inward sensitivity with precision and objectivity in the treatment of concrete reality, of personal vision with general themes. It is a far cry from the totally individual orientation and continuous, dynamic forward movement of the 'Mailied' to this consciously shaped and balanced production. In both, love is the central element and in both, all the strands are united in one individual consciousness. But now, the plurality of the outside world is not swallowed up in the overwhelming feelings of the individual Self. The world of ancient classical culture is present; admittedly, primarily as part of the poet's experience, but its independent identity is not swallowed up in his. Past and present time, for example, are kept carefully apart. The references to the books whose pages the poet turns, to the marble of ancient statues, the use of the hexameter, all these keep the world of antiquity separate and give it an objective presence. Subjective feeling can bridge the gap, but does not obscure it. The contrast with the forgetting of this time-gap in 'Wandrers Sturmlied', with a consequent loss of the objectivity which the classical references might have brought with them, is striking.

No less striking is the contrast in the treatment of the beloved between this elegy and the 'Mailied'. Whereas in the latter, the flash and sparkle of the girl's eyes is all that we are given of her presence beyond the lover's emotional response to her, the elegy presents the beloved tenderly, but also objectively observed. She gives the poem much of its undoubted plasticity. Conscious planning, which is meant to be recognized and savoured, is apparent particularly in the way in which the present love-scene is framed by references to the classical past, and in which dualism is constantly manipulated and referred to (past and present, day and night, spiritual gain and physical 'Genuss') and often brought out in balance and contrast in individual lines (e.g. lines 6: 'halb nur gelehrt' – 'doppelt beglückt', and 11–12: 'Stunden des Tages' – 'Stunden der Nacht').

But it is not opposition, separateness, or any other kind of intellectualistic impression that the poem aims to leave at the end, even if it is not afraid to include such things. If the writer is detached, even humorous at times, he is also deeply involved emotionally. The girl may help him to 'understand marble properly for the first time', but if his eye and hand are active (line 10), his heart is no less so. He is 'beglückt'; her bosom is 'lieblich', and she is 'die Liebste'. And spirituality and tender feeling are allowed the last word in the description of the sleeping girl, whose breathing 'glows through me into the deepest part of my breast'.

There is a balance, then, even a certain fusion of objective and subjective, and the two sides are so closely knit together that it is difficult to say whether this is movement in order or order in movement. That is particularly true of the handling of metre. By comparison with that of 'Mailied', of course, it is settled and orderly, with regular, recurrent patterns and clearly marked points of rest. But it is also handled with great flexibility and just as the tone of the language varies from high and formal diction (e.g. line 1) to cleverly balanced formulation (line 10), delicate and poetic (17–18), or conversational (6, 9, 13), so pace and accentuation vary constantly, though without ever upsetting the overall impression of balanced smoothness. From whatever angle one approaches this poem, one comes to a final impression of duality resolved in harmony.

The elegiac form continued to be a fruitful one for the Classical Goethe and a number of fine examples were produced in the nineties. One of the finest is 'Euphrosyne', written when, on a visit to Switzerland in 1797, Goethe learned of the death of a talented young actress, a rising star of the Weimar theatre whom he had helped to train. One of her most successful roles had been that of Arthur in *King John*, in rehearsal for which Goethe had played opposite her as Hubert. She had appeared in a play as Euphrosyne shortly before her death. All these personal details play a part in this poem, particularly the Hubert–Arthur scene, which is the basis of the vital central episode (lines 43–96). It is, then, a poem of a directly personal nature. Goethe's relationship with the dead person is one of 'teacher and friend and father' (line 33); she is the 'much-loved creature' (line 90) whose youth and promising talent had moved the older man so deeply. All of this is included, and in no way depersonalized or robbed of its immediacy and individual force. Nor does Goethe play down the sharp personal grief he feels when the apparition of the dead Euphrosyne is gone and he is left alone amongst the nocturnal mountain scenery:

> Tiefer liegt die Nacht um mich her, die stürzenden Wasser
> Brausen gewaltiger nun neben dem schlüpfrigen Pfad.
> Unbezwingliche Trauer befällt mich, entkräftender Jammer,
> Und ein moosiger Fels stützet den Sinkenden nur.
> Wehmut reisst durch die Saiten der Brust; die nächtlichen
> Tränen
> Fliessen, und über dem Wald kündet der Morgen sich an.[19]

All this must be seen in context, of course. The poem as a whole is not presented so directly, or written in such a personal tone, as might have been the case in earlier years. The device of putting all but the opening and closing lines into the mouth of the dead girl, who, in antique fashion, appears to him and begs that he should immortalize her before her descent to the shadows, does much to temper the subjectivity of the material. Even the highly emotional passage just quoted has its stabilizing as well as its dynamic elements. There is the steady regularity of the metre, and in particular the way in which the sharper expressions tend to be placed in the first half of the line, where the pace is usually more measured and the accentuation more firm (as, for example, 'Brausen gewaltiger nun', or 'Unbezwingliche Trauer befällt mich'). The Alpine scenery, which gave such a grand and solemn introduction to the whole poem, is infected to some extent by the emotion which rages and rends inside the poet, but is still felt as something outside him, something solid which contains him and provides static, as well as dynamic elements: the path, even if it is slippery, the rock which prevents him from falling, and finally, the forest, over which he sees the coming dawn.

So there is distance as well as immediacy and in the same way, the death of one person, tragic as it is in itself, is primarily the occasion for a serious confrontation with the theme of death in general. The heart of the poem is in fact, not impersonal but general in nature, and it leads us to consideration of another aspect of the Classical poetry of Goethe, namely his handling of images. Goethe aims to maintain their force and beauty, while giving them a clarity and solidity which the subjective approach of earlier poetry tended to miss. Ideally, they should combine a sensuous reality in their own right with a wider significance. Sometimes the element of objective description is dominant, as for example in the lines concerned with Dora's gift of fruit to Alexis.[20] A fine example of symbolic use of an image is that of the ivy on the apple tree in 'Amyntas' to render the element of self-giving in the love-relationship, though for some, calculation may be felt to play too obvious a part here.[21] The balance of emotional involvement and objectivity in 'Euphrosyne' is exemplary:

Ach, Natur, wie sicher und gross in allem erscheinst du!
Himmel und Erde befolgt ewiges, festes Gesetz:
Jahre folgen auf Jahre, dem Frühlinge reichet der Sommer,
Und dem reichlichen Herbst traulich der Winter die Hand.
Felsen stehen gegründet, es stürzt sich das ewige Wasser
Aus der bewölkten Kluft schäumend und brausend hinab.
Fichten grünen so fort, und selbst die entlaubten Gebüsche
Hegen, im Winter schon, heimliche Knospen am Zweig.
Alles entsteht und vergeht nach Gesetz; doch über des Menschen
Leben, dem köstlichen Schatz, herrschet ein schwankendes Los.
Nicht dem blühenden nickt der willig scheidende Vater,
Seinem trefflichen Sohn, freundlich vom Rande der Gruft;
Nicht der Jüngere schliesst dem Älteren immer das Auge,
Das sich willig gesenkt, kräftig dem Schwächeren zu.
Öfter, ach! verkehrt das Geschick die Ordnung der Tage:
Hilflos klaget ein Greis Kinder und Enkel umsonst,
Steht, ein beschädigter Stamm, dem rings zerschmetterte Zweige
Um die Seiten umher strömende Schlossen gestreckt. (*Luke*, p. 143.)

The parallel between the death of Christiane Becker and that of Arthur in *King John* leads Goethe to project this reflection back, through the reminiscence of Euphrosyne, to the episode at the rehearsal in which he had played Hubert. But its force is such that it can overcome the elaborateness of such an arrangement, and this artificially contrived distance in fact lends just the right element of detachment to the view. Nature, which actually surrounds the poet in the time of Euphrosyne's appearance to him (the 'Brausen' of the water, for example, is in his ears and will in fact return at the end of the poem), can more easily function as nature in general, the nature of 'eternal' laws, just as the water itself becomes 'the eternal water'. One notices again the finely judged blend of individual descriptive detail with generalizing words, in the description of the 'foaming and roaring' but 'eternal' water, or in the cycle of the seasons where 'abundant' Autumn 'holds out a friendly hand' to Winter. As in 'Amyntas', clear plan and arrangement is not sacrificed in favour of a denser symbolic quality, as happens, for example, in the *West-östlicher Divan*, in a poem like 'Selige Sehnsucht'. The comparison, which is there left implicit, is here openly made, though the intellectualistic tenor which is a potential effect of this is less strong than it might be, owing to the deeper emotional disturbance expressed in the second half of the passage (and reflected in a more disturbed rhythm). The recurrence of natural imagery in the last two lines also helps to blur somewhat the distinction between animate and inanimate nature.

Regretfully, we must pass quickly by the ballads of 1797, with only a brief registration of such things as the blending of individual and ideal in 'Der Gott und die Bajadere' and the containment, in 'Die Braut von Korinth', of fiery, not to say Romantic material (the vampire-legend) in coolly polished and eminently clear language and a strophic form which is a particularly striking balance of rest and movement. Our last port of call in this chapter must be the philosophical-cum-scientific 'Lehrgedicht', in which Goethe set out to expound the laws of life as he saw them in a systematic way, though without forgetting the need to give them individual relevance. Indeed, it would have been difficult for him to have forgotten this in any case, since a balance of respect for the general and the individual, and a harmonious working relationship between the two, lie at the heart of these very laws. The poem in which he found the form in which he could best do justice to such a thought-content is the 'Metamorphose der Pflanzen' (1798), which arises out of the desire to balance the rather dry and grey character of the prose-treatise on botany, *Versuch die Metamorphose der Pflanzen zu erklären* (1790), with a version which shows that science has links with poetry, indeed with all other branches of human activity. Christiane, with whom he always, quite rightly, associated the qualities of straightforward, healthy natural being, and whom he characterized as a simple flower in the charming lyric 'Gefunden', is appropriately called in to be the recipient of an affectionate lecture on the nature of the plant and the laws governing its growth.

The scientific context enables Goethe to enunciate, in a more or less objective and sensuously appreciable form, truths which were basic to his own life and which enabled him to feel the whole realm of nature and of human activity as a unity, without undermining the validity of each individual being or form. With the wisdom of hindsight, one can see the patterns which emerge here influencing the direction taken even by the 'Sturm und Drang' Goethe, though he is not then conscious of them, and there is inconsistency and confusion. In the search for truth without rigid system, for God without theology and a wider order without loss of freedom, there is certainly something which preserves the young Goethe, who has no obvious star to guide him, from becoming imprisoned in a dogmatic rut or losing himself in complete relativism.

In some respects, the outlook we shall shortly be describing is not so very different from that reflected in the *Urfaust* of the early 1770s, when the hero contemplates the sign of the Macrocosm (lines 94 ff.) and sees 'all things weaving themselves into one whole, each living and working in the other' and a harmony 'sounding through the universe'. But here, this is only capable of being conceived in relatively vague terms, and the way to complete knowledge of these ultimate truths seems barred along anything but mystical or magical paths (lines 101 ff.). The passage in which Faust can claim that he has understood nature through study of it in the 'stern [i.e. strictly disciplined] pleasure of contemplation'[22] could not have been, and was not written until the Classical period (in fact, in 1788).

Confusion is also the starting-point of the 'Metamorphose der Pflanzen', a confusion caused by the variety and multiplicity of the apparently disordered tangle ('Gewühl') of flowers in the garden. The framework of the poem is the removal of this confusion by explanation of the 'secret law' (line 6) to which similarities between the different forms seem to point, even in the preparatory stage, before the explanation proper has begun. This is important, for the aim is not to diminish the variety and multiplicity in any way: in the final stage, when the aspect of the garden is 'no longer confusing', it is still as varied as ever. The word 'Gewühl', with its suggestion of a jungle-like, disorderly mass, has gone, but the expression that replaces it, 'bunte(s) Gewimmel' (a variegated teeming), is no less indicative of a profusion of different forms and shapes. There is a unity, in that each plant 'proclaims the eternal laws' (line 65), but this in no way undermines the independent being of the individual plant. The order obtained is no restrictive or lifeless one: instead of uniformity, it aims at unity in multiplicity.

This applies also to the parts of the single representative plant which is observed in the central part of the poem. Goethe conceives it as a unity, just as he conceives nature as a unity, developed out of certain primal, basic forms (in the case of plants, this is the leaf). But what slept 'in simple form' in the seed (line 15) develops in different forms in the plant. The original form is always repeated, but it is not always the identical one (lines 24–5).

So the one and the many are brought together in a coherent view. And the context in which they are interrelated is also one which exhibits a polarity of freedom and order. It is the context of metamorphosis, of growth and development, in which a strong creative impulse is involved, an impulse which, like the 'Kraft' of the 'Sturm und Drang', needs to express and fulfil itself and seems to have infinite longings in it. But here it is fitted, without losing its essential character, into a pattern of law and – in the widest sense – order. Just as the impulse seems to be 'free and infinite' (line 32), so we see it 'gently guided' (line 34) by nature. It still moves and has its being, but within an order: it is now a progressive development in which the nature of the individual thing changes, not from forcible, external intervention, but through an intensification of its own essential nature to a higher perfection ('in das Vollkommnere' line 34). The sequence of different stages, then, through which the plant goes, is one which combines the dynamic with a stable element of law and unity. This way of understanding change and growth is what Goethe elsewhere calls 'Steigerung' (intensification), which is, for him, one of 'the two great driving wheels of nature',[23] the other being polarity, the term which embodies his concept of opposition with unity.

It was not, perhaps, until after the Classical period proper that Goethe perfected the working-out of this philosophy, in terms of both systematic thought and of literature. In the 'Metamorphose der Pflanzen' and contemporary works, he still tends to stress the element of order a shade the more strongly. One can observe this in the style of the poem, which is clear-cut to a degree, though certainly not unpoetic, and often enlivened by a sensitive or imaginative touch and an emotional shading. Similarly, the arrangement is planned for clarity and balance, with the central expository section framed by corresponding introductory and concluding passages, the second often picking up phrases or motifs from the first (e.g. 'Dich verwirret, Geliebte' (line 1) and 'Wende nun, o Geliebte' (line 63) and 'verwirrend nicht mehr' (line 64), or the motif of 'Gesetz' (law)).

The Classical Goethe is a little less open to wonder than the older man, less inclined to indulge the individual impulse towards the infinite to the full. So that the conclusion of *Faust*, Part Two is more indistinct and open-ended in dealing with the individual's development than is *Wilhelm Meisters Lehrjahre*. The exact blending of the synthesis of the nineties and early 1800s was not the final stage for Goethe, nor would it have been for Schiller had he lived beyond his forty-sixth year. But just as Schiller would certainly have remained true to its general principles and kept himself distinct from the Romantic Movement, so we can say that the theoretical and practical achievement of the Classical Goethe is the indispensable foundation for his later works, which can therefore, in a sense, be called the finest flower of the eighteenth century.

13
Synthesis in Literature (II): Schiller

After *Don Carlos* (1787), there followed a more than ten-year gap in Schiller's serious dramatic production, until *Wallenstein*. In the interim, he was going through the period of self-training and self-discipline which finally put him into a position to realize the Classical ideal, which he had meanwhile consolidated in himself in theoretical form, in terms of practical drama. *Carlos*, the product of a long period of gestation, had, admittedly, begun to show the signs of a firmer approach in the change to blank verse and in greater objectivity in the treatment of issues and characters. But it is still predominantly a subjective play and the elements of order (e.g. the objective portrait of the king, the self-discipline of the queen) are not by any means an equal counterweight to the rampant idealism and passion of Posa and Carlos, to the impulse towards freedom in general. The extreme degree of self-identification with his hero which led Schiller in the initial stages to refer to him as 'to a certain extent, taking the place of a sweetheart'[1] was certainly modified, but not to the extent of providing a sufficient counterweight to the – to our taste – excessive warmth of his emotions. True, Posa shows him a less self-indulgent outlet for these, but the heat of passion is not abated. In the scene (Act II, scene 2) in which the young and passionate Carlos confronts the old and chilly king, there is nothing to indicate that Schiller disapproves of the extravagance of his hero's feelings. Goethe, in the exchange between the subjective idealist Tasso and the objective realist Antonio maintains a much better balance, though his sympathies are largely on Tasso's side. In the period that elapsed between *Don Carlos* and *Wallenstein*, Schiller achieved much greater objectivity. In the confrontation between Wallenstein and Max in Act II scene 2 of *Wallensteins Tod*, he even allows the former to administer a chastening rebuke to Max, the apple of his eye:

> Schnell fertig ist die Jugend mit dem Wort,
> Das schwer sich handhabt, wie des Messers Schneide,
> Aus ihrem heissen Kopfe nimmt sie keck
> Der Dinge Mass, die nur sich selber richten.[2]

Schiller's ability to see Wallenstein objectively and with understanding is the best symbol of the advance he has made since *Don Carlos*. There, the king, even if he was given some measure of humanity, remained in the last analysis a tyrant, seen from the outside, and without deep sympathy. That the new objectivity was not entirely easy to achieve or maintain is certainly true and we shall look, together with *Wallenstein*, at the play in which the Classical balance was most seriously threatened by the by no means extinct volcano within, namely *Die Jungfrau von Orleans*.

Throughout his Classical period, Schiller worked on his subjects with great conscientiousness, using historical sources wherever appropriate, seeking to build up his plays with solidity and individual life while at the same time serving the other master, the ideal. He was never a realist in the proper sense of the word, not even in *Wallenstein*, which was written in the consciousness that 'the poet, like the artist in general, must distance himself in a public and honest way from actuality',[3] but he did not wish altogether to lose contact with 'nature' and with the sense of objective reality. Thus he took considerable trouble to maintain the 'objective and definite'[4] quality which attracted him to historical material in the first place. He sought works on astrology from Körner to help him with the figure of Seni in *Wallenstein*[5] and read the seventeenth-century preacher Abraham a Sancta Clara in order to find the right tone for the Capuchin's harangue in *Wallensteins Lager*, the prelude to the tragedy. Plays like *Maria Stuart* have more of a sense of locality about them than had *Die Räuber*, even though the locality in question was much further removed from Schiller in space and time.

In addition, characters of what Schiller would have called an 'unpoetic' type and function, like Burleigh in *Maria Stuart* or Illo and Terzky in *Wallenstein*, are given a degree of independent life and colour that they would never have had in the 'Sturm und Drang' plays, where the dominance of the central figures is much more marked. The 'poetic' quality here, i.e. the quality which conforms to the higher, ideal demands of art, would have to come from the 'form', the manner in which the material was presented. The main characters and action of the latter play had never had an appeal for him in themselves: it was, as he wrote to Goethe (1 December 1797), a 'prosaic' material. The tug-of-war between this and his own innate idealizing tendency may have been what led here to the best example in all his dramatic work of synthesis between freedom and order, or, to use his own formulation in a letter to Körner, power and control.[6]

The situation was very different with *Die Jungfrau von Orleans*. While the play still demanded long and hard work from him, it was not, in this case, because of any lack of spiritual sustenance in the material. This was, as he put it to Körner,[7] 'poetic to a very high degree', and it buoyed him up through the donkey-work of his historical researches. In his poem 'Das Mädchen von Orleans', Schiller addresses Joan: 'The world loves to blacken that which shines and to drag the sublime in the dust; but have no fear! There are still hearts of unsullied spiritual beauty ('schöne Herzen') which are fired with love for what is high and glorious.' Schiller's was such a heart, and in this play he wrote more directly from the heart than in any other Classical drama. As a result we find that, if the Classical balance is upset anywhere, it is here, in favour of freedom. Figures like Countess Terzky and Buttler in *Wallenstein* have their grandeur and 'beauty', but this has nothing to do with their moral characters. In the *Jungfrau*, the figure most nearly corresponding to the Countess, Queen Isabeau, is allowed a moment of self-justification (Act II scene 2), but is mainly a negative contrast-figure. Talbot has one speech, his dying lament for reason (as *he* conceives it), in which he expresses a philosophy with which Schiller disagreed in a way which gives it dramatic dignity and conviction, but in general, he is prevented from achieving real dramatic stature. We shall be discussing these two plays in more detail later as examples of the two main trends in the Classical Schiller, but before that, it is necessary to look at the underlying principles of his Classical drama as a whole.

Man is the measure of all Classical German literature.

Schiller's natural tendency towards the idealistic leads him to see his subject in general terms, rather than the individual ones of Goethe. Even if he had not been already inclined in that direction by temperament, this alone would have impelled him to seek a wider stage than that inhabited by Goethe's characters, to go for the heroic atmosphere, the 'great' issue. As the prologue to *Wallenstein* has it: 'only the great object is capable of arousing the furthest depths of humanity'.[8] What particularly interested Schiller the dramatist was, in the words of 'Shakespeares Schatten', 'that great, gigantic Fate which elevates man when it crushes him'. All that is not 'human', then, is alien to Schiller's drama – which distinguishes him from the Romantics – but his concept of what is human is considerably wider than that of the 'Aufklärer'. It has at least one foot in the camp of metaphysics, in rather the same way that Kant's philosophy has, and its root, as with Kant's moral philosophy, is the concept of freedom. Only as a vehicle for demonstrating the essential moral freedom of man is history of real intrinsic interest for Schiller.[9]

Schiller's dramatic characters realize the ideal of freedom either in the state of moral 'beauty' (complete harmony of their desires with the moral law) or 'sublimity' (when they rise, by virtue of their moral freedom, above the compulsion of outside forces to which, as physical beings, they are inevitably subject).[10] No one character is shown as being constantly in one or other of these states, nor is any one shown to be totally incapable of them, as Franz Moor, for example, had been. Schiller was more objective now, and he was also more clearly aware of the difference between the aesthetic and the purely philosophical, as he showed in 'Über das Pathetische'. At the same time, some characters are so much inclined to the morally beautiful as to deserve the title of 'schöne Seelen' (e.g. Max and Thekla in *Wallenstein*) and others, even if not painted entirely black, are flawed in such a way that it is hard to conceive of their achieving sublimity in adversity as is the case with Wallenstein himself.

Schiller's Classical dramas show considerable variation of form, and on the more general level, they all reflect the interplay between freedom and control. After some hesitation, Schiller decided to use verse for *Wallenstein* and then, finding that it corresponded to the spiritual qualities he wished to cultivate, retained it for all his other plays. Its formality helps to temper the variegated and often turbulent nature of his plots. Schiller's verse is, broadly speaking, firm and regular, with occasional interludes in lyric metre. The language shows the same balance of orderly homogeneity and individual freedom. Illo, Wallenstein and Countess Terzky speak in styles graded according to their natures, and all fall short of the somewhat exalted language in which Max, the 'poetic' character, expresses himself. In *Wallensteins Lager*, there is even some colloquial speech, again distributed in degrees relating to the standing of the character. But when one looks more closely at them, one sees that the range of the colloquial usages employed is not really wide: omissions, elisions, familiar use of the definite article with proper names, idiomatic use of 'tun' and so on. By comparison with the raciness and richness of idiom to be found in Grimmelshausen's *Courasche* or Brecht's *Mutter Courage*, the equivalent here, the 'Marketenderin' of Scene 5, is a rather pale figure:

> Der Spitzbub! der hat mich schön betrogen.
> Fort ist er! Mit allem davon gefahren,
> Was ich mir tät am Leibe ersparen.
> Liess mir nichts als den Schlingel da![11]

Schiller wants a certain amount of the sap and colour of colloquial speech, but not enough to disturb the ordered regularity of his whole concept.

Dramatic form and construction show broadly the same picture. Schiller paints on a wide canvas, with a large and socially differentiated cast, but his technique is still broadly classicistic. He infringes the unities of time and place in their strict definition, but handles these elements with firm control. The sequence of scenes is never so rapid as to confuse, or so disjointed as to produce the dynamic, kaleidoscopic effect of a 'Sturm und Drang' play. And while there is action, action tends to speak less loudly than words. The drama is carried by verbal exchanges, often in long, set-piece speeches.

As has been said, the Classical Schiller works on wide canvases, but he always maintains unity and order. These canvases are not chosen for themselves alone. They are normally demanded by the central theme, which in turn gives the play integrity. In *Wilhelm Tell*, for example, the theme of justifiable revolution demanded a portrait of a whole people. In the case of *Wallenstein*, Schiller realized that the understanding of his hero's actions demanded full knowledge of the whole range of factors which conditioned them, and accordingly embarked on a unique expansion of the traditional five-act tragedy. Certainly the action and the detail interested him, but by comparison with Arnim's practice in a typical Romantic historical work like *Die Kronenwächter*, Schiller's background remains very much *subordinate* background.

It was the powerful and enigmatic figure of the historical Wallenstein which first fascinated Schiller, as it has many another historian of the Thirty Years War. Schiller was never entirely at home with the character, but during the composition of his *History* he came gradually to feel less absolute hostility towards him. Among other factors, one feels here the growing appreciation of the point of view of the realist, so that while he still could not condone treachery, he arrived at the more understanding formulation: 'Wallenstein did not fall because he rebelled, but he rebelled because he was falling.'[12]

Wallenstein is conceived in the image of the realist, the man whose horizon is bounded by the world of nature. Universal abstract ideals are alien to his way of thought, and moral imperatives having their origin in pure reason would be meaningless to him. This does not necessarily shut him off from all contact with law and morality, however, since these things can be seen as present in nature, taken as a whole. Further, Schiller believes that the realist is capable of feeling the justice of the ideal and the beauty of morality, even if it may be at the expense of a logical inconsistency in his outlook: he will claim that he knows these things from nature, but they are ideals.[13] Wallenstein is only partially aware of the deeper roots of his way of acting, but his conscious belief in Fate as the agency which shapes our ends is a reflection of his general tendency.

The belief in astrology, which Schiller handles with detachment, does reflect something positive: the feeling that the world is not without law, and the desire to be in harmony with what law exists. Illo sees only the argument of practical personal interest, which he has in mind in the phrase 'the stars that govern your fate are in your breast'.[14] The astrological view of life which Wallenstein develops in reply to this view of the man who can only 'grub, gloomy and blind, in the earth' is superior for Schiller, for it reflects, however distortedly, a recognition of considerations above everyday practicality. Even when the capture of his secret messenger seems to have forced his hand, Wallenstein needs a great deal of persuading. He *can* act decisively, as he later proves, when he is convinced that he is doing so in accordance with the ruling principle of nature, necessity. But this necessity is not 'blindly commanding chance',[15] which seeks to propel him like a will-less piece of driftwood.

Wallenstein's revolt against such a demeaning state is expressed in the monologue of *Wallensteins Tod*, Act I, Scene 4. Even after he has at last agreed terms with the Swedish emissary, he still feels that fidelity is a factor of real importance and is inclined to step back from treason (Scene 6). Not until Countess Terzky has articulated the realist's belief in necessity on the highest level, appealing to Nature herself,[16] can he see the way forward. He is still taking a wrong path, certainly, but Schiller makes him do this in a way which is clearly distinct from that of the opportunist who can see no further than material gain or self-preservation, and with a higher degree of freedom.

Similarly, his heart is open to the beautiful to some extent. The key is the character of Max Piccolomini. Himself a person of great beauty of soul, he is an indicator both of Wallenstein's imperfection (in his refusal to stay with him) and of the fact that there is good in him, in that he clearly prefers the general to his own father, Octavio. Wallenstein's reaction to his loss is stronger evidence still. Quite apart from the importance that his standing among the soldiers gives him, Max is of great value to Wallenstein for the very moral qualities which in fact part them. On hearing of Max's death, he expresses clearly for the first time the side of his character which distinguishes him from 'common' realists of the type of Terzky and Illo. Max was the 'flower' of his life and wove beauty round 'the common ('gemein') clarity of things'. To his own astonishment, he had found 'the flat everyday shapes of life' exalted by the fire of Max's feeling.[17] Max and Thekla are crushed by Fate, but their freedom is never in doubt, even if they are not spared the pain and in Max's case (since the crucial decision is his) even confusion of violently opposed inclinations. By the light which they cast and which it is their primary function to cast, we see that all the other characters are flawed to a greater or lesser extent, and to that extent not free. No one is painted as black as was Franz Moor, who, we recall, had emancipated himself to such a degree that he was completely a prisoner. Wallenstein and Gräfin Terzky achieve echoes of sublimity, Buttler, the murderer, assumes a degree of grandeur in his role of Nemesis; even Illo dies fighting bravely.

Freedom, then, in the context of man's ability to remain man even in the face of the overpowering force of Fate, is a key concept in *Wallenstein*. Schiller's outlook and mood show a greater stability and balance than was observable in the hectic 'Sturm und Drang' works. The primacy of the ideal is maintained, but the claims of practical reality, when they conflict with it, are not simply swept aside, nor are they felt as an entirely negative, crushing weight. In a Germany which has not changed radically from what it was in the first half of the century as far as social structure and conditions are concerned, and in which injustice, restriction and the other material and psychological pressures are still present, there is a feeling that one can preserve spiritual integrity without adopting a totally negative attitude to the real world.

But there is something of the precariousness of compromise about the Classical balance, however well it is worked out in Goethe and Schiller, which makes us hesitate to think of it as a true and final solution. The fact that they are the only two writers who can be called Classical in a really full sense is itself significant. And there is an element of stress and strain observable even in them. It is easier to see in the case of Schiller, who, for all his more rationalistically coloured and generalized approach to art, was probably temperamentally and emotionally closer to the Romantics than Goethe. Our last example, *Die Jungfrau von Orleans*, is chosen with this in mind.

Deep personal involvement is both a strength and a weakness of Schiller as a dramatist. The warmth of his heart gave his works a strong impetus, but it was in need of discipline. He had sought and achieved this discipline in large measure, and *Wallenstein* and *Maria Stuart*, his best completed Classical plays, are fine monuments to it. A certain amount of the spirit of discipline had gone over into his inner nature; even *Die Jungfrau von Orleans* is careful to cultivate the sense of the historical period as far as possible in the scheme, to characterize secondary figures in the round, and so on. But all the time one senses a force which is putting considerable strain on the balanced and objective form in which he still wishes to work. We are asked to see this as drama in the real human world and its problems as human problems. Yet there is an undercurrent of the operatic which comes to the surface strongly at times, as in the Prologue, the long and metrically varied first scene of Act IV, or the ending. The verse often has great beauty, but as often, it seems to be there as much to create beauty as to carry dramatic import. The characters surrounding the heroine are nothing like as solid and rounded as, say Elizabeth, Leicester, Mortimer, Burleigh, Paulet and the others in *Maria Stuart*. The play has great movement, light and colour, but it lacks the elements of stillness, and containment and management of this ubiquitous light and colour, which would give the Classical balance.

Schiller has *attempted* to anchor it in this way, for example by avoiding a true sense of the mysterious. His wonders are not the 'sweet wonders' of which a Romantic like Brentano speaks and which are incompatible with the clear daylight of rationalism: quite the contrary. He uses the Christian framework, but in a spirit much more in tune with the Greek culture. The very echoes of the New and Old Testament which are sprinkled quite liberally through the text in fact enhance this impression. They tend to be generalized and human-ized in the form in which they appear, just as the vision of the Virgin described by Johanna in Act I, Scene 10 (lines 1072 ff.) is numinous only in so far as that is compatible with a Classical mood. There is too much distinctness, both visually and in the language spoken. It is all reduced to the level of what the eye can see and the reason comprehend. The ascent of the Virgin into Heaven has none of the real wonder of a Transfiguration or Ascension:

> Und also sprechend liess sie das Gewand
> Der Hirtin fallen und als Königin
> Der Himmel stand sie da im Glanz der Sonnen,
> Und goldne Wolken trugen sie hinauf
> Langsam verschwindend in das Land der Wonnen[18]

The root of the trouble seems to be that this play is in large measure a superior kind of escape-literature. The idealist can maintain his faith in the higher reality while living in the imperfect actual world, he can even show it triumphant within corrupted human nature. The Classical Schiller, as Melitta Gerhard says, had 'matured in the acceptance and the overcoming of the inevitable'.[19] And as we have seen, he still desires an anchorage in reality even in this play. But the strain of his position was severe. Not only was he physically, and perhaps to some extent even economically under strain, his temperament was less able to adapt and take a cool or humorous view than was Goethe's. His Classical balance contains much more deliberate restraint than Goethe's and he must have felt the need to relax it at times, to let his heart have its way.

In *Die Jungfrau von Orleans*, Schiller indulges his desire for the light to the extent that he causes it to flood more or less unchecked by what he once called, in a letter to Wilhelm von Humboldt of 30 November 1795, 'the filth of actuality'.[20] He was speaking there of the idea of a 'sentimental idyll': 'All that is mortal' was to be 'extinguished', there was to be 'nothing but light, nothing but freedom, nothing but capacity – no shadow, no limitation, nothing more of all that to be seen.'[21] All who have experienced the exaltation of the ending of Beethoven's Choral Symphony will recognize this mood and accept its genuineness, even perhaps the possibility that Schiller might have been able to express it in literary form. But it could hardly have been in conventional dramatic form, certainly not in one which will not detach itself from the motivation of real life on the one hand, or a secularized humanist view on the other.

Schiller went some way towards the operatic in this play, as he also did towards the wondrousness of the fairy-tale. He felt the attraction of both these genres, no doubt because, at the expense of the solidity and credibility of the more realistic genres, they have freed themselves from the shackles which reality places on the ideal. Schiller is even reported to have exclaimed, when close to death: 'Give me fairy-tales and tales of chivalry: that is where the stuff of all goodness and greatness lies.'[22] In these circumstances, one can sympathize with Schiller's desire to relax the controls. It is less easy to do so in the case of *Die Jungfrau von Orleans*.

Here, Schiller uses a real historical personage in a real setting, to write what is primarily a hymn of praise to pure spirit. Johanna's actual mission is less important than the fact and the conditions of mission: the special relationship in which she stands to the 'Geisterreich' and the need for unsullied purity in her spirituality. Johanna must be human; Schiller insists on this at all times, not only in her fall from grace. The theme of love and her relationship with men form the symbolic vehicle of her ordinary humanity, as the mission is a symbol of her participation in the highest, ideal humanity. In the case of both love and mission, we feel that these things are of no real validity in themselves, but are simply being used. This gives them an emptiness which does not adhere to Maria Stuart's religious faith or to the love of Max and Thekla. But the objective control is not strong enough to enable Schiller to make Johanna human in the straightforward sense. She is given no hint of sensuality, of quickness of temper or pride; indeed, no hint of a clear individuality. Thekla may be a 'schöne Seele', but she is also 'Friedland's daughter', and can hold her own with Countess Terzky when the latter cross-examines her. Well before the great glory of the ending, Johanna has the flawless and unvarying light, the complete freedom, of the idyllic state. The formula is that she is the human vehicle for the divine power and glory, a kind of Samson-figure, perhaps. But the Samson of the Bible, for all his superhuman exploits, is much more convincing as a human, and therefore corruptible being. We can distinguish between what he is of himself, and what God works in him.

Schiller lacks the religious feeling to make the spiritual factor in his play truly superhuman and this means that he is also unable to make his heroine ordinarily human. Her reply to Karl in Act III, Scene 4, in which she rejects the idea of marriage, remains the best indication of what she is:

> Dauphin! Bist du der göttlichen Erscheinung
> Schon müde, dass du ihr Gefäss zerstören,
> Die reine Jungfrau, die dir Gott gesendet,
> Herab willst ziehn in den gemeinen Staub?[23]

The one word 'gemein' is enough to show us where we are. Schiller allows Johanna to 'fall', so that she shall rise again in sublime glory, but there is no suggestion that she has involved herself in 'das Gemeine'. Indeed, in the scene (Act IV, Scene 1) in which Johanna analyses her 'crime' to herself, he is not at all explicit about what she actually felt when she saw Lionel. That it was love we must assume, but there is no suggestion of a parallel to what Samson felt for Delilah.

The triumph of free spirit over the reality which seems to imprison it could well be the best formulation of Schiller's intention in the play as it stands. But to attain that triumph, one needs to feel the resistance of reality, one needs flesh and blood, and all the ties and conditions of actual, practical life. Schiller was able to portray these, and preserve his faith in the ideal and the beautiful. He can show its moral superiority, but also its destruction, sometimes in ugly circumstances, as in the death of Max Piccolomini, who is trampled to death beneath horses' hooves. 'That,' as Thekla says, 'is the lot of the beautiful on this earth.'[24] As a citizen of this earth, Schiller recognized that. But he could not entirely reconcile himself to life's imperfections and needed at times to compensate himself for the strains it imposed on him. *Die Jungfrau von Orleans* is a play in which he does this more openly and more obviously than in any other, with the possible exception of *Don Carlos*, in which he indulges himself in the portrait of Posa, who describes himself as a citizen, not of his own age, but of 'the centuries which are to come'.[25] But Posa, after all, lived in the present and strove to realize his ideals within it. So it was with Schiller in general, and the play on which he was working at his death, *Demetrius*, would have been much closer to *Wallenstein* than to *Die Jungfrau von Orleans* in character. In the latter play, he had placed himself in danger of the mistake against which he had warned the 'sentimental' poet, i.e. of 'leaving human nature completely behind' and thereby becoming 'überspannt'.[26]

'Nature', the concept which links the material and spiritual and the individual and general, is probably the one in which the balance of freedom and order in the outlook of the major Classicists is best expressed. Modern society is not in harmony with it, as that of the Greeks had been. The impulses of modern man towards freedom for reason and desire lead, as Schiller puts it in 'Der Spaziergang', to unhappiness and confusion.[27] Here,

Synthesis

as elsewhere, the Classicist rejects the path of revolution. But
there is no need to flee into some kind of restrictive stockade, or
to despair of all harmony. The greater order of nature still exists
and offers to the individual at least (and for the Schiller of the
Ästhetische Erziehung, to society as well) a path to true harmony
and fulfilment within reality:

> Und die Sonne Homers, siehe! sie lächelt auch uns.[28]

Notes

CHAPTER *1*

1 e.g. in such a work as Thomas B. Clarke's *A Statistical View of Germany* . . . etc., London, 1790.
2 J. Möser, *Über die deutsche Sprache und Literatur*, p. 177.
3 J. G. Seume, *Werke*, vol. 10, p. 160.
4 See P. Wiedeburg, *Der junge Leibniz*, Wiesbaden, 1962, vol. 1 (e.g. pp. 107 ff.), and F. H. Hertz, *The development of the German public mind*, vol. 1, pp. 115 ff.
5 See *Briefe zur Beförderung der Humanität, Werke*, vol. 5, p. 93, or his plan for an all-German institution of the Academy type, *Ideen zum ersten patriotischen Institut für den Allgemeingeist Deutschlands, Werke*, vol. 3.
6 *The Hapsburg Monarchy*, p. 25.
7 *Werke*, vol. 3, p. 267.
8 He wrote to J. D. Salzmann that he had set out to honour 'one of the noblest Germans' (*HA, Briefe*, vol. 1, p. 128). The play was widely received in this spirit. Lenz, in his *Über Götz von Berlichingen*, writes: 'let us first consider with a warm heart the character of this ancient (!) German and, if we find it good, make it our own, so that we may again become Germans, a state from which we have degenerated so far' (Lenz, *Werke und Schriften*, vol. 1, pp. 380–1).
9 The word is practically untranslatable in this context and has a strong Rococo flavour. It conveys the idea of the ability to please through mastery of sophisticated manners, appearance and so on: charm with polish. Neatly turned polite compliments, for example, would be 'Artigkeiten'.
10 Op. cit., p. 181.
11 *De la littérature allemande*, p. 83.
12 See *Sebaldus Nothanker*, pp. 34–5.
13 See F. Strich, *Goethe und die Weltliteratur*, Berne, 1946, and H. Kohn, *The Mind of Germany*, pp. 38 ff. Goethe's most important utterances on this subject are collected in *HA*, vol. 12, pp. 361–4. They are clearly opposed to nationalistic antagonisms, but in no way deny national differences.
14 Paul Hazard shows that there was a similar sense of national

233

identity, of 'Italianitas', in the politically fragmented Italy of the eighteenth century (cf. *European Thought in the Eighteenth Century*, pp. 483 ff.).

15 Cf. as an example A. G. Kästner's epigram 'Hippokrene' (a play on Rossbach) in Horner, *Politische Dichtung*, p. 34.

16 *Campagne in Frankreich*, *HA*, vol. 10, p. 318, and the letter to his mother of 24 December 1792.

17 Cf. his speech of 1792: 'Über das Verhältnis der Mainzer gegen die Franken', *Werke*, vol. 1, pp. 85 ff.

18 This is confirmed by G. P. Gooch in *Germany and the French Revolution*, pp. 475 ff. Horner (see bibl.), pp. 189 ff. and 192–5) prints some popular songs of the time which express strong anti-French sentiment in this connection.

19 P. 87. Cf. also such a work as his *Nöthiger Vorrath zur Geschichte der deutschen dramatischen Dichtkunst* (1757), which calls on the reader's love of his 'Vaterland' in the very first sentence and attempts to further German self-awareness and pride of achievement at every opportunity.

20 *Critische Dichtkunst*, p. 734.

21 In a satirical travel-book of 1789, quoted by Jost Hermand in the 'Nachwort' to Geiger's *Reise eines Erdbewohners in den Mars*, p. 17.

22 Cf. the account of his *Teutscher Engelländer*, ibid., p. 24. Nor was the turn to English literature a substitution of a new subservience for the old one: cf. Klopstock's poem 'Die beiden Musen'.

23 Schubart, *Werke*, pp. 93–6.

24 *Werke*, vol. 3, p. 269.

25 Ibid., p. 267.

26 For an account of Herder's political thought, see Barnard, *Herder's Social and Political Thought*.

27 *Vanished Supremacies*, p. 50.

28 Ibid., p. 63.

29 Op. cit., p. 84. Cf. also p. 108.

30 See the plan for a 'Gedicht zur Jahrhundertswende', *Werke*, vol. 9, pp. 204–8, especially pp. 208 and 206.

31 Hertz, *The Development of the German Public Mind*, vol. 2, p. 46.

32 Op. cit., vol. 1, pp. 278–80.

33 Cf. the letter (dated 17 February 1788) to Karl August of Weimar by J. H. Merck (*Briefe*, pp. 607–8).

34 *Werke*, p. 117.

35 Hertz, op. cit., p. 359. Hertz lists among others who did not desire political unification, Kant, F. von Moser, the historian Johannes Müller and Möser.

36 Ibid., p. 227.
37 F. Perthes: *Memoirs*, vol. 1, pp. 2 and 137.
38 J. Campbell, *The Present State of Europe* ..., London, 1750, p. 232.
39 Cf. A. Fauchier-Magnan, *The Small German Courts in the Eighteenth Century*, p. 199. This work gives a full, if perhaps a slightly lurid picture of conditions in Württemberg.
40 *Amtliche Schriften*, vol. 2 (i), p. 188.
41 'Ich ersterbe in tiefsten Respect ...' writes C. F. Schnauss to the Duke of Weimar in 1793 'und mit dem danckbarsten Herzen, Ew. Hochfürstl. Durchl. unterthänigster treu gehorsamster Diener' (Goethe: *Amtliche Schriften*, vol. 2 (i), p. 316).
42 *The Age of Absolutism*, p. 22.
43 Cf. Wraxall, *Memoirs*, vol. 1, pp. 114–15. A similar description is given by Wraxall of the routine of Maria Theresa of Austria.
44 *Memoirs*, vol. 1, pp. 174–5. I have retained the spelling of the eighteenth-century translation, for its period flavour. In spite of the datings in the text, Pöllnitz's actual experience of what he describes relates to the period 1710–23.
45 See Goethe, *Amtliche Schriften*, vol. 2 (i), p. 80.
46 *Bureaucracy, Aristocracy and Autocracy*, pp. 57 ff.
47 In his letter to Nicolai of 25 August 1769 (*LM*, vol. 17, p. 298). Lessing goes so far as to call Prussia 'the most slavish land in Europe'.
48 Biedermann, op. cit., p. 81. Even if, as Biedermann suggests, the story has lost nothing in the telling, it would have required a pretty Gilbertian state of affairs to produce an *apocryphal* tale of this kind.
49 *Werke*, p. 437.
50 Cf. Biedermann, op. cit., vol. 1, p. 80.
51 W. Martens, *Die Botschaft der Tugend*, especially p. 337.
52 Biedermann, op. cit., vol. 1, p. 99.
53 *Politische Dichtung*, pp. 16–17.
54 *Werke*, vol. 3, pp. 568–9.
55 Quoted by Olga Smoljan, *Friedrich Maximilian Klinger. Leben und Werk*, Weimar, 1962, p. 13
56 Hertz, op. cit., vol. 1, p. 228.
57 Martens, op. cit., pp. 330 ff.
58 Op. cit., p. 17.
59 *Europe, 1780–1830*, p. 96.
60 Biedermann, vol. 1, p. 146. Moses Mendelssohn, writing in 1758, considered the Germans to be 'admittedly not as free as the English, but also not everywhere so restricted as the

French' (cf. H. Hettner, *Geschichte der deutschen Literatur im achtzehnten Jahrhundert*, vol. 1, p. 584).

61 J. Kemp, *The philosophy of Kant*, p. 88.

62 Namier, *Vanished Supremacies*, p. 218, where the 'truly German Masslosigkeit' of Hitler is spoken of.

63 *Campagne in Frankreich, HA*, vol. 10, p. 235. His derogatory remarks about the Jacobins in many letters to Schiller need to be balanced by his very reasonable view of the French Revolution as a whole, as expressed to Eckermann (*Gespräche mit Goethe*, 4 January 1824).

64 *Leben und Schriften*, vol. 2, p. 316.

65 *Werke*, vol. 3, p. 720.

66 *Werke*, vol. 3, p. 708.

CHAPTER 2

1 See K. Berger, *Schiller* vol. 1, p. 600.

2 Cf. Anderson, *Europe in the Eighteenth Century*, p. 73.

3 P. E. Schramm, *Neun Generationen*, vol. 1, p. 79.

4 Cf., for example, Seume's account of the help given to poor people by Rector Mücke in Grimma (*Werke*, vol. 10, pp. 165–6). J. G. Sachse, in his autobiography, *Der deutsche Gil Blas*, in which he describes a life spent largely moving from place to place in search of a living, gives frequent examples of charity received.

5 For this aspect of eighteenth-century German life, cf. particularly Schilfert, pp. 131 ff. Schiller gives a more factual treatment of the theme than that of *Die Räuber* in *Der Verbrecher aus verlorener Ehre*.

6 *Memoirs*, vol. 1, p. 202. Sachse recounts having seen five men on one wayside gibbet near Fulda much later in the century (op. cit., p. 116).

7 *Werke*, pp. 140–1. Prison conditions could also be appalling (e.g. the description of Ehrenbreitstein in Forster's *Ansichten vom Niederrhein*) and military discipline was often brutal, not least in Prussia.

8 See Goethe, *Amtliche Schriften*, vol. 1, p. 249. The occasion was a memorandum on the retention of the death-penalty for infanticides. It was retained, but it is significant that Karl August did raise the question.

9 In 'Der Menschenfreund', *Werke*, Teil 1, p. 225.

10 A. Lafontaine, *Die Familie von Halden* (Berlin, 1797), vol. 2, pp. 352 and 353.

11 *HA*, vol. 11, p. 398 ('. . . wo ich mich nur abarbeite und nichts fruchte').

12 Letter of 8 February 1790, quoted by E. Kessel, *Wilhelm von Humboldt*, p. 41.

13 Cf. W. Martens, op. cit., pp. 377 f.

14 *Dichtung und Wahrheit*, Book 7, *HA*, vol. 9, p. 265. Another critic who attaches what seems to us excessive importance to this military pageant is Breitinger, in his *Critische Dichtkunst* (vol. 1, Abschnitt 10). It will be noted that neither of these two observers was a Saxon.

15 See F. Sengle, *Wieland*, pp. 141–50.

16 *Culture and Society*, p. 85.

17 Gellert, *Lustspiele*, p. 316.

18 Cf. the description of Leipzig in A. Jericke, *Es ist ein klein Paris. Die Wirkung der Stadt Leipzig auf Persönlichkeit und Werk Goethes*, Weimar, 1965.

19 *Der Biedermann*, Blatt 15: *Schriften*, vol. 3, p. 122. There is no doubt that the manners (in the broadest sense) of university students in the eighteenth century left much to be desired. Criticism of their drunkenness, brawling, duelling and so forth continue to be voiced well into the century.

20 *Dichtung und Wahrheit*, Book XIII, *HA*, vol. 9, pp. 569 f. For the play in question, cf. Bruford, *Theatre*, pp. 225–7.

21 Cf. Fauchier-Magnan, op. cit., pp. 125 ff., especially pp. 184–211.

22 Biedermann, op. cit., vol. 2, pp. 87 f. The philosopher Wolff also considered it to be a part of the proper princely dignity (see Hertz, op. cit., vol. 1, p. 230).

23 *Critische Dichtkunst*, vol. 2, p. 18.

24 Wraxall: *Memoirs*, vol. 2, p. 175.

25 In his essay on Oeser, *Werke*, vol. 10, p. 151.

26 Biedermann, op. cit., vol. 2, p. 165.

27 Pöllnitz, *Memoirs*, vol. 1, p. 93.

28 The achievements of the Rococo in music and architecture, in which fields it was at its best in Germany, have long since been fully recognized. In the literary field, the best general accounts are by Sengle (in his study of Wieland) and Anger (see Bibliography).

29 In its eighteenth-century sense of a particularly close affinity of souls. The lines quoted occur in Merck's *Werke*, p. 115.

30 *Werke*, p. 592. Seume, in an interesting account of an 'Excursion to Weimar', speaks warmly of the kindness with which he was received and says of the relationship between two aristocratic

Notes

ladies: '. . . unless I am very much mistaken, they are soul-mates ('Herzensfreundinnen') in the best "Bürger" sense' (*Werke*, vol. 10, p. 175).

31 *Neun Generationen*, vol. 1, pp. 268f.

32 *Werke*, vol. 7, p. 50.

33 *Letters*, vol. 1, p. 253.

34 Biedermann, op. cit., vol. 4, p. 1081. The notorious snobbery of German aristocrats is mercilessly pilloried in the opening chapters of Voltaire's *Candide*.

35 *Memoirs*, vol. 1, p. 359.

36 Cf. Rosenberg, op. cit., p. 70.

37 *CMEH*, vol. 8, p. 429

38 Op. cit., vol. 2, p. 84. Cf. A. Köster, 'Aber das mattherzige Bürgertum duckte und fügte sich' (*Die deutsche Literatur der Aufklärungszeit*, p. 246).

39 E.g. Rebmann, as quoted by Bruford (*Germany*, p. 101), on the way in which 'when the servant of some bankrupt count strikes out with his torch amongst well-dressed people at a gate, because the crowd has held up the carriage a little, they wipe the burning pitch off their clothes and go quietly home.'

40 Sir John Littleman in Geiger's *Teutscher Engelländer*; cf. *Reise*, 'Nachwort', p. 26.

41 Cf. Martens, op. cit., pp. 370 ff.

42 Even in the privacy of his diary, as in the entry for 22 April 1808: 'Abends bei Durchlaucht der Herzogin gelesen . . . etc.'

43 Cf. Turner, *Mozart*, p. 158 (letter of 16 February 1778). The case for Leopold is forcefully put on pp. 153–4 of this work.

44 E.g. H. A. Korff in *Geist der Goethezeit*, vol. 1, p. 237. Luise is 'die zaghafte und an das Herkommen gebundene unfreie Seele.'

45 *Heinrich Stillings Jugend*, p. 167. Cf. earlier C. F. Gellert: 'Ich will mit meinem Gut . . . Mein reinliches Gemach nicht glänzend überziehen' (*Werke*, Teil 1, p. 225).

46 *Memoirs*, vol. 1, p. 15. Moritz had a similar experience. Jung-Stilling's patron, the merchant 'Herr Spanier' who in fact wished him well, nevertheless felt him to be a social inferior. When another merchant, a man of Pietistic and therefore more democratic leanings, invited Stilling to be godfather to his child, Spanier 'could not understand how one merchant could ask another merchant's servant [in fact, he was a tutor] to stand godfather' (op. cit., p. 258).

47 Ibid., pp. 30–31. Seume also recounts how his father, a peasant farmer, suffered under clerical 'Bonzenwesen' (*Werke*, vol. 1, p. 8).

48   Cf. Feuerbach, *Uz und Cronegk*, p. 154.
49   *Heinrich Stillings Wanderschaft*, p. 244.
50   *Memoirs*, vol. 1, pp. 7 ff.
51   *Memoirs*, vol. 1, p. 221.
52   *Revolutionary Europe*, p. 49.

CHAPTER 3

1   Cf. Bruford, *Germany*, p. 276. Part Four, Chapter One of that work gives a fairly detailed survey of writers' conditions. For the theatre, see the same author's *Theatre, Drama and Audience in Goethe's Germany*.
2   Bruford, *Germany*, p. 279. Further to this question, see F. C. Perthes, *Der deutsche Buchhandel als Bedingung des Daseins einer deutschen Literatur* and the accompanying essay by G. Schulz, 'Die Entwicklung des Urheberrechts in Deutschland im 19. Jahrhundert', Stuttgart, Reclams Universal-bibliothek, 1967.
3   *Campagne in Frankreich, HA*, vol. 10, p. 291.
4   *Sebaldus Nothanker*, ed. cit., pp. 65–6.
5   Cf. his submission to the Hanover provincial government of 1784, *Werke und Briefe*, pp. 273 ff.
6   Cf. Bielschowsky, *Goethe*, vol. 2, pp. 448–9.
7   Bruford, *Germany*, p. 250.
8   *Werke*, p. 400 (article in the *Teutsche Merkur* of 1779).
9   *Anton Reiser*, p. 141. Cf. also p. 343.
10   'Vom Einfluss der Regierung . . . etc.', *Werke*, vol. 3, p. 318.
11   *Schriften*, p. 100.
12   *Critische Dichtkunst*, vol. 1, p. 323.
13   *Werke*, vol. 5, pp. 130 and 142.
14   *Werke*, p. 22.
15   In the *Humanitätsbriefe, Werke*, vol. 5, p. 90.
16   Cf. the 'Proktophantasmist' in *Faust* I, for example, or in the 'Xenien', 'Empiriker' and 'Empirischer Querkopf'.
17   'Zum ewigen Frieden', *DLER* (Klassik), vol. 11, p. 64.
18   *Belphegor*, p. 305.
19   Ibid., p. 308.
20   *Werke*, vol. 1, p. 124.
21   Bruford, *Theatre*, p. 362. Cf. pp. 360–3 of this work and the Preface for more discussion of this problem.
22   Ibid., p. 361.
23   *Werke*, vol. 1, p. 265. ('You must flee from the stress of life into the sacred, quiet spaces of the heart. Freedom exists only in the realm of dreams and beauty lives only in song.')
24   *Goethe und seine Zeit*, pp. 42–3. Lukács believes that classical

Notes

German literature is a reflection of what are, for the Marxist, the great practical political issues of the time, but that political and social conditions caused this to happen in a very indirect manner.

25 'Your nature, that miserable one'.

26 *HA*, vol. 10, pp. 321 ff., especially pp. 324–5 and 329–33.

27 E. Kessel, *Wilhelm von Humboldt*, p. 70.

28 Ibid., p. 103.

29 Ed. cit., pp. 81–2.

30 'Würde des Menschen', *Werke*, vol. 1, p. 143.

31 *DLER* (Klassik), vol. 11, p. 258.

32 Siegfried Schmid (1774–1825), a very minor talent who contributed some pieces to Schiller's *Musenalmanach*. He had failed to impress Goethe, who links him, in his letter of 9 August, with Hölderlin, whom he had also found unimpressive. As Goethe points out, Schmid, who was the son of a well-to-do merchant was 'kein gedrückter Mensch'.

33 Jean Paul Richter. In the epigram entitled 'Richter', Goethe attributes Jean Paul's imperfect cultural development to the fact that he is surrounded by the unpoetic environment of the small provincial town of Hof, in Bayreuth. London would have made a different man of him, Goethe feels.

34 'Das Absolute, aber nur innerhalb der Menschheit', *Werke*, vol. 8, p. 384.

35 I.e. a firm, systematic profile, giving consistency and definite form, something very different from the ever-developing 'progressive universal poetry' which was the Romantic ideal, as stated by Friedrich Schlegel. It is interesting that, in the intermediate stage of his development to conscious Romanticism, Schlegel defines the essential quality of modern (as against Greek) literature as 'lack of character' (cf. his essay 'Über das Studium der griechischen Poesie').

36 *Siebenkäs*, p. 60.

37 Ibid., p. 150.

38 'And as a trembling pupa hung beside him, dreaming its way, as it still slept in the wrinkled half of its shell, towards its calixes – and as the soul's eye of Fantasy looked over from the mound of the last hay-harvest into the evening splendour of the month of the new hay-harvest – and as every many-coloured tree blossomed, as it were, for the second time – and as the multicoloured mountain-tops, like enlarged tulips, drew a rainbow across the haze of autumn – so now it was the earlier breezes of May which chased the fluttering leaves and blew upon our friend in trembling waves and rose up with him and

bore him aloft over the Autumn and over the mountains. And he could see away over the mountains and the lands, and Lo! he saw all the Springs of his life, waiting for him in their buds, like gardens one beside the other, and in each Spring, there stood his friend!'

CHAPTER 4

1   Cf. 'Gott, der Weltschöpfer', *Sämtliche Poetische Werke*, no. 96.
2   Stanza 18: '... der mit Vernunft genösse Was deine Huld hervorgebracht.'
3   See *Weltweisheit*, vol. 1, pp. 87 and 581.
4   Cf. Cassirer, ch. 4, section 1, pp. 137 ff.
5   For secularization, see works like A. Schöne, *Die Säkularisation als sprachbildende Kraft* (Göttingen, 1958) and Requadt, *Lichtenberg*, pp. 22 ff.
6   *Allgemeine Theorie*, vol. 3, p. 507.
7   Cf. Cassirer, *The Philosophy of the Enlightenment*, p. 281: 'Truth and beauty, reason and nature, are now but different expressions for the same thing.'
8   Bodmer, *Brief-Wechsel*, p. 13.
9   Ibid., Preface ('... Verstand, der nicht mehr als einer ist').
10   Book I, Chapter 8; *Werke*, vol. 2, p. 165.
11   Ibid., pp. 163 ff.
12   *Werke*, p. 316.
13   Op cit., vol. 3, p. 508. See also Stück 34 of Lessing's *Hamburgische Dramaturgie* which, in addition to the element of purpose, particularly stresses 'das Unterrichtende' (the instructive).
14   Gottsched, *Schriften*, vol. 3, pp. 8–9.
15   Cf. Breitinger's acceptance of the original meaning of the Greek 'poietes' in his *Critische Dichtkunst* (vol. 1, p. 60), and Lessing's thoughts on the Genius, *Hamburgische Dramaturgie*, Stück 96 and particularly Stück 34, where he compares the genius to God, (or rather, God to the genius) but allows neither to break through the limits of 'nature' as he conceives it.
16   *Versuch in scherzhaften Liedern*, p. 71. Cf. also Lessing's *Rettung des Horaz*.
17   In the *Gelehrtenrepublik*; *Werke*, p. 356.
18   E.g. Gottsched, *Critische Dichtkunst*, p. 103.
19   Cf. *Ars Poetica* in *The Collected Works of Horace*, translated by Lord Dunsany and Michael Oakley, London, 1961, p. 290: 'It isn't enough for poems to have mere beauty; they must also have charm and lead the soul of the hearer Wherever they will ... if you would have me weep, You must first feel sorrow yourself ... etc.' Very early on in the 'Aufklärung' Hagedorn adopts

this attitude: 'Was hilft es, Reim und Reim und Wort und Wort verbinden? . . . etc.' (*Versuch einiger Gedichte*, p. 60).

20 Cf. Bodmer's *Critische Abhandlung von dem Wunderbaren in der Poesie* and Breitinger's *Critische Dichtkunst*, vol. 1, particularly Sections 5, 6 and 7.

21 E.g. in the matter of Satan's artillery, pp. 71 ff.

22 *Critische Dichtkunst*, vol. 1, p. 130.

23 I.e. a world which can be conceived, just as, for Leibniz, God created the best of 'possible' worlds.

24 Op. cit., vol. 1, p. 131. To be 'probable', a thing must 'square with our normal concepts' (p. 136). 'Inventions' lacking probability, like those in *Amadis*, arouse only disgust (p. 133).

25 'Von der heiligen Poesie', *Werke*, p. 311.

26 Schleiden, op. cit., p. 112.

27 In *Die Gelehrtenrepublik*, quoted by Schleiden, ibid., p. 97.

28 See 'Die Ratgeberin', ibid., pp. 90 ff., and the essay 'Von der Sprache der Poesie', in which he warns that 'after the fiery hour of composition must follow the cooler one of revision' (*Werke*, p. 326).

29 Quoted by J. Murat in *Klopstock*, p. 347.

30 'Kein Übermass, mein Freund, ich bitte sehr', Book III, line 1250.

31 'Glück und Genuß sind in dem Mittelstande' ('Horaz'; *Poetische Werke*, vol. 1, p. 103).

32 Cf. *Hamburgische Dramaturgie*, Stück 1.

33 Examples are Gellert's 'Epiktet', Uz's 'Der standhafte Weise', Wieland's presentation of Kleanth in *Musarion* (cf. also his *Theages*). One exception to the general rule, interestingly enough, is Gottsched.

34 *DLER*, Aufklärung, vol. 8, pp. 238–9 and 224.

35 *Schriften*, p. 198: 'Bewundert will ein Held und nicht bedauert sein'.

36 Act V, Scene 10: '. . . Diese Heilige befahl mehr, als die menschliche Natur vermag'.

37 *Weltweisheit*, vol. 2, pp. 236 ff.

CHAPTER 5

1 Letter to Ebert of 21 April 1773, *Briefe*, p. 247.

2 Letter to Herder of 5 May 1773, ibid., p. 249.

3 Letter to J. J. Eschenburg, *LM*, vol. 18, p. 116; cf. also that to Karl Lessing of 30 April 1774, ibid., p. 109.

4 *Werke*, p. 50. For the review of Nicolai's parody, see ibid., pp. 902–3.

5 Cf. his letter to Lessing of 17 January 1775 (*LM*, vol. 21, p. 52), and the marginalia in his copy, quoted by Minor in his edition of *Die Freuden des jungen Werthers*, pp. 294–5.

6 *Die Freuden des jungen Werthers*, in *Lessings Jugendfreunde*, (*DNL* 72), ed. J. Minor, p. 376.

7 See his Introduction to the novel, reprinted by Brüggemann in *DLER*, Aufklärung, vol. 14, p. 21.

8 See, for example, Schiller's poem on the performance of Goethe's translation of Voltaire's *Mahomet* in *Werke*, vol. 1, pp. 259–61.

9 See *Versuch schweizerischer Gedichte*, pp. 318 ff. For Haller in general, see C. Sigrist, *Albrecht von Haller*, Stuttgart, Metzler, 1967, and on his poetry, my articles, Haller's 'Gedanken über Vernunft, Aberglauben und Unglauben: Structure and Mood', *Forum for Modern Language Studies*, 8 (1972), 95–106 and 'Order and Freedom in Haller's "Lehrgedichte": on the Limitations and Achievements of Strict Rationalism within the Aufklärung', *Neophilologus*, 56 (1972), 181–7.

10 'Begebenheiten', a word often used in these novels and sometimes in their titles. For a survey of the common run of novels in the period of the 'Aufklärung', cf. Marianne Spiegel, *Der Roman und sein Publikum im früheren 18. Jahrhundert*.

11 See his review of *Vie de Madame de Maintenon*, *LM*, vol. 5, p. 178: 'das Wunderbare des Romans'.

12 Ibid., p. 181.

13 Ibid., p. 427.

14 See his *Erziehung des Menschengeschlechts*, para. 73.

15 See *Hamburgische Dramaturgie*, section 15.

16 Ibid., section 11.

17 In his letters to Nicolai and Moses Mendelssohn of 1756 and the *Hamburgische Dramaturgie*, particularly sections 73 ff.

18 'A stormy young-man's head with grey hair', Act V, Scene 2.

19 See 'Literaturbrief' 49.

20 *LM*, vol. 5, p. 196.

21 'Verdruss': not a trivial and temporary burst of temper, but a corrosive inner state of irritation must be meant.

22 'Die schlafende Laura', *Werke*, vol. I, p. 20.

CHAPTER 6

1 V. -L. Tapié, *The Age of Grandeur. Baroque and Classicism in Europe*, London, 1960, p. 223. Vierzehnheiligen is illustrated in plates 178–80 of this work. A good example of a Rococo church (Wies, in Bavaria), is shown in plate 181. I would not agree

Notes

with the author's view that this building has a spirituality equal to that of the Baroque.

2   See *Hamburgische Dramaturgie*, Stück 18. For the theme in general, see W. Hinck, *Das deutsche Lustspiel des 17. und 18. Jahrhunderts und die italienische Komödie*, Stuttgart, 1965.

3   See M. Levey, *Rococo to Revolution. Major trends in eighteenth-century painting*, London, 1966, pl. 37 and pp. 62 ff.

4   'The night, the solitude, the moonlight, the magical effect of love which overcomes the reason, her own heart, which she resists only languidly, how much combines to kindle the lady's easily inflamed blood!'

5   J. N. Götz, 'Das Vergnügen'; Elschenbroich, p. 69.

6   *Sämtliche Poetische Werke*, p. 116.

7   'Die Poesie', *Versuch einiger Gedichte*, p. 37.

8   'The hills and the pastures are bathed in light, and fruitfulness and joy cover the field with flowers. The enamel of the flat green land shines full of splendour and the night retires from the clear brooks.'

9   Professor Dent (*Opera*, London, 1951, pp. 55–6) seems to suggest that in spite of the fact that the 'satirical element' of Beaumarchais was largely left out (p. 56), the general intention was still satirical. There is really no direct evidence for this assumption.

10   E.g. 'Lied des armen Arbeitsmanns' and others, in *DNL*, vol. 45 (I), pp. 299 ff.

11   See Lewis F. Feuer (ed.), *Marx and Engels. Basic Writings on Politics and Philosophy*, London, (Fontana Books), 1969, p. 242.

12   Among other activities in the literary field, Weisse published an Anacreontic collection of *Scherzhafte Lieder*.

13   *Sämtliche Poetische Werke*, p. 107. ('Murmur, when all is at rest, you trees with your gently swaying branches, lull me with your murmuring, as the water bubbles huskily, into voluptuous dreams.')

14   Cf. the stanza beginning 'Geht hin, die ihr nach Golde schnaubet...' *Sämtliche Poetische Werke*, p. 51.

15   'Heiterkeit des Geistes' and 'Ruhe des Gemüts' are seen as the essential qualities of the ideal state: cf. *Agathon*, p. 307.

16   In the dedication to C. F. Weisse, he states that he intended the poem to be 'a true depiction of the shape of my mind'.

17   'What good is resolution? At the moment when one has dedicated oneself to Minerva, Cytherea herself would come at an inconvenient time ... It was not she, it is true, but the beauty who did come would, perhaps, have been equally unafraid of the wager which Pallas once lost.'

18 '[She was] beautiful when the veil revealed only her black eyes, more beautiful still when it concealed nothing; pleasing when she was silent, and bewitching when she spoke: then, her wit would have found favour even for cheeks which had no roses. It was a wit which never lacked charm, equally ready to sting or to caress, but which smiled as it stung and had no poison in it. Never were the Muses and Graces seen in a more beautiful alliance, never did playful reason speak from fairer lips, or Cupid sport around a fairer breast.'

19 *Werke* (ed. Klee), vol. 1, p. 203.

20 *Agathon*, pp. 353–4: 'diesen enthusiastischen Schwung der Seele'.

CHAPTER 7

1 Cf. A. Lübbering (ed.), *Der Gedichtband des Göttinger Hains 'Für Klopstock'*, Westerstede, 1956, p. 17. ('Daughter of Eden, o Peace, thou who inhabitest the darkness of quiet groves, who tarriest with arms folded in the twilight of moon-silvered poplars . . . At last, thou who bringest joy to the heart, thou offerest me thy golden cup and embracest me, as thou dost the shepherd playing his flute or the shepherdess as she dances. A super-terrestrial feeling trembles through my breast, through my inmost being . . .')

2 Cf. Marianne Spiegel, op. cit., pp. 14 ff.

3 Gellert, *Werke*, Part 2, p. 24. Cf. also Gellert's *Lehren eines Vaters für seinen Sohn*, ibid., pp. 157 ff., especially p. 158.

4 The use of 'empfindlich' to mean 'sensitive', rather than 'touchy' was common in the eighteenth century.

5 *Schwedische Gräfin*, ed. cit., pp. 109–10. ('The Count was trembling so violently that he could hardly rise from his chair and we watched their embraces for a long time and with a thrill of joy. "Now," cried Steeley at last, "Now we receive our reward for all the misery we have endured." He tore himself free from the Count and I hurried towards him with outspread arms . . . O what a voluptuous delight is the pleasure afforded by friendship and how strongly are sensitive hearts impelled towards one another at such happy moments.')

6 Ibid., p. 138.

7 Sophie von Laroche, *Geschichte des Fräuleins von Sternheim*, ed. F. Brüggemann; *DLER*, Aufklärung, vol. 14, Leipzig, 1938, p. 104.

8 Ibid., p. 172.

9 Ibid., pp. 184–5.

Notes

10 *Lichtenberg*, chapter 1.
11 Ibid., p. 45.
12 *Andreas Hartknopf*, p. 126: 'Ich fühlte mein Daseyn zum ersten-male ... etc.'
13 Ibid., p. 122.
14 Ibid., p. 128.
15 See the essay 'Von der besten Art, über Gott zu denken', summarized in Murat, *Klopstock*, p. 114.
16 See her letter of 5 March 1757 to her sisters; *Briefwechsel*, vol. 2, p. 589.
17 *Werke*, vol. 9, p. 11 ('He wanders aimlessly in his arid wilder-nesses and digs for himself wells which yield no water').
18 *Briefe von und an Klopstock*, p. 82.
19 Ibid., p. 59.
20 See 'Von der Darstellung', *Werke*, p. 336. Klopstock talks at this point of 'apparent disorder', of an abrupt breaking-off of the thread of thought and the arousing of expectation. He is thinking of elevated, hymnic poetry, but the remarks have relevance to the lyric as well. All this is conceived as being part of a plan.
21 *Der Messias*, Canto IV, line 1071.
22 Lines 791–6, my italics. (Why do I *feel* then ... new *thoughts*, ... trembling *thoughts*, which quite dissolve into love ... [why does Cidli's voice] awaken my beating heart to *emotions* which *move* me so strongly?').
23 On Haller, cf. my article 'Haller's *Gedanken über Vernunft, Aberglauben und Unglauben*: Structure and Mood', *Forum for Modern Language Studies*, vol. 8 (1972), pp. 95–106.
24 Cf. the essay 'Über die Fülle des Herzens' (1777), reprinted in *DNL*, 50 (II), pp. 18–27.
25 E.g. K. L. Schneider, *Klopstock und die Erneuerung der deutschen Dichtersprache im 18 Jahrhundert*, Heidelberg, 1960.
26 See Klopstock, *Werke*, 'Nachwort', p. 455.

CHAPTER 8

1 *Journal meiner Reise im Jahr 1769*; *Werke*, vol. 1, pp. 113–14.
2 *Ardinghello*, p. 178.
3 'Über Götz von Berlichingen'; *Werke und Schriften*, vol. 1, p. 379.
4 See the beginning of Book 14. Lavater is also described in this Book (*HA*, vol. 10, pp. 15 ff.).
5 For Kaufmann, see also Hettner, *Geschichte der deutschen Literatur im achtzehnten Jahrhundert*, vol. 2, pp. 252–3. Goethe called him a 'Lügenprophet' (letter to Lavater of 6 March 1780) and

Müller satirized him in *Fausts Leben* (*Dichtungen,* 1 Theil, p. 201).

6 *Theatre,* p. 217.

7 'To love, to hate, to fear, to tremble, to hope, to despair to the depths of one's being, can certainly make life bitter, but without them, it would be worthless' ('An das Herz', *Werke und Schriften,* vol. 1, p. 108).

8 Cf. *Werke und Schriften,* vol. 1, pp. 484 ff.

9 *Dichtungen,* I Theil, p. 173.

10 'Die ganze Anlage zur Seligkeit', letter to Wilhelm von Wolzogen, 25 May 1783 (*NA,* vol. 23, p. 88).

11 Lenz, 'Eduard Allwills erstes geistliches Lied', *Werke und Schriften,* vol. 1, pp. 95–6 ('No, I cry: Father, Saviour! This heart desires to be filled, desires to be satiated. If it cannot be, then shatter thy image').

12 *Ardinghello,* p. 46.

13 *WA,* vol. 37, pp. 274–5.

14 See *HA,* vol. 12, p. 13.

15 For a discussion of this, the first important German park laid out in the 'English' style, see W. D. Robson-Scott, *The Literary background of the Gothic Revival in Germany. A Chapter in the History of Taste,* Oxford, 1965, pp. 30–32.

16 Cf. the poems 'An Belinden' and 'Lilis Park'.

17 'Auf dem See' ('And I suck in fresh nourishment, new blood from a free world. How lovely and kind is Nature, which holds me to its breast!')

18 *WA,* vol. 11, p. 289.

19 In the essay on Ossian, *Werke,* vol. 2, pp. 201–2.

20 Cf. his Letter to Frau von Klettenberg of 26 August 1770, quoted in *Begegnungen und Gespräche,* vol. 1, p. 138.

21 Müller, *Dichtungen,* I Theil, p. 189. ('Oh, they must all come out, all the gods which are silent within me.')

22 Rede zum Shakespeares Tag, *HA,* vol. 12, p. 226.

23 *Werke,* vol. 2, p. 248.

24 Ibid., p. 249 (my italics).

25 In *Aesthetica in Nuce, Sämtliche Werke,* vol. 2, p. 206.

26 E.g. those Marxist critics who wish to see the movement as a continuation of the 'Aufklärung'. Hans Mayer, for example, attempts to portray Lenz as an 'Aufklärer' ('Nachwort' to Lenz's *Werke und Schriften,* vol. 2, pp. 803 ff.). But the man who, among other things, prefers Herder's view of history to Voltaire's (vol. 1, pp. 403–4), who deliberately sets out his ideas 'in rhapsodic form' (ibid., p. 329) and likens reason to a long-sighted eye which can see things only from a half-hour's distance away (p. 485), hardly fills the bill.

Notes

27 *Aesthetica in Nuce*, p. 197.

28 *Werke und Briefe*, p. 321.

29 Both Bürger and Schubart, incidentally, had a stronger practical political consciousness and a closer relation to actuality than most members of the movement. Schubart, apart from his publicistic work, is best known for some forceful, but only moderately inspired political poems (e.g. 'Die Fürstengruft').

30 'Wolken', *Sämtliche Werke*, vol. 2, p. 96.

31 *NA*, vol. 23, p. 79.

32 *HA*, vol. 12, p. 13.

33 Cf. Götz von Berlichingen's account of the good old days (*HA*, vol. 4, p. 142), or the idealization of Patriarchal life in Herder's *Auch eine Philosophie* . . .

34 For this whole section on 'inner form', cf. 'Aus Goethes Brieftasche', *HA*, vol. 12, p. 22.

35 Ibid., pp. 13–14.

36 Ibid., p. 13.

37 *Sämmtliche Werke*, vol. 5, pp. 606–7.

38 *Anmerkungen übers Theater* pp. 244 and 246.

39 *Werke und Schriften*, vol. 2, p. 232.

40 *Anmerkungen übers Theater*, p. 245 ('mit einer Empfindung alle Wonne').

41 *The Idea of History*, p. 77.

42 *Werke*, vol. 2, p. 359 ('the confused mass of all ages, nations and tongues').

43 *Patriotische Phantasien*, pp. 65–6.

44 *Werke*, vol. 2, p. 358 ('Gang Gottes über die Nationen').

45 Ibid., p. 373.

46 *Werke*, vol. 2, p. 276.

47 Ibid., vol. 2, p. 284. ('See this man, full of power and the feeling of God, and yet whose feeling is as deeply inward and as peaceful as the sap moving through this tree, as instinct, that quiet, healthy, self-possessed natural urge which is distributed among creatures in a thousand forms and impels each single creature so powerfully, is capable of being! . . . Long life, enjoyment of himself in the most completely integrated way, division of his days through rest and exhaustion, learning and retaining – see! such was the Patriarch in himself alone. But how can I say "in himself alone"? The blessing of God through all nature, where was it deeper and warmer than in the image of mankind, as it went on feeling and developing: in the woman created for him, in the son who resembled his own image, in the divine race of beings which was to fill the earth around him and would go on doing so?')

CHAPTER 9

1   *Begegnungen und Gespräche*, vol. 1, p. 286.
2   Ibid., p. 214.
3   *HA*, Briefe, vol. 1, p. 57.
4   Ibid., p. 58.
5   Ibid., p. 120.
6   For an account of the revision, cf. W. Kayser in *HA*, vol. 4, pp. 492–4. The text of the 'Urgötz' is in *WA*, vol. 39.
7   Franz contrasts her 'fire' with the gentleness of Marie (*HA*, vol. 4, p. 104) and she speaks of her 'great' undertakings (p. 153).
8   *HA*, vol. 4, p. 175: 'Es kommen die Zeiten des Betrugs . . . etc.'
9   E.g. pp. 85 (Reiter), 90 (Weislingen) and 142–3 (Götz).
10 *HA*, vol. 4, p. 99: 'Du siehst nicht ganz frei, Adelbert' ('You don't look entirely free, i.e. at your ease').
11 Act V (ibid., p. 169). There is a similar fatalism in Werther, and in certain poems, e.g. 'Seefahrt'. Egmont has it to begin with but overcomes it in adversity.   *v. a Prometheus.*
12 Cf. especially *Clavigo* IV (1) and *Stella* V (2).
13 Cf. the scene 'Heilbronn. Im Thurm' in Act V: '*Sein* Wille geschehe' (p. 173).
14 Cf. the scene 'Weislingens Schloss' in Act V (p. 171).
15 'Goethes Werther'; cf. *Goethe im zwanzigsten Jahrhundert*, ed. H. Mayer, Hamburg, 1967, p. 14.
16 E.g. by making the character of Albert more sympathetic, as he wrote to Kestner on 2 May 1783. For the original version, cf. *WA*, vol. 19. A general account of the history of the text is in *HA*, vol. 6, pp. 593–5.
17 'Endlos', i.e. limitless, of metaphysical proportions. Goethe not infrequently uses this word, or others like it, in connection with love (for example, the 'grenzenlos' love of Eduard for Ottilie in the later novel *Die Wahlverwandtschaften*).
18 'Goethes Werther', p. 14.
19 *HA*, vol. 6, p. 12.
20 The phrase 'those few noble ones', which occurs just before the passage here discussed, is a very Klopstockian one (cf., for example, *Der Messias*, Canto I, line 19).
21 *HA*, vol. 6, p. 9.
22 Ibid., p. 22.
23 Cf. the 'Künstlergedichte' in *HA*, vol. 1, especially 'Künstlers Morgenlied'.
24 *HA*, vol. 6, p. 9.
25 Cf. *Emilia Galotti*, Act I, scene 4, where the painter, Conti, remarks: 'Ha! dass wir nicht unmittelbar mit den Augen malen

Notes

. . .' ('What a shame that we do not paint directly with our eyes . . . etc.').

26 Also known by the title of the later version, 'Mit einem gemalten Band'. Both versions are in *HA*, vol. 1.

27 'And yet, heaven, I would give you a thousand such nights if my sweetheart were to give me (just) one.'

28 *Werke* (ed. Klee), vol. 1, p. 275.

29 *HA*, vol. 1, p. 36 ('When the wheels rattled, wheel to wheel, swiftly around the marker and away [and] the whip-cracks of young men filled with the fire of victory flew high, and dust rolled as hailstorms roll down from the mountains into the valley, your soul glowed out courage, o Pindar, towards approaching dangers – Glowed – poor heart – up there on the hill – heavenly power, just [give me] enough warmth – my hut is up there – to wade up to it.')

30 Anacreon ('him playing, flower-happy') and 'the bee-singing, honey-murmuring, friendly-waving Theocritus'.

31 'How, in the shining morning light, you glow towards me, Spring, my beloved!'

32 *The Penguin Book of German Verse*, p. 193. Luke (p. 7) translates: 'How splendid is the brightness of Nature around me!', which may read more smoothly, but surely misses the force of 'mir'.

33 *HA*, vol. 12, p. 24.

CHAPTER 10

1 Cf. Schiller's preliminary announcement for the 'Rheinische Thalia' (1784), quoted in *NA*, vol. 3, p. viii.

2 Unless otherwise stated, discussion will be of the 'Schauspiel' version, which is probably aesthetically superior to, and certainly more typical of the 'Sturm und Drang' Schiller than the 'Trauerspiel', which was an adaptation for stage performance in Mannheim.

3 *NA*, vol. 3, p. 244: 'einen dramatischen Roman, und kein theatralisches Drama'.

4 *Schiller*, Darmstadt, 1967, pp. 61–2.

5 See the account of the drama's origin in *NA*, vol. 3, pp. 270 ff.

6 *Schiller*, p. 52.

7 *NA*, vol. 3, p. 87.

8 Franz's superhuman evil is considerably toned down in the 'Trauerspiel' version, as part of the general tendency towards 'enoblement' of the characters whose superficiality Herbert Stubenrauch rightly points out (p. xxviii).

9 Both Iago and Richard the Third figure among the literary parallels cited by Schiller himself (cf. first Preface, p. 244, and Preface to the 'Schauspiel', p. 7).

10 *NA*, vol. 3, p. 18.

11 Ibid., p. 19.

12 Ibid., p. 95 ('Man arises out of slime, he wades through slime for a span and makes slime and then melts back into slime until in the end, he is a piece of filth which sticks to the soles of his grandson's shoes.') This monologue does not occur in the 'Trauerspiel' version, where an unconvincing scene (IV, 9) is substituted, in which Franz decides against fratricide, in deference to 'the convulsions of dying virtue'.

13 *Werke*, vol. 1, p. 12. ('Who is it who, trembling on his crutch, with gloomy, downcast backward glance, consumed in a howling cry of grief, heavily struck by iron fate, wavers along after the silently-borne coffin? Did the word 'Father' come from the youth's lips? Damp shivers shiver fearsomely through his bones, dissolved in grief. His silver hair rears up. . . .').

14 See Lenz, *Gesammelte Schriften* (ed. Blei), vol. 5, pp. 3–47 and 385–8.

15 Quoted by Blei, ibid., pp. 385–6 ('. . . ihm konnte nicht wohl werden, als wenn er sich grenzenlos im Einzelnen verfloß und sich an einem unendlichen Faden ohne Absicht hinspann').

16 Quoted by Pascal, op. cit., p. 33.

17 *Werke und Schriften*, vol. 2, p. 174; 'Diese Grillen sind mir heilig, heiliger als alles'.

18 Cf. his letter to Goethe of 2 February of that year.

19 Cf. Lenz, *Der neue Menoza*, pp. 87 ff., especially p. 89.

20 Op. cit., p. 13.

21 *Gespräche mit Goethe*, 2 April 1829. ('The Romantic I call the Unhealthy'.)

CHAPTER 11

1 Cf. his *Gespräch über die Poesie*.

2 For the relationship between Moritz and Jean Paul, see H.-J. Schrimpf's 'Nachwort' to *Andreas Hartknopf*, pp. 11 ff.

3 *Anton Reiser*, p. 349.

4 Cf. particularly the section beginning 'Aber abseits, wer ist's?'

5 *HA*, *Briefe*, vol. 2, p. 24 (2 Dec. 1786).

6 Cf. the opening lines of the fifth and seventh elegies.

7 Ibid., Rome, January 1787.

8 Cf. the letter to Goethe of 23 August 1794: 'von innen heraus ein Griechenland zu gebären'.

9 I.e. the fallibility (both intellectual and moral) of man and all

Notes

his works, the uncertain, 'fragile' state of his knowledge and his goodness.

10 *HA*, vol. 8, p. 288. Here again we come up against the problem of Goethe's highly concentrated, poetic 'Altersstil'. The 'durchaus gesteigerte Gegenwart' to which he refers is a particular problem. 'Steigerung' (literally, 'intensification') was for Goethe a process of growth in which opposing and interlinked forces worked upon each other, and the intrinsic quality of the being undergoing the process developed to the point at which quantitative gave way to qualitative change.

11 *HA*, vol. 11, p. 369.

12 Cf. 'Metamorphose der Tiere'.

13 'Ihre Form als moralische Grösse', cf. ed. cit., p. 7. For the Kantian basis of this use of the term 'moral' i.e. the appeal of nature to our capacity for 'practical' (moral) ideas, cf. Mainland's note 30, ibid., p. 100.

14 *Werke*, vol. 5, p. 100 (*Briefe zur Beförderung der Humanität*).

15 'Die gottgedachte Spur'; cf. the poem 'Im ernsten Beinhaus war's . . .' (1826).

16 'Parteiischer Enthusiasmus'; cf. letter to Schiller of 14 June 1796.

17 'Ins Nützlich-Platte', into that which, in its concern to be morally justifiable and 'useful', loses the nature of art. It may be true of, or of use in ordinary human life, but it lacks all connection with man's higher spiritual nature, his 'Humanität'.

18 *Über naive und sentimentalische Dichtung*, ed. cit., pp. 46–7.

19 Ibid., pp. 22–3.

20 *HA*, vol. 12, p. 48.

21 Cf. Winckelmann's *Gedanken über die Nachahmung der griechischen Kunstwerke* (1754), which already sets up the ideal of harmony (e.g. *Werke*, p. 20), Lessing's *Laokoon*, Herder's *Humanitätsbriefe* (see *Sämmtliche Werke*, vol. 17, p. 351) and Schiller's 'Über das Pathetische' (*Werke*, vol. 8, pp. 130 ff.)

22 'Über Laokoon', *HA*, vol. 12, p. 58. On the 'softening principle of beauty' in the context of literary tragedy, cf. 'Der Sammler und die Seinigen', ibid., p. 80.

23 Ibid., p. 96.

24 *HA*, vol. 12, p. 133.

25 *HA*, vol. 8, p. 483.

26 Part Two, line 10,176: 'Schlecht und modern! Sardanapal!'

27 *Winckelmann, HA*, vol. 12, p. 98.

28 Cf. above, pp. 49–56.

29 *HA*, vol. 12, p. 42.

30 Cf. above, pp. 55–6.

31 *HA*, vol. 12, p. 471: 'Das ist die wahre Symbolik, wo das Besondere das Allgemeinere repräsentiert, nicht als Traum und Schatten, sondern als lebendig-augenblickliche Offenbarung des Unerforschlichen.'

32 *Foundations of the Metaphysics of Morals*, p. 44, text and note 11.

33 E.g. the *Metakritik*, and *Kalligone*. For the 'campaign against Kant', cf. R. T. Clark jr., *Herder. His Life and Thought*, Berkeley and Los Angeles, 1955, chapter Twelve.

34 *Werke*, vol. 5, p. 96 (*Briefe zur Beförderung der Humanität*).

35 'Ernst ist das Leben, heiter ist die Kunst.' See the ending of the prologue to *Wallenstein*.

36 Cf. Therese's letter to Natalie, *HA*, vol. 7, pp. 531–2.

37 Cf. his *Ideen zu einem Versuch, die Gränzen der Wirksamkeit des Staats zu bestimmen* (1792), *Werke*, vol. 1.

38 *Werke*, vol. 1, p. 67.

39 Ibid., p. 64.

40 Ibid., p. 69.

41 Cf. the first paragraph of his letter to Schiller of 6 January 1798.

42 Cf. Schiller's letter of 12 January 1798 and his reply of the 13th.

43 'Metamorphose der Tiere', lines 50–2. ('May this beautiful concept of [the interplay of] power and limitation, of untrammelled fancy and law, of freedom and measure, of mobility in order, excellence and defect gladden you deeply!').

CHAPTER 12

1 E.g. by E. M. Wilkinson, 'Goethe's Tasso, the tragedy of the creative artist', *Proceedings of the English Goethe Society*, vol. 15 (1946).

2 Line 969: 'So fühlt man Absicht, und man ist verstimmt.'

3 *HA*, vol. 5, pp. 130–1 ('Then he wants to grasp and hold everything; then he demands that whatever ideas he may have be put into effect ... his spirit wishes to draw together the ultimate ends of all things.')

4 E.g. the entirely personal 'Gesetz' which gives order and form to Ottilie's life in *Die Wahlverwandtschaften* and whose disruption leads to her tragedy. It is not a set of maxims of a general, impersonal character and can therefore never be formulated, only observed in actions and utterances. Cf. also the reference by the 'Gerichtsrat' in *Die natürliche Tochter* (*HA*, vol. 5, p. 271) to 'meiner Bahn Gesetz' which the appearance of Eugenie, like a meteor, has disrupted.

5 HA, vol 5, p. 242 ('It is a long time, my heart, since you expressed in such measured terms the emotion which moves you').

Notes

6 'The wave flees, and wavers, and swells, and bends over foaming.'

7 'And if by chance a *clear* spring should show me, in its *pure* mirror, a man . . . etc.'

8 E.g. the *Unterhaltungen deutscher Ausgewanderten*, or the plays *Der Bürgergeneral* and *Die Aufgeregten*.

9 *HA*, vol. 5, p. 245 ('How rich and how sweet is the glittering of the silver and the colours as their pure flashes move one through the other').

10 'The soft light of the pearls' and 'the gleaming force ('Gewalt', a word which often includes the idea of violence) of the jewels'; ibid., p. 246.

11 *HA*, vol. 7, p. 489.

12 Ibid., p. 554.

13 Ibid., p. 531.

14 Ibid., p. 71. Cf. the Abbé's remarks on p. 121, where he expresses the preference for human reason over experience as a guide in life.

15 Cf. particularly the remarks of the Uncle in Book Six (p. 405: 'Des Menschen grösstes Verdienst . . . etc.')

16 Ibid., p. 222. (A large, gently sloping stretch of grassland in the forest invited them to stay awhile. An enclosed spring afforded most pleasant refreshment, and on the other side, seen through gorges and wooded ridges, the distant prospect was beautiful and full of hope. There were villages and mills in the hollows, small towns on the plain and fresh hills, appearing in the distance as a no more than moderate limitation, made the prospect more hopeful still.).

17 Letter to Goethe of 8 July 1796.

18 Letter to Schiller of 9 July 1796.

19 'The night lies more deeply about me. The falling waters roar more violently now beside the slippery path. An unconquerable sadness comes upon me, a debilitating misery, and only a mossy rock supports me and prevents me from falling. Melancholy tears its way through the strings of my breast, the night tears flow and over the forest, morning announces its coming.'

20 'Alexis und Dora', lines 85 ff.

21 Schiller (letter of 28 November 1797), refers to Goethe's 'playful use of the object' (i.e. the tree-image), though without obvious disapproval. He is thinking, no doubt, of the conscious 'Spiel' of art.

22 'Der Betrachtung strenge Lust', *Faust*, Part One, line 3239.

23 See *HA*, vol. 13, p. 48.

CHAPTER 13

1 See the letter to Reinwald of 14 April 1783: 'Ich muss Ihnen gestehen, dass ich ihn gewissermassen statt meines Mädchens habe.'

2 'Youth is quick to come out with words which, like the knife's edge, are difficult to handle. It is bold enough to take from within its own hot head the measure for things which can only be judged by their own criteria.'

3 Cf. his letter to Goethe of 24 August 1798.

4 'Objective Bestimmtheit'; cf. the letter to Goethe of 5 January 1798.

5 Letter of 9 March 1797.

6 Letter of 8 January 1798: '. . . die kraftvolle Ruhe, die beherrschte Kraft.'

7 Letter to Körner of 28 July 1800: 'Poetisch ist der Stoff in vorzüglichem Grade.'

8 'Denn nur der grosse Gegenstand vermag Den tiefen Grund der Menschheit aufzuregen'. Cf. also 'Shakespeares Schatten', lines 31–2.

9 See his remarks in the essay 'Über das Erhabene' (Werke, vol. 8, p. 430).

10 These ideas are developed in 'Über das Erhabene' (Werke, vol. 8, pp. 419–20). Schiller conceives the process as a kind of dynamic resignation, in which the inevitable is accepted, but positively, as a matter of free choice, as something which is willed (for man is only man when he is 'the being which wills').

11 NA, vol. 8, p. 16. ('The villain! He tricked me properly. He's gone! Run off with all I managed to scrape together. Left me nothing but that ruffian there' (her son)). Grimmelshausen's Lebensbeschreibung der Ertzbetrügerin und Landstörzerin Courasche is a picaresque novel of the Thirty Years' War whose 'heroine' is, for a period, a sutler-woman.

12 Quoted in NA, vol. 8, p. 357.

13 Über naive und sentimentalische Dichtung, p. 79.

14 Die Piccolomini, II, 6; NA, vol. 8, p. 98.

15 Ibid., p. 183. Cf. again Über naive und sentimentalische Dichtung, p. 79: '. . . denn jene zwingt dich bloss blind . . . etc.'

16 Scene 7, pp. 199–201.

17 Ibid., pp. 333–4 (Tod, V, 3).

18 NA, vol. 9, p. 208. ('And so saying, she allowed her shepherdess's garb to fall away and stood there as Queen of the Heavens, in the brilliance of the suns, and was borne up on

golden clouds, slowly disappearing from view into the land of bliss.')

19 M. Gerhard, *Schiller*, Berne, 1950, p. 373.

20 'Unrat der Wirklichkeit', quoted in *NA*, vol. 9, p. 437.

21 '... lauter Licht, lauter Freiheit, lauter Vermögen – keinen Schatten, keine Schranke, nichts von dem allen mehr zu sehen', ibid., p. 437.

22 Reported by Schiller's sister-in-law, Caroline von Wolzogen, *Gespräche*; *NA*, vol. 42, p. 430.

23 *NA*, vol. 9, pp. 253–4. ('Dauphin! are you so tired already of the [earthly] appearance of the divine that you wish to destroy its vessel, to drag the pure virgin whom God has sent you down into the common dust?')

24 *Wallensteins Tod*, Act IV, scene 12; *NA*, vol. 8, p. 318.

25 *Don Carlos*, Act III, Scene 10.

26 *Über naive und sentimentalische Dichtung*, pp. 63–4.

27 Cf. *Werke*, vol. 1, p. 131, lines 141 ff.

28 'And see! The sun which shone on Homer smiles also on us.'

Bibliography

No attempt at a systematic Bibliography of the period is made here. What follows is simply a list of works cited in the text, with a short title given in brackets where appropriate. If some outstanding works of scholarship (e.g. many excellent studies of Goethe, such as those of Friedrich Gundolf, Karl Viëtor and Emil Staiger) are not mentioned, that does not mean that they have not been of great value to me in the writing of this book. Those who seek fuller bibliographical information are referred to the bibliographies in works mentioned below (e.g. those by Bruford, Sengle (for Wieland) or Murat (for Klopstock)), or to standard reference works such as Dahlmann and Weitz, *Quellenkunde der deutschen Geschichte* (7th edition, Leipzig, 1906); K. Goedeke, *Grundriss zur Geschichte der deutschen Dichtung*, 2nd edition, Dresden, from 1884; or H. W. Eppelsheimer, *Bibliographie der deutschen Literaturwissenschaft*, Frankfurt, from 1945. Specialist bibliographies include the *Goethe-Bibliographie* of H. Pyritz, continued by H. Nicolai and G. Burkhardt, Heidelberg, from 1965 and the *Schiller-Bibliographie* of W. Vulpius, Weimar, from 1959.

List of Abbreviations

CMEH   Cambridge Modern European History.

DNL   Deutsche National-Literatur. Historisch-Kritische Ausgabe. herausgegeben von Joseph Kürschner.

DLD   Deutsche Litteraturdenkmale des 18. und 19. Jahrhunderts.

DLER   Deutsche Literatur. Sammlung literarischer Kunst- und Kulturdenkmäler in Entwicklungsreihen. (Series: 'Aufklärung', 'Irrationalismus', 'Klassik', 'Politische Dichtung'.)

DVLG   Deutsche Vierteljahrsschrift für Literaturwissenschaft und Geistesgeschichte, Stuttgart.

HA   Goethe, *Werke* (Hamburger Ausgabe), see Goethe.

HAMBURGER   Hölderlin, *Selected Verse*, see Hölderlin.

LM   Lessing *Sämtliche Schriften* (Lachmann-Muncker), see Lessing.

LUKE   Goethe, *Selected Verse*, see Goethe.

NA   Schiller, *Werke* (Nationalausgabe), see Schiller.

WA   Goethe, *Werke* (Weimarer Ausgabe), see Goethe.

Bibliography

1. *Primary Sources*

BODMER, J. J. *Brief-Wechsel von der Natur des Poetischen Geschmacks*, ed. W. Bender, Stuttgart, 1966 (= *Brief-Wechsel*).
Character der teutschen Gedichte in *Vier Critische Gedichte*, ed. J. Baechtold, Stuttgart, 1883; *DLD*, 12.
Critische Abhandlung von dem Wunderbaren in der Poesie und dessen Verbindung mit dem Wahrscheinlichen, ed. W. Bender, Stuttgart, 1966.

BRÄKER, U. *Leben und Schriften Ulrich Bräkers, des armen Mannes im Tockenburg*, ed. S. Voellmy, Basle, 1945, 3 vols.

BREITINGER, J. J. *Critische Abhandlung von der Natur, den Absichten und dem Gebrauche der Gleichnisse*, ed. M. Windfuhr, Stuttgart, 1967 (= *Gleichnisse*).
Critische Dichtkunst . . . etc. ed. W. Bender, Stuttgart, 1966, 2 vols. (= *Critische Dichtkunst*).

BÜRGER, G. A. *Werke und Briefe*, ed. W. Friedrich, Leipzig, 1958.

CLAUDIUS, MATTHIAS *Werke*, ed. U. Roedl, Stuttgart, 1954.

CRONEGK, J. F. VON *Schriften*, Carlsruhe, 1776.

ECKERMANN, J. P. *Gespräche mit Goethe in den letzten Jahren seines Lebens*, ed. E. Merian-Genast, Basle, 1945, 2 vols.

ELSCHENBROICH, A. (ed.) *Deutsche Dichtung im achtzehnten Jahrhundert*, Munich, n.d.

FORSTER, G. *Ansichten vom Niederrhein* in *Georg Forsters Werke* (German Academy of Sciences edition), vol. 9, ed. G. Steiner, Berlin, 1958.
Werke, ed. G. Steiner, Berlin and Weimar, 1968, 2 vols.

FREDERICK II ('THE GREAT') OF PRUSSIA *De la littérature allemande*, ed. L. Geiger (Hamburg 1902), reprint by Wissenschaftliche Buchgesellschaft, Darmstadt, 1969.

GEIGER, C. I. *Reise eines Erdbewohners in den Mars*, ed. J. Hermand, Stuttgart, 1967 (= Sammlung Metzler, 61).

GELLERT, C. F. *Lustspiele*, ed. H. Steinmetz, Stuttgart, 1966.
Werke, ed. F. Behrend, Berlin-Leipzig-Vienna-Stuttgart (Bongs goldene Klassiker-Bibliothek), n.d. (two parts in 1 vol.).

GLEIM, J. W. L. *Versuch in scherzhaften Liedern*, ed. A. Anger, Tübingen, 1964 (= Neudrucke deutscher Literaturwerke, 13). (Cf. also Muncker: *DNL*, vol. 45.)

Bibliography

GOETHE, J. W. VON *Amtliche Schriften*, vols 1 (ed. W. Flach) and 2 (i) and (ii) (ed. H. Dahl), Weimar, 1950, 1968 and 1970.

Begegnungen und Gespräche, vol. 1, ed. E. and R. Grumach, Berlin 1965.

Briefe, ed. K. R. Mandelkow, 4 vols, Hamburg, 1962–7 (= *HA, Briefe*).

Selected Verse, ed. D. Luke, London, 1964 ('Penguin Poets').

Werke ('Hamburger Ausgabe') ed. E. Trunz and others, 14 vols, Hamburg, from 1948 (= *HA*).

Werke ('Weimarer Ausgabe'), im Auftrag der Grossherzogin Sophien von Sachsen, Weimar, from 1887, 50 vols. (= WA).

GOTTSCHED, J. C. *Erste Gründe der gesamten Weltweisheit* (Leipzig, 1733–4), reprint, Frankfurt, 1965 (= *Weltweisheit*).

Gesammelte Schriften, ed. E. Reichel, Berlin, Gottsched-Verlag, n.d., 6 vols.

Versuch einer Critischen Dichtkunst . . . etc. (4th edition, 1751), reprint, Darmstadt, Wissenschaftliche Buchgesellschaft, 1962 (= *Critische Dichtkunst*).

HAGEDORN, F. VON *Poetische Werke* (1757), reprint, Berne, 1968. *Versuch einiger Gedichte*, ed. A. Sauer, Heilbronn, 1883; *DLD*, 10.

HALLER, A. VON *Versuch schweizerischer Gedichte* (9th edition of 1762), reprint, ed. J. Helbling, Berne, 1969.

HAMANN, J. G. *Sämtliche Werke*, ed. J. Nadler, Vienna, 1949–57, 6 vols.

HEINSE, J. J. W. *Ardinghello und die glückseligen Inseln* (2nd edition, 1794), Berlin, Propyläen-Verlag, n.d.

HERDER, J. G. *Sämmtliche Werke*, ed. B. Suphan, Berlin, from 1877, 33 vols.

Werke, ed. W. Dobbek, Weimar, 1963, 5 vols.

HÖLDERLIN, F. *Selected Verse*, ed. M. Hamburger, London ('Penguin Poets'), 1961.

HORNER, E. (Ed.) *Vor dem Untergang des alten Reichs, 1756–95*; *DLER*, Politische Dichtung, 1, Leipzig, 1930.

HUMBOLDT, W. VON *Werke*, ed. A. Flitner and K. Giel, vol. 1, Stuttgart, 1960. Cf. also *DLER*, Klassik, vol. 11 (see Kant).

JUNG, J. H. (JUNG-STILLING) *Heinrich Stillings Jugend, Jünglingsjahre Wanderschaft und häusliches Leben*, ed. D. Cunz, Stuttgart, 1968.

259

Bibliography

KANT, I. *Foundations of the Metaphysics of Morals* and *What is Enlightenment?*, translated and ed. L. W. Beck, Indianapolis and New York, 1959.
Zum ewigen Frieden in *Gegenwart und Altertum*, ed. W. Muschg, Leipzig, 1932 (*DLER*, Klassik, vol. 11).

KLOPSTOCK, F. G. *Der Messias* in *Werke*, Carlsruhe, im Bureau der deutschen Klassiker, 1825, vols 1–2.
Werke in einem Band, ed. K. A. Schleiden, with 'Nachwort' by F. G. Jünger, Munich, 1954 (= *Werke*)
Briefe von und an Klopstock, ed. J. M. Lappenberg (1867), reprint, Berne, 1970.

KLOPSTOCK, META *Briefwechsel mit Klopstock und ihren Verwandten und Freunden*, ed. H. Tiemann, Maximilian-Gesellschaft, 1956, 3 vols (= *Briefwechsel*).

LENZ, J. M. R. *Anmerkungen übers Theater* in *Von deutscher Art und Kunst*, ed. H. Kindermann; *DLER*, Irrationalismus, vol. 6, Leipzig, 1935.
Der neue Menoza, ed. W. Hinck, Berlin, 1965 (Komedia, 9).
Gesammelte Schriften, ed. F. Blei, vol. 5, Munich and Leipzig, 1909.
Werke und Schriften, ed. Britta Titel and H. Haug, Stuttgart, 1966–7, 2 vols.

LESSING, G. E. *Sämtliche Schriften*, ed. K. Lachmann, 3rd edition, revised by F. Muncker, Stuttgart, from 1886, 23 vols (= *LM*).

MERCK, J. H. *Briefe*, ed. H. Kraft, Frankfurt, 1968.
Werke, ed. A. Henkel, Frankfurt, 1968.

MILLER, J. M. *Siegwart. Eine Klostergeschichte*, Frankfurt and Leipzig, 1777, 2 vols.

MORITZ, K. P. *Andreas Hartknopf . . .* etc., ed. H.-J. Schrimpf, Stuttgart, 1968 (Sammlung Metzler, 69).
Anton Reiser. Ein psychologischer Roman, ed. H. Henning, Leipzig, 1906.

MÖSER, J. *Patriotische Phantasien*, ed. S. Sudhof, Stuttgart, 1970.
Über die deutsche Sprache und Literatur in *De la littérature allemande* (see Frederick the Great).

MÜLLER, F. ('Maler') *Dichtungen*, ed. H. Hettner (1868), reprint, Berne, 1968, two parts in 1 vol.

NICOLAI, C. F. *Das Leben und die Meinungen des Herrn Magister*

Sebaldus Nothanker, ed. F. Brüggemann; *DLER*, Aufklärung, vol. 15, Leipzig, 1938 (= *Sebaldus Nothanker*)

PERTHES, F.   *Memoirs of Frederick Perthes*, translated from the German of C. T. Perthes, Edinburgh and London, 1856.

PFEIL, J. G. B.   *Lucie Woodvil* in *Die Anfänge des bürgerlichen Trauerspiels in den Fünfziger Jahren*, ed. F. Brüggemann; *DLER*, Aufklärung, vol. 8, Leipzig, 1934.

PÖLLNITZ, K. L.   *The Memoirs of Charles-Lewis, Baron de Pollnitz*, 2nd edition, London, 1739 (translation of 2nd edition of 1734), 2 vols (= *Memoirs*).

RICHTER, JEAN PAUL   *Siebenkäs*, ed. F. Burschell, Hamburg, 1957 (Rowohlts Klassiker, 17–18).

SACHSE, J. G.   *Der deutsche Gil Blas . . . etc.*, ed. W. Segebrecht, Munich, 1964.

SCHILLER, F.   *Die Horen*, reprint, Stuttgart, 1969, 12 vols in 6.

Über naive und sentimentalische Dichtung, ed. W. F. Mainland, Oxford, 1957.

Werke, ed. L. Bellermann, Leipzig, Bibliographisches Institut, from 1895, 14 vols.

Werke ('Nationalausgabe'), ed. J. Petersen, H. Schneider and others, Weimar, from 1943 (= *NA*).

SCHLEGEL, J. E.   *Ästhetische und dramaturgische Schriften*, ed. J. von Antoniewicz, Heilbronn, 1887; *DLD*, 26.

SCHUBART, C. D.   *Werke in einem Band*, ed. H. Böhm, Weimar, 1962.

SEUME, J. G.   *Werke*, Berlin, G. Hempel, n.d., 10 vols in 4.

STOLBERG, F. L. VON   Selection in *DNL*, vol. 50 (2) ed. A. Sauer, Stuttgart, n.d.

SULZER, J. G.   *Allgemeine Theorie der schönen Künste*, with Introduction by G. Tonelli, Hildesheim, 1970 (= *Allgemeine Theorie*).

UZ, J. P.   *Sämtliche Poetische Werke*, ed. A. Sauer (Stuttgart, 1890). *DLD*, 33–8; reprint, Darmstadt, Wissenschaftliche Buchgesellschaft, 1964.

WEZEL, J. C.   *Belphegor oder die wahrscheinlichste Geschichte unter der Sonne*, ed. H. Gersch, Frankfurt, 1965.

WIELAND, C. M.   *Geschichte des Agathon* (reprint of 1767 edition), ed. K. Schaeffer, Berlin, 1961.

Bibliography

Musarion, ed. A. Anger, Stuttgart, 1964.

Werke, ed. G. Klee, Leipzig, Bibliographisches Institut, 1900, 2 vols.

Werke, ed. F. Martini and H. Seiffert and others, Munich, from 1964, 5 vols.

WINCKELMANN, J. J. *Werke in einem Band*, ed. H. Holtzhauer, Berlin and Weimar, 1969.

WORTLEY MONTAGU, LADY MARY *The Complete Letters*, ed. R. Halsband, vol. 1, Oxford, 1965.

WRAXALL, N. W. *Memoirs of the Courts of Berlin, Dresden, Warsaw and Vienna in the years 1777, 1778 and 1779*, London, 1799, 2 vols (= *Memoirs*).

2 *Secondary Sources (i) Historical, Political and Social Background*

ANDERSON, M. S. *Europe in the Eighteenth Century. 1713–1783*, London, 1961.

BIEDERMANN, K. *Deutschland im achtzehnten Jahrhundert*, 2nd revised edition, Leipzig, 1880, 4 vols.

BRUFORD, W. H. *Germany in the Eighteenth Century. The Social Background of the Literary Revival* (1935), Cambridge, 1965 (= *Germany*).

FAUCHIER-MAGNAN, A. *The Small German Courts in the Eighteenth Century*, translated by M. Savill, London, 1958.

FORD, F. L. *Europe, 1780–1830*, London, 1970.

GLEICHEN-RUSSWURM, A. VON *Das galante Europa. Geselligkeit der großen Welt 1600–1789*, Stuttgart, 1919.

GOOCH, G. P. *Germany and the French Revolution* (1920), London, Frank Cass, 1965.

HERTZ, F. H. *The Development of the German Mind*, vol. 2, London, 1962.

KOHN, H. *The Mind of Germany. The Education of a Nation*, London, 1965.

MARTENS, W. *Die Botschaft der Tugend*, Stuttgart, 1968.

NAMIER, L. *Vanished Supremacies. Essays on European History, 1812–1918*, London, 1962.

NEW CAMBRIDGE MODERN EUROPEAN HISTORY (*CMEH*) Vol. 7, *The Old Regime, 1713–63*, ed. J. O. Lindsay, Cambridge, 1957.

Vol. 8, *The American and French Revolutions, 1763–93*, ed. A. Goodwin, Cambridge, 1965.

NICOLSON, H. *The Age of Reason, 1700–1789*, London, 1968.

ROSENBERG, H. *Bureaucracy, Aristocracy and Autocracy. The Prussian Experience, 1660–1815*, Boston, 1966.

RUDÉ, G. *Revolutionary Europe. 1783–1815*, London, 1964.

SCHILFERT, G. *Deutschland, 1648–1789*, 2nd edition, Berlin, 1962.

SCHRAMM, P. E. *Neun Generationen. Dreihundert Jahre deutscher 'Kulturgeschichte'* . . . *1648–1948*, vol. 1, Göttingen, 1963.

STREISAND, J. *Deutschland, 1789–1815*, 2nd edition, Berlin, 1961.

TAYLOR, A. J. P. *The Hapsburg Monarchy*, London, 1961 (paperback edition).

(*ii*) *Literary History and Criticism, Culture and Thought*

ANGER, A. 'Deutsche Rokokodichtung. Ein Forschungsbericht', *DVLG*, vol. 36 (1962).

BARNARD, F. M. *Herder's Social and Political Thought*, Oxford, 1965.

BERGER, K. *Schiller. Sein Leben und seine Werke*, Munich, 1918, 2 vols.

BIELSCHOWSKY, A. *Goethe. Sein Leben und seine Werke* (revised by W. Linden), Munich, 1928, 2 vols.

BRUFORD, W. H. *Culture and Society in Classical Weimar. 1775–1806*, Cambridge, 1962 (= *Culture and Society*).
Theatre, Drama and Audience in Goethe's Germany, London, 1950 (= *Theatre*).

CASSIRER, E. *The Philosophy of the Enlightenment*, Translated by F. A. Koelln and J. P. Pettegrove, Boston, 1951.

COLLINGWOOD, R. G. *The Idea of History*, Oxford, 1961 (paperback edition).

ENGELS, F. and MARX, K. *Basic Writings on Politics and Philosophy*, ed. L. F. Feuer, London, 1969.

FEUERBACH, NELLY *Uz und Cronegk*, Leipzig, 1886.

HAZARD, P. *European Thought in the Eighteenth Century*, translated by J. L. May, London, 1965.

Bibliography

HEITNER, R. R. *German Tragedy in the Age of Enlightenment*, Berkeley and Los Angeles, 1963.

HETTNER, H. *Geschichte der deutschen Literatur im achtzehnten Jahrhundert*, revised edition by G. Erler, Berlin, 1961, 2 vols.

KEMP, J. *The Philosophy of Kant*, Oxford, 1968.

KESSEL, E. *Wilhelm von Humboldt. Idee und Wirklichkeit*, Stuttgart, 1967.

KORFF, H. A. *Geist der Goethezeit*, reprint of 4th edition, Leipzig, 1958, 4 vols.

KÖSTER, A. *Die deutsche Literatur der Aufklärungszeit*, Heidelberg, 1925.

LUKÁCS, G. *Goethe und seine Zeit* in *Werke*, vol. 7, Neuwied and Berlin, 1964.

MAY, KURT *Friedrich Schiller. Idee und Wirlkichkeit im Drama*, Göttingen, 1948.

MURAT, J. *Klopstock. Les thèmes principaux de son oeuvre*, Paris, 1959.

NEWALD, R. *Vom Späthumanismus zur Empfindsamkeit; Geschichte der deutschen Literatur* (with H. de Boor), vol. 5, 4th edition, Munich, 1963.

PASCAL, R. *The German Sturm und Drang*, Manchester, 1953.

SCHLEIDEN, K. A. *Klopstocks Dichtungstheorie als Beitrag zur Geschichte der deutschen Poetik*, Saarbrücken, 1954 (= *Klopstocks Dichtungstheorie*).

SCHNEIDER, F. J. *Die deutsche Dichtung der Aufklärungszeit. 1700–1775*, 2nd edition, Stuttgart, 1948.

SENGLE, F. *Wieland*, Stuttgart, 1949.

SPIEGEL, MARIANNE *Der Roman und sein Publikum im früheren 18. Jahrhundert 1700–1767*, Bonn, 1967.

TURNER, W. J. *Mozart. The Man and his Work* (edition revised by C. Raeburn), London, 1965.

Index

Figures in bold type indicate pages on which a subject is treated at length

Index

Index

Index